INFORMAL COMMERCIAL IMPORTERS IN CARICOM

INFORMAL COMMERCIAL IMPORTERS

IN

CARICOM

ROGER HOSEIN *and*
MARTIN FRANKLIN

THE UNIVERSITY OF THE WEST INDIES PRESS
Jamaica • Barbados • Trinidad and Tobago

The University of the West Indies Press
7A Gibraltar Hall Road, Mona
Kingston 7, Jamaica
www.uwipress.com

A catalogue record of this book is available from
the National Library of Jamaica.

978-976-640-464-2 (print)
978-976-640-472-7 (Kindle)
978-976-640-480-2 (ePub)

Cover design by Robert Harris
Typesetting by The Beget, India
Printed in the United States of America

Contents

Figures

Tables

Preface

The informal economy has been a feature within many countries world-wide, with its earliest documentation in 1973 by Keith Hart. Aside from a few notable studies, there still exists a wide gap in the literature of the relative size and contribution of the informal sector to the Carib-bean region. This text attempts firstly to help fill this empirical gap, and secondly to provide theoretical and empirical support that higgling is a response to market failure and price differentials. Further, this text pre-sents some of the underlying issues that may arise if formalization of the informal sector is to be undertaken and outlines some of the poten-tial features and systems that should be considered if formalization is to occur. Due to the nature of activities conducted in this sector, data is largely unavailable and where data does exist, it is minimal to say the least. In this regard, we saw a need to conduct data gathering exercises, conducting surveys in various Caribbean islands. This book is in fact the first of its kind as it presents the most comprehensive study of the underreported informal economy in the Caribbean hemisphere to date. Therefore, it is the intention that this book will provide the foundation for further studies in this area and serve as a point of departure for the review of the evolution of the shuttle trade in the Caribbean and so reflect a changing national and global dynamic.

This book is comprised of eight chapters. Chapter 1 focuses on the macroeconomic climate of the Caribbean, specifically its trade and investment framework and the implications for shuttle trading. Chap-ter 2 looks at the role of women in the shuttle trade, how they became involved in the trade and their growing membership in sector, while chapter 3 looks at the persistence of the shuttle trade in the Caribbean. As it is the purpose of this book to attach quantitative support for the existence of shuttle trading in the Caribbean, as well as the sector's increasing share of the aggregate economy, the next three chapters (4, 5 and 6) provide a detailed discussion of three empirical surveys conducted in the study: the shuttle trade between Guyana and Trinidad and Tobago, hucksters in agricultural produce operating between Dominica and some of the small surrounding islands, and the informal commercial importing activities of Jamaican traders. Chapter 7 provides a case study of the suitcase trade in prescription medicine. Finally, chapter 8 offers a summary of the empirical results associated with shuttle trading in the Caribbean and details some of the stylized issues that may arise if formalization of the shuttle trade is to occur.

Acknowledgements

I would like to acknowledge my wife, Denise Hosein, and my children, Amartya, Daniel and Jayelle. This book would not have been completed without the assistance of Rebecca Gookool, Rishi Singh, Jeetendra Khadan and Justin Joseph, all diligent research assistants. Most significantly, though, I would like to acknowledge the research assistance of Ranita Seecharan, a truly dedicated researcher and a very bright young scholar.

Roger Hosein

I would like to acknowledge my wife, Martha, and my children, Maxine, Mendel and Michelle. This book would not have been completed without the assistance of Ashley McFarlane, a research assistant with an eye for detail.

Martin Franklin

Abbreviations

ACP	African, Caribbean and Pacific Group of States
CARICOM	Caribbean Community
CSME	Caribbean Single Market and Economy
DEXIA	Dominica Export and Import Agency
DHA	Dominica Hucksters' Association
ECLAC	Economic Commission for Latin America and the Caribbean
FDI	foreign direct investment
IDB	Inter-American Development Bank
ICI	informal commercial importer
ILO	International Labour Organization
IMF	International Monetary Fund
OECS	Organisation of Eastern Caribbean States
RoSCA	Rotating Savings and Credit Association
SITC	Standard International Trade Classification
SME	small and medium enterprise
UVA	United Vendors Association
WHO	World Health Organization
WTO	World Trade Organization

INTRODUCTION

The informal economy plays an important role in economies throughout the world. While there is no agreement in the literature on the definition of the informal economy, terms such as *underground, shadow, black, unofficial, unrecorded, hidden, parallel, clandestine* and *second* economy are frequently used by researchers to describe the informal economy. Differences in terminologies and definitions reflect to a great extent the differences in research objectives (IDB 2006).

The informal sector was introduced to academia by Hart (1973) as part of his International Labour Organization (ILO)–based research on the Kenyan economy in 1973. He noted that the informal sector consisted of a wide range of activities generating both employment and income for its participants. Hart introduced the informal sector to describe the urban labour force that was not employed in the formal labour market. He treated the informal sector as being virtually the same as all categories of small self-employed workers.

Other researchers became interested in the informal sector over time. For example, Hernando de Soto, a Peruvian economist in the 1980s, noted that in many developing economies the high level of taxes, bribes and other types of administrative hassles by the bureaucracy within an economy push some entrepreneurs into the informal sector. De Soto noted that as a consequence, bootstrap enterprises were created. Specifically, de Soto noted that "the informal economy is the people's spontaneous response to the state's incapacity to satisfy the basic needs of the impoverished masses" (de Soto 1989, xiv–xv). From de Soto's perspective, the legal status of a business was the main element that distinguished the formal sector from the informal sector. He emphasized that the informal sector existed on account of the various policies and regulations imposed by the authorities and the associated transaction costs involved. Other researchers, such as Portes,

Castells and Benton (1989, 12), have defined the informal economy as "a process of income generation characterized by one central feature: it is unregulated by the institutions of society in a legal and social environment in which similar activities are regulated".

In 1993, International Labour Conference statisticians provided the following definition for the informal sector: "all unregistered or unincorporated enterprises below a certain size, including: microenterprises owned by informal employers who hire one or more employees on a continuing basis; and own account operations owned by individuals who may employ contributing family workers and employees on an occasional basis" (ILO 2002, 11).

Gërxhani (2004) identified that authors often define the informal sector in the context of political, economic and social criteria or perspectives. Inter-American Development Bank (IDB) (2006), for example, cites the following subdefinitions of the informal sector from the economic perspective:

- Labour market – The informal sector is the combination of all activities that do not involve contractual or legally regulated employment but that also allow individuals to earn an income.
- Tax evasion – The informal sector is made up of all income that individuals do not list in order to avoid taxation.
- Size of activity – Businesses within the informal sector all have one similar feature and that is that they typically engage in business activity on a small scale.
- Regulation or registration of the activity – Based on the work of de Soto (1989), the main characteristic widely accepted of the informal sector is the fact that the activities of businesses are unregistered and unlicensed.
- National statistics – The informal economy involves all activity that is not captured by official economic statistics such as the gross domestic product.

Although the definitions provided above are generally tractable, some researchers indicate that the informal sector tends to be more easily described than defined (Hussmanns 2001). The informal sector can be typically observed in urban hubs, on streets and in train stations. A wide cross-section of people participate in the sector, including petty traders, barbers, shoeshine boys and shoemakers. The sector is characterized by undertrained and unskilled workers, many of whom benefit only from on-the-job training or some form of traditional apprenticeship system. A substantial number of the workers in the informal sector migrate from rural to urban communities and are generally lacking in skills and basic education (Lund and Nicholson 2006). Additionally, the children of the urban-based poor may not all attend school and so may not have received a formal education and thus remain in the informal sector in something of a vicious cycle (Lund and Nicholson 2006).

Osarenkhoe (2009) describes the essential characteristics of the informal sector as:

- Employment – he noted that this describes the characteristics of the people engaged within the sector. Some of the points he highlighted were "Absence of official protection and recognition; Non-coverage by minimum wage legislation and social security system; Predominance of own account and self-employment work; Absence of trade union organization; Low income and wages; Little job security; No fringe benefits from institutional sources."

- Enterprise – this characteristic describes the activities involved within the informal sector. He highlighted that they include "Unregulated and competitive markets; Small-scale operation with individual or family ownership; Ease of entry; Reliance on locally available resources; Family ownership of enterprises; Labour-intensive and adapted technology; Absence of access to institutional credit or other supports and protections."

- Habitat – this characteristic focuses on the land and housing issues within the informal sector. According to Osarenkhoe, this involves "Unauthorized use of vacant public or private land; Illegal subdivision and/or rental of land; Unauthorized construction of structures and buildings; Reliance on low cost and locally available scrap construction materials; Absence of restrictive standards and regulations; Reliance on family labour and artisanal techniques for construction; Non-availability of mortgage or any other subsidized finance."

- Credit – the final characteristic pointed out by Osarenkhoe is the involvement of credit markets within the sector. He highlighted some factors about these markets, which include "Unregulated and non-subsidized; Easy accessibility; Availability in very small size and for short terms; Low administrative and procedural costs; Little to no collateral requirements; Flexible interest rates (from very high to no interest at all); Highly flexible transactions and repayments tailored to individual needs."

Financial markets are central to the functioning of productive markets as they help in sustaining longer run investments and also facilitate shorter run exchanges by providing short-term credit (Pagano 2001). The efficiency of these financial institutions is critically dependent on the efficiency of various supporting institutions in the economy, which allow lenders to benefit from a reasonable rate of repayment from borrowers. This helps to reduce the default on loans and is aided by a judicial system that facilitates the recovery of loans. Standard operating procedures for these institutions include the requirement that borrowers of funds present credible information regarding their stock of assets, flow of revenues and physical location, as reflected in credible records. The informal sector does not archive credible information and as a consequence is squeezed out of the formal financial sector and has to seek financial aid elsewhere.

The use of capital by the informal sector is often shared by the household, a good example being the use of motor vehicles such as cars and small vans. Even so, the United Nations Economic and Social Commission for Asia and the Pacific (2006, 3) notes that "economic entities operating in the informal sector generally operate on a small scale and don't make a significant distinction between labour and capital as factor inputs into the production process. In reality though, the main factor of production owned by the informal sector is its labour skills."

Most regions of the world have relatively large informal sectors. In particular, informal employment contributes to more than 75% of non-agricultural employment in sub-Saharan Africa and southern and eastern Asia, and more than 50% in Latin America and western Asia (see table 0.1). Kar and Marjit (2001) argue that the large number of people employed by the informal sector in developing economies is not surprising as the sector produces a wide category of goods and services and also

Table 0.1: Share of Informal Employment in Non-Agricultural Employment (%)

Region	%
Sub-Saharan Africa (SSA)	78
Southern and Eastern Asia	75
Latin America	52
Western Asia	50
Northern Africa	43
Transition countries	21

Source: OECD (2009).

a significant number of them produce goods and services that are really import substitutes. Informality also serves to exclude large chunks of many developing economies from important developmental opportunities acquired via education, health care and access to redress in the judicial system.

The informal sector, in contrast to the formal sector, is typically less vocal on matters pertaining to public expression and opinion. Indeed, figure 0.1 shows that in societies where the size of the informal economy does not account for the dominant share of gross national product, there tends to be high levels of inequality in terms of their participation in national governance issues.[1]

Services represent the greater proportion of economic activity within the informal sector, with the manufacturing sector accounting for only a small share of informal sector activity (Olofin and Folawewo 2009). The concern with the size of the informal sector stems from the understanding that workers in the informal sector are generally poorer and work under harsher conditions than workers in other parts of the economy (Lund and Nicholson 2006). This relationship, however, is not trivial or simple, and without the informal sector, the poor would become so marginalized that they could even become destitute (Charmes 1998; Thomas 1995). Even

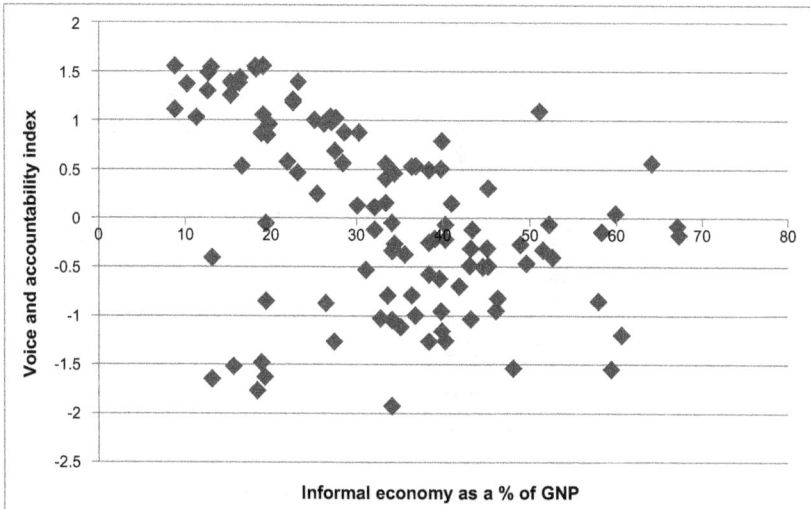

Figure 0.1 Scatterplot between voice and accountability (2009) and size of the informal economy in total GNP, 1999/2000
Source: World Bank (various years); Schneider (2002).

so, the Organisation for Economic Co-operation and Development (2009, 96) notes that "a strong link exists between informality and poverty; most of the working poor in the world work informally, either in self-employment or as wage earners. Many of these people lack basic social protection and are locked into low productivity activities, with scant opportunities for economic mobility."

Informal sector workers generally operate from their homes, on sidewalks or on streets and alleys (Alderslade et al. 2006). When informal sector businesses operate from sources other than the entrepreneur's home, they struggle for basic infrastructural access such as electricity, water and sanitation services. This is one of the big disadvantages of firms operating in the informal sector. Limited access to electricity, for example, constrains the amount and type of electric tools to which informal sector workers have access. For this sector, a generalized improvement in physical infrastructure can thus go a long way toward improving economic outcomes.

Since the identification of the informal sector by Hart (1973), a number of criteria have been used to classify the informality of firms, including the degree of compliance of the firm with government regulations and the size of the firm (Hussmanns 2004). Figure 0.2 provides evidence of economies

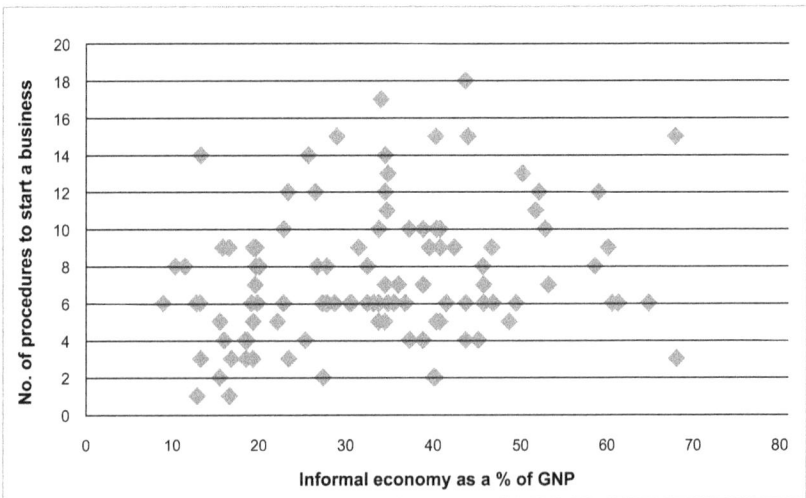

Figure 0.2 Scatterplot of the relative size of the informal sector 1999/2000 and the number of procedures to start a business
Source: World Bank (2010); Schneider (2002).

with both a heavy element of government regulation and a large informal sector. Specifically, data has shown that as the number of bureaucratic processes increase, there is a higher propensity for persons to venture into the informal economy.

There are distinct differences and diversities when comparing the activities and participants of the informal sector to the formal sector. Informal sector activities can be located in various markets, such as the input markets and the labour market. They can also be found in the financial system and the sale of final goods and services. This classification is important because there is nothing inherent in goods and services that make them informal; informality is derived from the different activities involved in production and commerce. From the perspective of an individual or a firm, informality is viewed as a continuum rather than a dichotomy. Most individuals or firms comply with some laws and regulations while ignoring others: "Informal activities can provide a much needed source of income for a great number of people. At the same time, informality motivated by regulatory distortions, tax evasion, or in the pursuit of illegal activities can be a development trap that deprives governments of needed funds and leaves participants without legal protection" (IDB 2006, ii).

The IDB (2006) approached the rationale for participating in the informal sector by citing the work of Loayza (1996), who used a cost benefit approach to highlight the reasons for individuals being more inclined to participate in the informal sector. Loayza noted that "economic units choose to be partially or completely informal by weighing the costs and benefits that a legal status entails and considering their particular institutional and resource constraints. In this sense, the choice to be informal is a rational one, a fact which does not imply that some firms are not forced by their constraints to be either formal or informal." He also noted that access to the formal sector comes at a cost that reflects the time and financing needed to obtain licences and registrations, as well as the cost of taxes, regulations and bureaucratic requirements normally related to operating within the sector. He based this on the research done by de Soto in Peru, which showed "that the ten-month waiting period to settle a small garment business cost US$1,037, much more than the US$195 in direct costs for licences and permits. As a result, the total cost of legal registration was equivalent to 32 times the minimum monthly salary. In looking at the costs of staying in the formal sector, Loayza [1996, 10–11] points out that costs 'related to workers' welfare [minimum wages, fringe benefits, social security, etc.] are the most restrictive and costly in underdeveloped countries (and in many developed countries as well)' " (IDB 2006, 11).

The IDB (2006, 1) cites Loayza (1996) as pointing to two kinds of costs of participating in the informal sector:

> penalties when informal activities are detected and the inability to take full advantage of government-provided goods. In the case of the latter, the roles played by the legal system and law enforcement are very important. In Peru, informal sector entrepreneurs report that their main constraints include an inability to expand their customer base to include those engaged in more formal activities and the disincentive to grow (which means becoming more visible).

Commenting on the costs associated with the informal sector, Osarenkhoe (2009) makes the point that the informal sector in low-income countries is usually born out of a heavily bureaucratic environment. While it is not unusual for the informal sector to account for over half of gross domestic product for these countries, it still comes at a cost. He points to the work of Barrientos and Barrientos (2002), who noted that

> small tax bases constrain fiscal authorities to raise revenues through inefficient means and to delay necessary investments in infrastructure and education. Furthermore, resources are not likely to be directed to their most efficient uses if production is carried out in an environment where formal mechanisms of contract enforcement and dispute resolution are not available. Governments in developing nations resort to a variety of policies to try and bring more economic units into the tax-paying fold. These range from sporadic crackdowns on undeclared economic activities, to subsidies and tax breaks for firms that agree to register legally and maintain legitimate tax accounting practices.

Results from Previous Studies

The informal sector is a sizable and growing portion of the economy of many Caribbean countries. Estimating the size of the informal sector in the Caribbean has not featured prominently in the literature, with only a few studies to date carried out in the economies of Guyana, Jamaica, Trinidad and Tobago, and Barbados. The following paragraphs provide a brief review of some of the empirical results from these studies.

Jamaica

One of the first studies to actually attempt to measure the size of Jamaica's informal sector was that of Witter and Kirton (1990). These authors estimated that the size of the informal sector in Jamaica increased from 8% of formal GDP in 1962 to 24% in 1984. In terms of employment, these researchers estimated that in 1985 about 20% of the population above fourteen years was employed in the informal sector.

In 2006, the IDB examined the size and characteristics of the Jamaican informal economy and noted that the informal economy helped elevate many Jamaicans, as shown by a decline in poverty levels in Jamaica from 44% in 1991 to 17% in 2001. Four methods were used to estimate the size of the informal economy in Jamaica: the monetary or currency demand approach, the electricity consumption approach, the expenditure/income discrepancy approach and the monetary additions approach. The informal economy was shown to have experienced a rate of growth superior to that of the formal sector, irrespective of the method used to measure the size of the informal sector.

Table 0.2 reports some of the findings of the IDB on the characteristics of the informal sector in Jamaica.

The IDB (2006, 13–14) applied the indirect monetary model to data for the period of 1966 to 2000 and found that over the two earlier decades, there was discontinuous growth of either registered or total GDP that makes up the informal sector. The report found that "while the relative importance of informal sector activity in Jamaica first declined from 7% in 1966 to 1% in 1978, it increased in subsequent years and reached its maximum value in 1989, with a share of 52%. After that, it fell to 15% in 1991, followed by another period of expansion with a share of 40% in 2000." Witter and Kirton (1990), using Gutman's monetary approach to study the period 1966–84, found similar results for the size of the informal

Table 0.2: Selected Findings of Inter-American Development Bank on the Informal Economy in Jamaica

Type of activity	Low productivity, labour intensive Wholesale or retail trade and agriculture
Type of work	Mostly part-time
Gender	Women dominate the informal sector, comprising 57% of workers in the sector
Education	Informal sector workers are on average better educated than their counterparts in the formal sector
Motivation	Motivation to enter the sector dominated by the desire to be independent and earn more income

Source: IDB (2006).

economy (as a percentage of total GDP). The researchers found that there was an upward trend from 9% in 1966 to 19% in 1984. The IDB (2006) estimated informal activities for the year 2001 as representing around 43% of official GDP, which was double the share of the previous decade. The report noted that this rapid growth in the informal economy contributed significantly to the decline in poverty during the decade. Such reduction in poverty occurred amid declining economic growth, and the researchers concluded that this could be attributed to the recovery of real wages, falling inflation and growing remittances.

Trinidad and Tobago

Maurin et al. (2006) applied two models (the structural cointegrated vector autoregression [SCVAR] model and an alternative model) to estimate the size of the informal economy in Trinidad and Tobago in the period 1974–98. Both models yielded a similar pattern: an increase in the period 1974–81 and a decrease in the period 1982–98. The increase in the former period was 14% to 36% of official GDP from the SCVAR model and 15% to 41% from the alternative model. The decrease in the latter period was 36% to 22% of official GDP from SCVAR model and 41% to 24% from the alternative model. Further to this, Vuletin (2008) estimated the size of the informal sector in Trinidad and Tobago to be around 25% of official GDP. Vuletin argued that as a percentage of non-energy GDP, the informal sector of the Trinidad and Tobago economy was around 33%. He noted that the output of the energy sector is not easily informalized so that ideally the size of the informal sector should be measured against the size of the non-energy GDP.

Barbados

In 1998, the Barbados Statistical Service Department conducted an enquiry into the informal sector in Barbados with the objective of determining the situation of workers and eventually making appropriate policy recommendations to help increase the productivity of this sector. It was estimated that in Barbados there were 5,720 informal small businesses in operation with 6,904 employees, compared to 117,575 workers in the formal sector. Feige (2005) estimated informal employment in Barbados to be 12.8% of total employment. Vuletin (2008) found that the size of the informal sector in 2000 was around 36% of GDP. In another paper, Greenidge et al. (2009) investigated the size of the informal sector for the Barbadian economy based on data for the time period 1972–2007. These researchers used an unrestricted error correction model and found that the informal sector in Barbados is large and has grown to reach one-third the size of the official economy.

Greenidge et al. (2009) provided data on the size of the informal economy for the period 1973–2007. From this data, the researchers distinguished among five episodes in the evolution of the informal economy. The first episode refers to the period 1973–86 in which it fluctuated around 30% of official GDP; the second refers to the 1987–88 period when it declined sharply to 21% of official GDP; the third episode refers to the 1989–92 period when it increased steadily to 36% of official GDP; the fourth period is 1993–99 when it hovered around 33% of official GDP; and the fifth period is 2000–7 when it fluctuated around 38% of official GDP.

Guyana

The informal sector of the Guyanese economy has been inferred by several researchers to be as large as the formal sector. One researcher, Thomas (1989), argued that the informal sector during the 1980s hovered between 80% and 100% of the official economy. Using trend line analysis of income velocities with respect to currency, he obtained estimates of the size of the underground economy in Guyana ranging from 26% to 99% of the official economy in the period 1982–86. Another study on the Guyanese economy by Bennett (1995), which covered the time period 1977–88, used a currency ratio model and found that the size of the informal economy in Guyana ranged from 22.7% to 54.4% of official GDP, with an average of 34.93%.

Faal (2003) used a Tanzi-type currency demand model to provide an estimate of the size of the informal economy. Faal found a very large informal economy that was approximately 27% of GDP in 1970 and averaged 39.7% of GDP in 1970–79. It increased to an average of 76% of GDP in 1980–89, but thereafter decreased to an average of 47% in 1990–2000 as various macroeconomic reforms were implemented in the economy. Vuletin (2008) estimated the size of the informal sector in Guyana at 57%.

After reviewing the approaches of Thomas (1989), Bennett (1995) and Faal (2003), Thomas-Hope et al. (2009, 13) concluded that "by any standards the underground economy[2] accounted for a considerable share of the value of economic transactions in Guyana". By applying a dataset for the 2001–2008 period to the methodology of Bennett, Thomas and other researchers were able to extend Bennett's estimates to a range of 10.7%

to 40% of GDP, with an average of 22.44% over the period 2001–8. The researchers also applied a modified econometric methodology to that of Faal and estimated the underground economy in 2001–8 as ranging between 31.7% and 111%, with an average of 61%. These estimates confirm that the underground economy in Guyana remains significant in the context of the country's formal economy.

Thomas, Jourdain and Pasha (2011) estimated the size of the informal economy for the period of 1979 to 2008 in terms of five episodes. The first episode is in the 1974–84 period when it increased steadily from 15% to 68% of GDP; it decreased to 16% in the second episode which corresponds to the 1985–94 period; the third episode is in the 1992–97 period when it increased to 110% in 1996 before falling to 91% of GDP in 1997; the fourth episode is in the 1998–2000 period when it increased to 127% of GDP; and the fifth episode is the 2001–8 period when it decreased steadily to 32% of GDP.

Other Caribbean Countries

Vuletin (2008) measured the informal economy in thirty-two Latin American and Caribbean countries by using the Multiple Indicators, Multiple Causes approach to estimate the size and the factors contributing to the informal economy.[3] This approach models the informal economy as a function of its indicators and causes and can be used to make absolute comparisons across countries (see methodology in Vuletin 2008). This approach has the specific advantage over other methods of estimating the size of the informal sector (for example, surveys, currency demand approach, transaction approach, electricity consumption approach) in that it considers more than one indicator of the informal economy. In particular, the approach "explicitly considers several causes, as well as the multiple effects of the informal economy" (Vuletin 2008, 7). In this study, Vuletin referred to both cause and indicator variables. Cause variables impact the size of the informal economy, while the indicator variables are correlated either positively or negatively with the size of the informal economy. The cause variables considered included tax burden, labour rigidities, agricultural sector, inflation and the strength of the enforcement system. Increased tax burden strengthened the incentive to work in the informal economy, and labour rigidities (legal restrictions on the labour market) are suggested to increase the size of the informal economy. Greater prominence of the agricultural sector is argued to be accompanied by a larger size of the informal economy. In addition, the higher the rate of inflation, the larger the informal economy (because inflation alters income distribution and this may induce disrespect for tax law). The strength of the enforcement system – characterized by quality of bureaucracy, corruption in government and the rule of law – was also considered. Vuletin showed that stronger enforcement capability of a government tended to lower the expected size of the informal economy.

Vuletin (2008) set Jamaica's informal economy at 35% of GDP in 2000–2001 based on the estimates in de la Roca et al. (2002) and used that value as a benchmark to estimate the absolute sizes of the informal economies of other countries in the Caribbean. He found that the sizes of the informal economies in the respective countries varied greatly with the Bahamas, Cyprus, Grenada, St Kitts and Nevis, Trinidad and Tobago, and Barbados falling in the lower spectrum with informal economy values ranging from 15% to 25% of GDP. Countries such as St Vincent and the Grenadines, Belize, and the Dominican Republic fell in the upper spectrum with values ranging from 45% to 51% of GDP.

The Informal Commercial Importer (ICI)

Among the participants of the informal economy in the Caribbean Community (CARICOM), particularly in Jamaica, Guyana, Dominica, and Trinidad and Tobago, the informal commercial importer (ICI) is by far the most visible. In Jamaica for example, Smikle and Taylor (1978) estimated that 115,006 higglers plied their trade in the markets or in close proximity to these markets, while a further 1,046 were estimated to sell in curbside markets in 1977. In many ways, the authors view informal commercial importing as representative of informal sector activity. Most of the existing literature on ICIs are at least a decade old (for example, Le Franc et al. 1985; Taylor 1988; Holder 1988; Witter and Kirton 1990; Lagro and Plotkin 1990; Mulakala 1991) and confirm the dominance of women among ICIs. Given the dominance of female heads of family in the English-speaking Caribbean and the increases in unemployment arising out of the global financial crisis, it is fitting that the role of ICIs be revisited. Accordingly, the objectives of this book are to update the sociological dimensions of ICIs in CARICOM, to explore whether this activity can be formalized, and if so, how it may be formalized.

ICIs are the modern day higglers in CARICOM countries. The term *higgle* is a verb that is possibly derived from the term haggle, which has been associated with higgledy-piggledy, an adverbial term that is used colloquially to mean mixed up or without order (*Oxford Advanced*

Learner's Dictionary 1974). This usage may be linked to the economic concept of regulated and unregulated markets, where higgle can be associated with the unregulated market demand and supply conditions referred to elsewhere (for example, see Pigou 1938; Peltzman 1976).

When used as a noun, higgler is possibly derived from haggler or one who seeks to get a better price. Higgling itself and the use of oratory and linguistic rhetoric to secure gain are inferior to the use of objectivity and facts, but achieve the market objective of disposing of one's goods (Brown 1994). Higgling and bargaining were recognized early on by Adam Smith (1776, 1.5:4) in *The Wealth of Nations* where he noted that in the marketplace, adjustment occurs: "Not by any accurate measure, but by the higgling and bargaining of the market, according to that sort of rough equality which, although not exact, is sufficient for carrying out the business of common life."

Smith argues that different jobs require different labour inputs – physical, social, human, and so on – and ingenuity. It is reasonable, Smith notes, that these differences in labour input, time, effort and quality are reflected in the product prices and that this adjustment takes place in a process of higgling. From this standpoint, higgling becomes invisible and achieves what must be achieved. In the words of Brown (1998) "the language of the markets may be seen as a transport medium by which the true outcome is realized".[4]

The modern day higgler crosses borders in search of goods and to sell goods. They are referred to as informal commercial importers and hucksters within CARICOM, but exist in virtually all modern economies, selling a wide category of goods ranging from shrimp to cloth to electric items and processed goods. The practice of ICIs and their country-to-country trading within the Caribbean sphere, however, remains a vastly understudied area.

ICIs help to meet the needs of domestic consumers that are unmet by domestic producers or distributors.[5] They sell their wares from their homes or on the streets, and are self-employed without any formal benefits. They are generally most visible in the airports, carrying bulging suitcases. To avoid crossing their own weight limitation, these traders typically beg and badger other travellers for the use of any unused baggage allotment that they may have at their disposal. Informal commercial importing, also referred to as shuttle trading by the International Monetary Fund (IMF) in some regards, is also opportunistic, and partly depends on failure and rigidities in the economic system and various anomalies in the system that allow this type of trade to be advantageous. The IMF (1998) has noted that the shuttle trade generally follows one of two practices:

1. Travellers carry goods from country A, sell it in country B and return with cash to country A to buy more goods.
2. Same as 1, but travellers now buy goods in country B and return to country A where they sell the goods purchased in B and then the cycle restarts.

In economies that are connected by a land bridge, shuttle trade is referred to as border trade. The thriving nature of the international shuttle trade is such that it was recognized by the IMF (1998) as encouraging grassroots capitalism. Table 0.3 provides a summary of the key terms used to describe the shuttle trader mainly within the Caribbean hemisphere. Indeed, it alludes to an important point that, regardless of the titles used, the presence of the shuttle trader is certainly easily discernible within these territories.

ICIs play an important role in the development process of small capital starved economies. Caribbean ICIs generally purchase commodities from the more urbanized centres within the region, such as Port of Spain in Trinidad, Panama and Caracas, and sell them to other parts of the region. ICIs that are in possession of United States or Canadian visas bring in some of their goods from extra regional perimeters. Many of these ICIs transport their goods back to their home countries in their personal suitcase (hence the alternative term "suitcase traders"). ICIs engage in the importation of goods outside of the official procedure for such imports.

Table 0.3: Terms Used in Various Countries to Describe the Shuttle Trader

Terms	Country of Origin
Higgler or informal commercial importer (ICI)	Jamaica
Machanta	Dominican Republic
Madansara or marchande	Haiti
Peddling/peddler	Britain
Speculator	St Lucia and Nevis
Trafficker	St Vincent
Turn hand	St Kitts
Huckster or hawker	Dominica, Antigua and Guyana

ICI traders in the Caribbean traditionally have two options for shipping goods by air: air freight or checked baggage. With air freight, the actual shipment of their goods depends on the airline's schedule for cargo flights (which can often take up to a week), and clearance of the goods may require the services of a customs broker. In addition, shipping by air freight requires traders to invest in tamper-free shipping containers to reduce the risk of their shipments being rummaged by cargo handlers. Checked baggage, on the other hand, is generally faster as traders enjoy a higher probability of having the goods travel on their flight. Traders can then clear customs promptly without contracting the services of a customs broker. Accordingly, the goods are available for sale immediately upon arrival in the destination country, and this translates into a greater level of working capital for traders.

This study investigates the attributes of ICIs in CARICOM and argues that higgling in the region is a response to market failure and price differentials. Further, it is argued that informal commercial trading is playing an increasingly significant role in individuals' lives. In addition, their national economies and CARICOM can maximize the associated benefits by not treating shuttle trading as a mere fringe activity but rather as a legitimate economic activity that could be formalized. Rather than definitively supporting this proposition, this book outlines some of the main benefits and challenges associated with formalization of the trade, and further presents some potential features and systems that should be considered if formalization is to occur. The study is built around three substantive pieces of empirical work. The first empirical study investigates the shuttle trade between Guyana and Trinidad and Tobago. The second empirical study focuses on providing an understanding of the hucksters in agricultural produce operating between Dominica and some of the small islands in its vicinity. The last empirical block of research is built on the informal commercial importing activity of traders operating out of Jamaica.

This book has eight chapters. Chapter 1 discusses various facets of the trade and integration process in CARICOM and its attendant implications for informal sector activity (of which shuttle trading is a subset) in the Caribbean. The arguments for trade liberalization at the regional level and at the international level have much in common. Implicit in both sets of arguments is a close correlation between trade and economic growth. Caribbean economies have embraced a greater degree of trade liberalization in the last few decades. A major part of the trade policy of the countries on which this study is based is the formation of the regional integration arrangement – the Caribbean Community (CARICOM). This chapter provides an overview of trade and investment policies in the Caribbean and also an overview of the macroeconomic conditions. The chapter concludes by focusing on how some of the recent global changes that affect CARICOM economies, such as the erosion of banana preferences and the global financial crisis, can potentially affect informal sector activity in the region.

Chapter 2 discusses the evolution of women from slave traders or slaves who traded goods to ICIs in the Caribbean. In particular, this chapter traces the lineage of ICIs back to their early days as slave traders through the period of emancipation. It highlights the details associated with the emergence of ICIs in the three different settings of Guyana, Dominica and Jamaica. Three principal reasons are discussed in the chapter regarding the evolution of the suitcase traders: the process of import substituting industrialization adopted by many economies in the Caribbean, the globalization of labour markets and the generalized de-agriculturalization of economic activity.

Chapter 3 discusses various reasons associated with the persistence of the shuttle trade, while chapters 4, 5 and 6 discuss the three substantive empirical surveys conducted in the study. All three studies use the same methodology and survey instrument. Each of these chapters details the specifics of the trade associated with the relevant traders. Chapter 7 provides a case study of the suitcase trade in prescription medicine and chapter 8 concludes the study.

1 TRADE AND INVESTMENT IN THE CARIBBEAN: IMPLICATIONS FOR THE INFORMAL SECTOR

The post-war experience has offered useful insights into the causes of growth and development without producing a coherent set of principles that can be universally applied as a formula in all cultures and situations. Differing levels of poverty and the capacity to adjust to policy changes reflect differences not only in economic progress, but also in the social and institutional factors that have emerged from varying historical and cultural experiences. Based on per capita income, CARICOM countries are generally ranked as middle-income countries with average incomes exceeding that of a large number of other developing states. But growth has been erratic, depending on movement in the volume and prices of a narrow range of exports, tourism and foreign investment. Changes in the level of well-being tend to depend heavily on foreign exchange availability. National policies have failed to deal effectively with the issues of unemployment, sustained development and poverty eradication. Integration as a strategy to fuse the politically distinct units into a viable economic entity has largely been a failure, as national programmes continue to take precedence over collective action and collaboration.

Fundamental changes in the global economy have not only made foreign aid more difficult to access, but have created a more competitive environment by eliminating preferential trading arrangements. The end of the cold war and the acceleration of the globalization process have increased competition for aid, markets and foreign investment, exposing weaknesses in post-independence economic policies and the integration strategy that has been hampered by an insular nationalism and a failure to implement regional decisions. The persistence of irrelevant political systems, outdated institutions and failing economic policies have contributed significantly to a situation where the Caribbean has been left behind on many fronts, and remains ill-prepared in some regards to cope with a global open trading system. To this end, the implications for informal traders in the Caribbean sphere are indeed great, as increased globalization promotes informalization by creating more marginalization. Indeed, as it becomes more difficult to compete with falling unit costs, innovation, greater productivity and other competitive advantages, economic agents are drawn toward the informal sector that operates on flexible and less than optimal trading practices.

This chapter provides a macroeconomic backdrop against which to better understand the past, present and future realities with which suitcase traders need to cope.

1.1. Population of CARICOM Economies

The population of the Caribbean countries listed in table 1.1 has increased from 10.8 million in 1980 to 16.6 million in 2008, an increase of 53%. Belize had the fastest increase in population growth in the listed time period of 113%, followed by Haiti with 79% and the Bahamas, 60%. Small economic size results in a relatively high cost of production which in the context of undiversified export baskets for the region limits the ability of the region to competitively engage in international trade. Although small market size tends to promote monopoly, because small Caribbean firms cannot spend significant funds on marketing and research and development, it affects their capacity to respond to international shocks.

1.2. Growth Performance

An important aspect of CARICOM is the difference in economic size of its thirteen member states. These member states have different levels of economic development, and over time the income gap between some member states has actually widened, as shown in the data on gross national income (GNI) per capita from the World Bank in table 1.2.

The main reason for the difference in income is the differential growth performance of member states. A glance at table 1.3 shows that economic performance varies widely not only among the constituent units of CARICOM, but also over time in individual member countries. In the

Table 1.1: Population of Caribbean Economies, 1980, 1990 and 2000–2008

	1980	1990	2000	2001	2002	2003	2004	2005	2006	2007	2008	% change 1980–2008
Antigua and Barbuda	72,280	61,922	76,781	78,274	79,609	80,816	81,947	83,039	84,097	84,814	85,536	18.34
The Bahamas	210,109	255,167	303,150	307,333	311,397	315,379	319,333	323,295	327,279	331,140	335,047	59.46
Barbados	249,044	271,267	286,437	287,600	288,732	289,834	290,901	291,933	292,930	293,942	255,203	2.47
Belize	146,000	189,000	249,800	257,300	265,200	273,700	282,600	291,800	297,600	303,991	310,520	112.68
Dominica	73,350	72,258	71,326	71,079	71,079	71,212	71,471	72,000	723,95	72793	73,193	-0.21
Grenada	88,929	95,879	100,411	101,307	102,398	103,540	104,533	105,237	105,597	105,668	105,552	18.69
Guyana	760,860	730,620	734,397	734,917	736,174	737,741	738,992	739,472	739,065	738,548	763,437	0.34
Haiti	5,452,940	6,867,328	7,938,791	8,053,271	8,169,525	8,287,465	8,406,941	8,527,777	8,646,850	8,732,563	9,780,064	79.35
Jamaica	2,133,000	2,390,000	2,589,389	2,604,789	2,617,495	2,625,700	2,638,100	2,650,400	2,663,100	2,675,800	2,689,133	26.07
St Kitts and Nevis	44,400	42,025	44,286	46,111	46,710	46,710	46,984	48,000	48,393	48,790	49,190	10.79
St Lucia	115,500	134,100	155,996	158,018	159,133	160,620	162,434	164,791	166,014	167,976	169,960	47.15
St Vincent and the Grenadines	100,402	109,359	115,949	116,567	117,201	117,847	118,494	119,137	119,772	120,325	109,117	8.68
Suriname	356,242	402,347	436,443	440,114	443,485	446,609	449,579	452,468	455,273	457,686	515,124	44.60
Trinidad and Tobago	1,081,764	1,223,563	1,300,545	1,305,464	1,310,124	1,314,639	1,319,139	1,323,722	1,328,432	1,333,050	1,337,684	23.66

Source: World Bank (various years); CDB (2006).

Table 1.2: GNI per Capita, Atlas Method (current US$)

Country	1990	2008
Antigua and Barbuda	5,430	13,200
The Bahamas	11,380	21,390[a]
Barbados	6,560	13,330[b]
Belize	2,100	3,740
Dominica	2,140	4,750
Grenada	2,130	5,880
Guyana	350	1,450
Jamaica	1,700	4,800
St Kitts and Nevis	3,420	10,870
St Lucia	2,660	5,410
St Vincent and the Grenadines	1,640	5,050
Suriname	1,440	4,760
Trinidad and Tobago	3,510	16,590

[a]2007
[b]2002
Source: World Bank, *World Development Indicators* (2010).

1960s, the average growth rate was estimated to be around 5% for the region as a whole. The growth of traditional exports, a favourable international environment, foreign aid, the expansion of the mining sectors and an intensification of the import substitution process contributed to this performance. In the 1970s, some countries performed well, but with high oil prices and the emergence of foreign exchange problems, a few economies (for example, Guyana and Jamaica) slowed down considerably. The 1980s was a disastrous period for the more developed countries of CARICOM, with real production experiencing a significant decline, particularly in Jamaica, Guyana, and Trinidad and Tobago. Falling production and prices in the export sectors, the emergence of fiscal and debt servicing problems, as well as the decline in consumer and capital spending, resulted in a reversal of some of the gains made earlier.

In Jamaica, real GDP in 1986 was 20% below the 1973 level, while in Trinidad and Tobago total production declined by some 25% between 1984 and 1990. Due to the expanding tourism industry, foreign investment inflows and increased earnings from banana exports, the less developed countries of CARICOM performed better in the 1980s, growing by over 5% per year on average. In the 1990s, the growth rate fell in the less

Table 1.3: Average Growth Rates of Real GDP, 1960s, 1970s, 1980s and 1990s

Country	1960–1969	1970–1979[a]	1980–1989	1990–1999	2000–2009	2009p	2010f
Antigua	n/a	5.76	6.74	3.32	3.44	−6.60	2.00
The Bahamas	9.85	2.31	3.60	1.47	0.91	−3.90	2.00
Barbados	6.36	3.35	2.23	0.74	1.40	−3.60	2.00
Belize	5.20	6.34	5.52	4.52	4.41	−0.50	2.00
Dominica	n/a	−3.30	6.28	2.28	1.49	−1.50	2.00
Grenada	n/a	5.71	5.00	3.51	1.39	−5.00	2.00
Guyana	3.66	1.67	−2.80	4.79	1.69	0.90	3.00
Jamaica	4.11	1.14	1.37	0.91	0.13	−3.00	1.00
St Kitts and Nevis	n/a	8.28	6.06	3.94	2.30	−8.50	2.00
St Vincent and the Grenadines	n/a	n/a	5.77	3.57	3.73	−0.20	2.00
St Lucia	n/a	n/a	5.85	4.89	1.72	−3.80	2.00
Suriname	n/a	2.47	−0.80	3.15	4.69	2.50	4.00
Trinidad and Tobago	5.84	6.03	0.57	2.87	6.27	−0.50	2.00

[a]Average for 1978 and 1979 for Antigua and Barbuda, Dominica, Grenada, St Kitts and Nevis, St Lucia, St Vincent and the Grenadines; ECLAC (2009).
p: preliminary, f: forecast
n/a Not applicable
Source: World Bank (various years); UNECLAC (2009).

developed countries as a result of the confluence of several factors, an important one being the decline of the banana industry. Economic activity, however, picked up in the more developed countries, with real income increasing by 40% between 1990 and 2000 in Trinidad and Tobago, although it was not until 1999 that this country attained the production level of 1983. Throughout the 1990s, however, the Jamaican economy stagnated, with growth averaging below 1% per year. The most aggressive growth was experienced by the Trinidad and Tobago economy, which averaged a whopping annual average growth per annum of 6.23%, with Belize following with 4.4%. Jamaica had the weakest growth performance for 2000–2009, averaging 0.13% per annum. Data for the year 2009 is provided to show the sharp negative effects of the global economic crisis on the region's economies. In 2010 it was forecasted that most of the economies in the region would return to a moderate real growth performance (IMF 2011).

Note that the falling production and prices in the export sectors, the emergence of fiscal and debt servicing problems, as well as the decline in consumer and capital spending constrain job creation and exacerbate the level of unemployment. It is in the context of rising unemployment that interest in the informal economy increases.

1.3. Structure of Economic Activity

Member states of CARICOM are also characterized by a dualistic economic structure with a strong agricultural sector co-existing alongside a small highly capital-intensive non-agricultural sector. For example, in Guyana, traditional rice and sugarcane practices co-exist with a capital-intensive gold and bauxite-mining sector. In Trinidad and Tobago, the traditional agricultural crops such as coffee and cocoa co-exist with a capitalized stream of resource-based industries clustered on crude oil and natural gas. In Jamaica, the once traditional banana crop now comprises one modern industry and exists with a highly capital-intensive bauxite sector. In general, the highly capital-intensive sectors of CARICOM are enclave in nature, and the main linkage of these enclave sectors to the rest of the economy is via government taxation and redistribution.

Table 1.4 shows the trend in the structure of income among CARICOM economies. Observe that in every CARICOM member state with the exception of Guyana, there was a decrease in the size of the agricultural sector. Manufacturing decreased in most CARICOM economies with the marginal exception of Grenada. Given the small size of national markets, the weak infrastructure and the lack of in-depth skills, the decrease in the manufacturing sector is no surprise as these factors present disincentives to investment in the sector.

The very clear indication from table 1.4 is that CARICOM economies are mainly service sector oriented economies. Between the listed beginning and end years for which data is recorded, there was an increase in the size of the services sector in every listed CARICOM economy except Trinidad and Tobago.

In general, for the listed economies in table 1.4, the ratio of the services sector output to GDP is over 70%, with the exception of Trinidad and Tobago and Guyana. No doubt this has been strongly influenced by the tourism sector; the abundance of sun, sand and sea allowed the tourism sector to flourish by attracting resources and attention away from sectors with less potential for development. Potential for linkages between

Table 1.4: Structural Composition of GDP in Caribbean Countries, Percentage Local Currency at Constant Prices, Various Years

Country	Period	Agriculture	Mining and Quarrying	Manufacturing	Services
Antigua and Barbuda	1981	6.59	0.44	4.57	88.40
	2005–2009	3.00	2.60	2.30	92.20
Barbados	1981	8.71	0.50	11.6	79.20
	2005–2009	4.50	0.80	5.60	89.00
Dominica	1993	23.79	0.77	7.60	67.80
	2005–2009	16.70	0.80	5.10	77.40
Grenada	1981	21.70	0.35	5.39	72.60
	2005–2009	5.90	0.80	5.80	87.50
Guyana	1981	24.90	16.10	18.10	40.70
	2005–2009	30.10	6.80	6.10	55.20
Jamaica	1982	6.57	10.70	17.40	65.40
	2005–2009	5.00	4.00	8.70	82.20
St Kitts and Nevis	1981	16.70	0.24	14.50	68.60
	2005–2009	4.20	0.30	11.30	84.20
St Lucia	1985	12.60	0.54	8.56	78.30
	2005–2009	3.50	0.50	6.20	89.90
St Vincent and the Grenadines	1981	19.32	0.28	10.41	69.90
	2005–2009	9.20	0.30	4.00	85.50
Suriname	1981	9.55	7.05	17.61	65.80
	2005–2009	7.70	8.40	12.60	71.40
Trinidad and Tobago	1980	1.91	23.50	9.76	64.80
	2006	0.50	40.50	8.10	51.10

Source: UNECLAC (various years); CDB (2006).

tourism, agriculture and manufacturing offers development opportunities for these CARICOM economies. With its resources of oil and gas, Trinidad and Tobago is among the most industrialized of the CARICOM countries, given the fact that most of its exports are oil- and gas-based. However, on the other side of this, issues such as labour shortages and high cost inflict the other sectors within the economy. Other resource-rich CARICOM states like Guyana, Suriname and Jamaica have been trying to capitalize on their bauxite resources by transforming them into higher local value-added products, but without success. The different production structures within

CARICOM have helped to promote different export structures and have made it challenging for CARICOM governments to agree on a common external strategy for their exports (World Bank 2009).

It is not surprising that informal sector activity has mirrored the trend in the formal economy, as discerned from table 1.4. The informal economy is also more visible in the services sector than in the agriculture, manufacturing, and mining and quarrying sectors. Recent research on the informal economy in Jamaica as published in IDB (2006, 2) found that "enterprises in the informal sector are concentrated in low-productivity, labour-intensive activities. Nearly 60% of Jamaicans in the informal sector work in the wholesale/retail trade or agriculture. Manufacturing is a distant third most important activity, involving only 9%."

1.4. Labour Force, Unemployment and Poverty

The data in table 1.5 indicate, not surprisingly, that the majority of employment opportunities among CARICOM economies exist in the services

Table 1.5: Labour Force by Sector in CARICOM Economies, 2006

Country	Services	Manufacturing	Agriculture
Antigua and Barbuda	82.0	11.0	7.0
The Bahamas	90.0	5.0	5.0
Barbados	75.0	15.0	10.0
Belize	62.3	15.2	22.5
Dominica	28.0	32.0	40.0
Grenada	62.0	14.0	24.0
Guyana	n/a	n/a	n/a
Haiti	66.0	9.0	25.0
Jamaica	64.0	19.0	17.0
Montserrat	n/a	n/a	n/a
St Kitts and Nevis	n/a	n/a	n/a
St Lucia	53.6	24.7	21.7
St Vincent and the Grenadines	57.0	17.0	26.0
Suriname	78.0	14.0	8.0
Trinidad and Tobago	65.6	12.9	4.0

Source: Wharton and Wasley (2009).

Table 1.6: Unemployment Rates in Various Caribbean Economies, Various Years

Country	1991	1995	1998	2001	2002	2003	2004	2005	2006	2007	2008
The Bahamas	12.3	10.9	7.8	6.9	9.1	10.8	10.2	10.2	7.6	7.9	12.1
Barbados	17.3	19.6	11.8	9.9	10.3	11.0	9.6	9.1	8.73	7.4	8.1
Belize	n/a	12.5	14.3	9.1	10.0	12.9	11.6	11.0	9.4	8.5	8.2
Grenada	n/a	17.0	15.2	11.5	11.5	11.5	15.0	18.5	–	–	n/a
Jamaica	15.4	16.2	15.5	15.0	14.2	11.4	11.7	11.2	10.4	9.9	10.6
St Lucia	n/a	16.3	21.6	18.9	24.6	21.0	22.3	18.7	15.7	–	n/a
Suriname	n/a	n/a	n/a	14.0	10.0	7.0	8.0	11.0	–	–	n/a
Trinidad and Tobago	15.9	14.7	12.6	10.8	10.4	10.5	8.4	8.0	6.2	5.6	2.5

n/a Not applicable
Source: CDB (various years); Downes (2000).

sector. Note the trends in agriculture, which was once the overwhelmingly dominant employment sector.

Although the Caribbean has benefited from economic growth and now has fairly high human development indicators, it has not drastically reduced unemployment rates, although in comparison with 1991, the unemployment rates in 2007 are considerably lower (see table 1.6). Unemployment rates in 2008, where available, were above 5% and the World Bank (2009) cites that this is on account of a mismatch between declining agricultural opportunities and the inability of the remaining sectors to absorb these workers. It is in these types of environments that workers will tend to turn to the informal sector for employment opportunities.

CARICOM's 2005 *Caribbean Trade and Investment Report* notes that one of the main labour market problems in the region is that of youth unemployment, where: (1) unemployment rates among females are in excess of that of males, and (2) young women in the age group 15–19 years are among the most vulnerable in the labour markets in the region. All things considered, a major challenge for Caribbean economies revolves around job stimulation, which can benefit an economy on two fronts: lowering unemployment rates and helping to reduce poverty levels. Although the region has benefited from higher growth rates, the progress toward reducing poverty has not been pronounced. Indeed, 80% of the Haitian population lives below the poverty line, while over one-third of the populace of many of the other Caribbean islands experience a similar predicament (see table 1.7).

Table 1.7: Population Living Below the National
Poverty Line (%), 2000–2006

Country	% of Population
Antigua and Barbuda	n/a
Barbados	13.9
Belize	33.0
Dominica	39.0
Grenada	32.1
Guyana	35.0
Haiti	80.0
Jamaica	18.7
St Kitts and Nevis	30.5
St Lucia	25.1
St Vincent and the Grenadines	37.5
Trinidad and Tobago	21.2

n/a Not applicable
Source: UN *Human Development Report* (2009); CDB
(various years); CIA, *The World Factbook*;
UNECLAC (various years).

Much of the literature on the informal sector in the Caribbean points
to the significant percentage of women among informal sector workers.
Recent research, for example as published for Jamaica in IDB (2006, 2),
revealed that "women make up a relatively large portion of the informal
sector, 57% compared with 50% in the formal sector of the economy".

1.5. Human Development Indicators

The favourable and generally positive real economic growth experienced
by CARICOM economies has helped to motivate favourable human development indicator trends in the region. Clearly, where data is available,
there have been improvements in these scores, even in Haiti. Specifically,
CARICOM member states are generally medium human development indicator economies. Barbados, the Bahamas, St Kitts and Nevis, Antigua and
Barbuda, and Trinidad and Tobago have human development indicator
scores in excess of 0.8 (see table 1.8).

The UN's 2009 Human Development Report ranked Barbados thirty-
seventh among all economies. These human development indicators are a

Table 1.8: Human Development Index Trends for Listed Caribbean Economies, Various Years

	1980	1985	1990	1995	2000	2005	2010
Very High Human Development Countries							
Barbados	–	–	–	–	–	0.775	0.788
High Human Development Countries							
The Bahamas	–	–	–	–	–	0.776	0.784
Trinidad and Tobago	0.656	0.660	0.660	0.662	0.685	0.713	0.736
Belize	–	–	–	–	–	0.690	0.694
Jamaica	0.589	0.590	0.620	0.648	0.665	0.676	0.688
Medium Human Development Countries							
Suriname	–	–	–	–	–	0.636	0.646
Guyana	0.500	0.483	0.472	0.522	0.552	0.585	0.611
Low Human Development Countries							
Haiti	–	–	–	–	–	0.406	0.404

Source: UN, *Human Development Report* (various years).

reflection of the effectiveness of human development strategies across both the formal and informal economies. The cost of implementing these strategies among participants of the informal economy and their dependents is borne in the most part by the formal economy, as the informal economy generally evades taxation.

1.6. Debt Situation

The tendency for governments to borrow both domestically and abroad comes out of a lack of sufficient local savings. Borrowed resources are sometimes spent inefficiently and ineffectively. Even when the resources are used effectively to expand the country's infrastructure, the returns from these investments are not immediate. Significantly, CARICOM economies have over time been characterized by a large debt burden. In the face of a vastly reduced amount of aid flows, increases in public investment were financed by commercial borrowing in the late 1990s and early 2000s. This type of approach led to a rapid buildup of debt in CARICOM economies to the extent that several member states rank among the most indebted economies in the world. In particular, CARICOM economies, including

Table 1.9: Public Sector Debt in Selected Emerging Market
Countries, Year Ending 2008 (in % of GDP)

Country	% of GDP
St Kitts and Nevis	175
Lebanon	160
Guyana	115
Grenada	110
Jamaica	108
Antigua and Barbuda	108
Barbados	100
Belize	90
Egypt	85
Dominica	85
St Lucia	75
St Vincent and the Grenadines	70
Brazil	68
Uruguay	65
Argentina	58
The Bahamas	53
Philippines	50
Mexico	45
Panama	45
Thailand	43
Turkey	43
Malaysia	40
Indonesia	40
Columbia	40
Haiti	40
Ecuador	40
Trinidad and Tobago	38
South Africa	37
Bulgaria	30
Suriname	20

Source: IMF (2010).

St Kitts and Nevis, Guyana, Grenada, Jamaica, Antigua and Barbuda, and Barbados, have all posted debt ratios in excess of 100% of GDP (see table 1.9).

The existence of relatively high levels of debt servicing among CARICOM countries constrains the availability of funds for capital spending after provisioning for recurrent spending. Limited capital spending constrains job creation and exacerbates the level of unemployment. It is in the context of rising unemployment that interest in the informal economy increases.

1.7. Fiscal Balances

Fiscal deficits can be worsened by debt servicing when there is a lack of proper debt management. Most Caribbean countries are plagued by current fiscal deficits. For instance, the fiscal balance as a percentage of GDP ranged from a deficit of 25% in Guyana to a surplus of 3.1% in Jamaica in the year 1990. By the period 2008–9, Jamaica had the largest region-wide fiscal deficit, averaging 9.2% of GDP, with all other CARICOM economies realizing fiscal deficits, except Belize, Dominica, St Kitts and Nevis, St Lucia, Suriname, and Trinidad and Tobago (see table 1.10).

Fiscal deficits in the Caribbean region may be eased by tightening expenditures by governments in the region. The World Bank (2008) notes that there is also need for improved expenditure allocation, greater transparency in expenditure and a reinforcement of revenue-enhancing measures to widen the fiscal base. The structures of public finances in the Caribbean are manifested in the burgeoning fiscal deficits of member states. The World Bank (2009) also notes that the Caribbean has a remarkable revenue performance. This performance of CARICOM economies is a result of improvements made in their revenue collection efforts, including improving tax rates and introducing value-added tax (VAT) measures where relevant. As the World Bank (2008) states, the Caribbean region's fiscal problem resides with their burgeoning fiscal expenses. Even more, the World Bank (2008, 7) states that "as the scope for increasing revenue may be limited, the issue is thus to what extent the region is able to mobilize additional resources, if only temporarily, in replacement of potential revenue foregone following a trade liberalization policy in the context of the EPA with the European Union".

In this regard, policymakers in the Caribbean find themselves faced with two key policy choices. One of these policy adjustments is to cut fiscal

Table 1.10: Fiscal Balance as a Percentage of GDP in CARICOM Member States, 1990–2009

	1990	1995	1996	1997	1998	1999	2000	2001	2002	2003	2004	2005–2007	2008–2009
Antigua and Barbuda	1.2	-3.3	-1.5	-3.2	-3.7	-4.0	-6.3	-0.4	-11.8	-8.3	-3.0	-7.1	-6.9
The Bahamas	n/a	-1.3	-2.9	-1.0	-1.9	-1.2	1.5	-1.3	-2.1	-1.8	-1.4	-2.2	-2.5
Barbados	-8.4	-0.7	-3.0	-1.1	-0.9	-1.2	-1.5	-3.5	-5.5	-2.2	-2.6	-2.7	-4.6
Belize	0.3	-3.1	-2.3	-2.5	-3.9	-6.6	-9.0	-11.0	-11.4	-9.0	-10.5	-2.5	0.8
Dominica	-10.0	-2.2	-2.0	-5.1	-0.7	-9.8	-6.1	-9.6	-5.1	-4.1	-1.5	1.7	1.5
Grenada	-15.0	0.3	-2.7	-2.2	-3.2	-2.8	-3.4	-8.5	-19.0	-4.8	-2.9	-3.1	-6.0
Guyana	-25.0	-3.3	-1.6	-6.9	-4.6	-2.7	-6.5	-5.6	-3.1	-7.1	-4.8	-11.4	-7.2
Jamaica	3.1	-3.1	-5.6	-6.7	-6.2	-3.7	-1.0	-5.5	-8.3	-5.4	-5.2	-4.5	-9.2
St Kitts and Nevis	-5.3	-5.6	-3.8	-4.1	-7.2	-11.9	-14.2	-11.8	16.6	-8.2	-7.9	-3.0	5.7
St Lucia	1.0	0.9	0.8	-0.8	3.6	3.2	-1.2	-3.4	-2.4	-6.5	-4.7	-4.9	0.6
St Vincent and the Grenadines	-0.8	0.6	0.6	-4.8	-3.7	-1.9	-0.1	-1.6	-2.3	-3.3	-1.4	-3.9	-2.2
Suriname	n/a	4.3	0.8	n/a	n/a	n/a	n/a	n/a	n/a	n/a	n/a	1.9	0.7
Trinidad	-1.2	0.2	0.5	0.1	-2.6	-0.6	-0.5	2.0	-0.2	1.4	2.0	4.4	1.3

n/a Not applicable
Source: CDB Social and Economic Indicators (2006); Cayman Islands Economic and Statistical Office (various years).

expenses to haul in fiscal deficits. Because it is difficult to reduce wages and salaries, the World Bank (2008) points out that the governments of these economies may need to reduce their expenditures on goods and services. The second policy choice comes in the form of the government expanding fiscal deficits by maintaining expenditure at unchanged levels. It seems unlikely that either of these policy choices could bring gain for the Caribbean. Thus, to support trade reforms in the Caribbean, foreign aid could play a key role.

Any reduction in goods and services is likely to negatively affect the formal sector in a direct way. Given that persons employed in the formal sector constitute a significant cohort of the customers of the informal sector, such a reduction in goods and services will also have a negative effect on the informal sector, but in an indirect way.

1.8. Foreign Direct Investment Flows

In 1916, Vladimir Lenin wrote an essay entitled "Imperialism: the Highest Stage of Capitalism". In this piece, Lenin argued that capitalists in the Western world would begin exporting their capital to developing countries to exploit their labour force, and they would then bring the profits back home. He noted that this will be done to forestall any workers' revolt within their own country. Many LDC governments have in the past taken heed of this type of advice and have sought to restrict their inflows of foreign direct investment (FDI).

However, by the early 1980s, as the international debt crisis deepened, most developing countries began to rethink their approach to FDI, as Western banks were not disposed to granting additional loans. In such an environment, developing countries, one might say, decided to woo and fawn upon private foreign capitalists. Barro et al. (1995) has provided sound empirical evidence that may point toward something of a consensus that for any given value of per capita GDP, the amount of economic growth experienced by an economy increases as the amount of human capital, the investment ratio, the quality of the rule of law and the degree of openness of the economy to international markets improve. In this context, wooing FDI becomes especially important to improve on the investment ratio in an economy.

Without a doubt, however, one of the more important contributions made by FDI to the overall process of economic development in the CARICOM region has been its role in financing domestic investment. In

Table 1.11: CARICOM Foreign Direct Investment Inflows, 1990–2008 (US$m)

Country	1980	1990	2000	2001	2002	2003	2004	2005	2006	2007	2008
CARICOM	303.4	395.1	1,661.0	2,007.9	1,750.0	2,256.5	2,343.8	3,027.8	3,713.5	3,868.0	3,208.3
Antigua and Barbuda	19.6	60.6	43.1	98.5	65.9	166.3	80.4	221.0	358.8	356.2	253.4
The Bahamas	4.1	−17.3	250.3	102.4	152.8	190.2	273.6	563.4	706.4	713.3	839.0
Barbados	2.8	11.2	19.4	18.6	17.4	58.3	−12.1	62.0	104.8	233.2	n/a
Belize	n/a	17.2	23.3	61.2	25.4	−10.9	111.5	126.9	108.8	140.4	190.1
Dominica	n/a	12.9	17.6	17.1	20.1	31.5	26.2	19.2	25.9	53.2	52.1
Grenada	n/a	12.9	37.4	58.8	54.5	89.2	65.0	70.2	89.8	174.2	161.2
Guyana	0.6	7.9	67.1	56.0	43.6	26.1	30.0	76.8	102.4	152.4	168.0
Haiti	13.0	8.0	13.3	4.4	5.7	13.8	5.9	26.0	160.6	74.5	29.8
Jamaica	27.7	137.9	468.3	613.9	480.8	720.7	601.6	682.5	882.2	866.5	1,436.6
Montserrat	n/a	10.0	2.0	1.0	1.0	2.0	3.0	1.0	1.0	n/a	n/a
St Kitts and Nevis	1.0	48.8	96.2	88.2	79.8	75.6	55.8	93.0	110.4	157.5	87.7
St Lucia	30.9	44.8	53.8	58.8	51.9	106.4	76.5	78.2	233.9	253.4	104.8
St Vincent and the Grenadines	1.1	7.7	37.7	21.0	34.1	55.2	65.7	40.1	109.1	109.8	119.3
Suriname	18.1	−76.8	−148.0	−26.8	−73.6	−76.1	−37.3	27.9	−163.4	−246.7	−233.6
Trinidad and Tobago	184.5	109.4	679.5	834.9	790.7	808.3	998.1	939.7	882.7	830.0	n/a

n/a Not applicable
Source: World Bank (various years).

general, CARICOM economies have tended to depend on FDI flows to reduce their two main financing gaps: the foreign exchange gap and the savings/investment gap. The amount of FDI flowing into the CARICOM sphere has also grown considerably since 1980 (see table 1.11). CARICOM received US$3,208.3 million in 2008 compared to US$303.4 million in 1980. To bolster its efforts, Caribbean economies would need to complement their trade policy with an even more aggressive policy to woo FDI. This is especially so in the medium term where, in the context of a global economic recession, FDI inflows to all economies are likely to fall.

FDI inflows are usually associated with capital spending, which allows for increases in employment in the formal sector, at least in the short term. A fall in FDI inflows results in a reduction in employment opportunities in the formal sector and increased participation in the informal sector.

1.9. Remittance Flows to the Caribbean

One of the constraints on CARICOM economic development is a shortage of capital. In this regard, worker remittances represent an important source of foreign exchange. At the macroeconomic level, the flow of remittances can directly ease the strain on the balance of payments when remittance flows are in hard foreign currencies, or indirectly by reducing the imports of capital goods when the inflows of remittances are of that nature. Typically, all CARICOM countries have at best fledgling capital sectors and as a consequence, import most of their capital requirements. In this sense, the flow of remittances can play an important role in terms of the financing of the developmental process.

Many poor people are unable to acquire loans from traditional financial institutions. For them, remittances can provide the relevant financial capital for middle- and lower-middle-income households to start up their productive activities. Remittances can be in the form of cash, capital goods, raw materials and inventory. Such remittance flows can then be used for industrial development and small business creation, which can increase the level of investment and by extension the capital stock of the country. Since not every household is interested in investing, remittances can provide a valuable source of savings (which can be channelled into productive investments through the operation of financial intermediaries) and hence, funds for investment, capital formation and development.[1]

It may be argued that remittances can be treated as an injection into the circular flow of income. Net remittances (remittance inflows minus outflows) are what really matters, and *ceteris paribus,* an increase in net real remittance, expands economic activity working through the multiplier. Negative net real remittance has the opposite effect, working through the demultiplier).[2]

Guyana, Haiti and Jamaica are the three member states of CARICOM that receive high levels of remittances. Among these three, Jamaica had the highest level of remittance flows peaking at US$2.22 billion in 2008 (IDB 2009). In the Organisation of Eastern Caribbean States (OECS), the three top recipients of remittances are Grenada, St Kitts and Nevis, and St Lucia, shown in table 1.12.

Developing countries incur many benefits from remittance inflows. One major benefit is that an investment of remittances can have a reducing effect on poverty at the household level by increasing the accumulation of capital within a country. This impact was noted by McCormick and Wahba (2003) in their study on remittances and poverty in Uganda, which showed that poverty levels fell by 11%. In their study focusing on Bangladesh and Ghana, Dillip and Mohapatra (2009) noted that poverty levels fell by 6% and 5% respectively. In his study of remittances and poverty in Jamaica, Alleyne (2007) found that remittances reduced the poverty headcount by 3.4%, while the poverty gap declined by 8.33%.

In a comparative survey of remittances in Trinidad and Tobago and St Lucia, Hosein et al. (2010) found that while 2% and 5% of the recipients of remittances in Trinidad and Tobago and St Lucia respectively were own-ers of small businesses, 6% and 5% respectively of recipients spent their cash remittances on small businesses in Trinidad and Tobago and St Lucia. (Most small businesses in the Caribbean operate within the informal sec-tor.) They also found that 27% and 11% respectively of the recipients used their cash remittances for home renovations in Trinidad and Tobago and St Lucia. In the Caribbean, home renovations very often involve the employ-ment of craftsmen such as masons and carpenters and a range of small contractors, most of whom operate within the informal sector. Note that the largest share of remittances in both countries was used for current con-sumption, health care expenses and education expenses, and the purchase of investment products, life insurance products, real estate and machinery. Almost all of these uses operate through the formal sector. However, over the years, migrants from the Caribbean have been engaging in a form of non-cash remittance referred to as the barrel trade. Basically, this involves members of the Caribbean diaspora annually sending millions of dollars' worth of goods in barrels or packages or as cargo to their friends and family members in the home country. Barrels are sent to the Caribbean for

Table 1.12: Workers' Remittances and Compensation of Employees (Current US$) for Caribbean Countries

Country	1995	1996	1997	1998	1999	2000	2001	2002	2003	2004	2005	2006	2007	2008
Antigua and Barbuda	3	3	6	12	12	10	16	6	8.55	20.9	22	23	23.5	26
Barbados	53	60	69	76	87	102	118	109	113	109	140	140	140	168
Dominica	3	3	2	3	3	3	4	4	4	23.2	25	25.4	26	30
Guyana	2	15	15	15	20	27	22	51	99	153	201	218	278	278
Haiti	109	152	256	327	422	578	624	676	811	932	985	1,063	1,222	1,300
Grenada	18	20	20	20	21	22	22	23	23	72.2	51.6	53.9	55.4	64
Belize	14	17	23	23	21	22	30	29	34	35	46.1	65.5	74.8	78.1
Jamaica	653	714	730	758	790	892	1,058	1,261	1,399	1,623	1,784	1,946	2,144	2,220
St Kitts and Nevis	2	2	3	4	4	4	4	3	3	31.3	33.5	36.2	37.3	37.3
St Lucia	2	2	2	3	3	3	2	2	2	28.7	29.5	30.3	31.1	31.1
St Vincent and the Grenadines	2	2	2	3	3	3	3	4	3.42	25.5	26.5	29.7	30.5	30.5
Trinidad and Tobago	32	28	30	45	54	38	41	79	87	86.9	92.4	91.2	109	109

Source: World Bank, *World Development Indicators* (2009).

the purpose of home consumption, as well as for informal trade at the level of the small businesses in the home country. A percentage of the money made from such sales is sometimes repatriated to the migrant for the purchase of more of these items. These barrels of goods form part of informal trade from the metropolitan countries to the Caribbean.

1.10. International Reserves and Public Debt as a Proportion of GDP

In terms of international reserves, Trinidad and Tobago, Montserrat, Guyana, and Barbados had reserves in 2008 that were greater than 20% of GDP. All other CARICOM countries shown in the table 1.13 had reserves of less than 20% of GDP.

A combined high external debt and a low level of international reserves render these CARICOM economies externally vulnerable. One immediate link is that of monetary policy within the economies. These policies not only impact trade transactions by the formal sector within these economies, but can create an environment in which the underground trade in

Table 1.13: Public Debt and International Reserves, 2008

Country	Public Debt (% of GDP)	International Reserves % of GDP
Antigua and Barbuda	89.7	13.0
The Bahamas	37.4	n/a
Barbados	108.8	21.3
Belize	82.7	12.4
Dominica	101.2	16.0
Grenada	110.6	16.0
Guyana	95.5	26.9
Jamaica	109.5	13.1
Montserrat	7.5	26.0
St Kitts and Nevis	173.7	16.0
St Lucia	70.0	13.0
St Vincent and the Grenadines	69.9	13.0
Suriname	32.9	16.2
Trinidad and Tobago	28.0	35.3

Source: UNECLAC (various years).

foreign currency flourishes. Such trade is considered to form part of the informal sector. ICIs generally require foreign currency for their trade and can resort to the underground foreign currency market to meet their needs.

1.11. Intra-regional Trade Performance of CARICOM

CARICOM[3] was formed after several failed attempts of economic integration in the region.[4] The early economic integration efforts in the region were strongly influenced by the work of Lewis (1950) who argued the case for rapid industrialization of the West Indies within a regional integration framework in his seminal paper "Industrialization of the British West Indies". This argument was based on the premise that Caribbean economies have peculiar features that distinguish them from developed economies in the world trading system.

CARICOM was established in 1973, succeeding the Caribbean Free Trade Association, which was formed in the mid-1960s by twelve English-speaking countries with a population of 4.6 million. Given the small size of the individual units, CARICOM was seen not only as a trading arrangement, but also as a mechanism to foster cooperation in a number of areas, including the coordination of foreign policies. Even though it was believed that CARICOM would bring additional development opportunities, the initiative has not generated the response originally expected. Member states have been slow not only to implement decisions, but also to actively compete in many areas, leading to wastage of resources. While the deepening process has been slow, the small size of the market itself has continually raised questions about the need to widen the movement to provide a larger space and take advantage of existing technologies.

From table 1.14, observe that there was an increase in the level of intra-regional exports from US$156.1 million in 1973 to US$2,205 million in 2008, an increase of 1,313%. Total export of CARICOM economies increased from US$1,544.3 million in 1973 to US$22,070 million in 2008, an increase of 1,329%. As a proportion of total exports, CARICOM's intra-regional exports declined marginally from 10.1% in 1973 to 10% in 2008, although in 1998 it had climbed to 18%. The average share of intra-CARICOM exports in total exports for the 1990s was 15%, and for the new century thus far is 15.4%.

One has to be careful, however, in reading too much into these results. Specifically, the share of intra-regional exports of Standard International Trade Classification (SITC) 3[5] in total intra-regional exports increased

Table 1.14: CARICOM Intra-Regional Trade (US$m), 1973–2008

	Intra-regional Exports	Total Exports	Intra-Regional Exports/Total Exports %	Intra-regional Exports of SITC 3/Intra-regional Exports %	Crude Oil Prices US$ WTI	Intra-regional Imports	Total Imports	Intra-Regional Imports/Total Imports %
1973	156.1	1,544.3	10.1	28.8	2.7	150.2	2,118.7	7.10
1974	283.0	4,928.4	5.7	45.8	9.8	302.7	5,604.3	5.40
1975	320.3	5,742.5	5.6	41.9	10.7	288.7	6,220.4	4.60
1976	337.3	6,384.2	5.3	40.9	11.5	273.0	6,965.8	3.90
1977	347.4	3,583.5	9.7	45.1	12.4	265.3	3,694.6	7.20
1978	367.7	3,536.7	10.4	41.7	12.7	292.7	3,968.3	7.40
1979	463.9	4,172.3	11.1	50.5	17.3	343.6	4,371.8	7.90
1980	599.6	10,447.6	5.7	60.9	28.7	418.7	12,844.9	3.30
1981	661.8	11,740.9	5.6	53.7	32.5	571.0	13,665.7	4.20
1982	573.3	8,769.4	6.5	55.6	33.5	409.1	12,276.0	3.30
1983	533.2	7,574.5	7.0	48.0	29.3	387.5	9,648.8	4.00
1984	403.2	6,744.4	6.0	62.3	28.5	267.6	8,013.8	3.30
1985	423.6	5,947.3	7.1	69.2	28.0	307.3	6,733.6	4.60
1986	279.4	5,241.9	5.3	40.4	15.0	227.4	6,698.7	3.40
1987	321.9	5,333.7	6.0	38.4	17.3	266.2	6,559.2	4.10
1988	367.2	5,463.0	6.7	29.2	17.0	326.8	6,360.6	5.10
1989	492.9	3,739.1	13.2	27.4	19.6	408.5	4,902.0	8.30

1990	506.7	4,396.6	11.5	31.5	24.1	444.4	5,056.5	8.80
1991	442.8	4,078.4	10.9	26.9	21.6	453.7	5,438.0	8.30
1992	425.0	3,764.6	11.3	28.7	20.6	423.8	5,287.0	8.00
1993	567.0	3,366.1	16.8	27.3	18.5	465.9	5,276.9	8.80
1994	599.2	4,268.4	14.0	30.2	17.1	572.9	5,545.8	10.30
1995	783.0	5,222.4	15.0	35.1	18.4	670.5	8,165.0	8.20
1996	863.7	5,080.6	17.0	37.0	20.2	741.3	7,401.7	10.00
1997	952.9	5,803.3	16.4	33.4	20.4	945.2	11,167.2	8.50
1998	960.4	5,308.1	18.1	33.1	14.4	917.9	10,933.5	8.40
1999	1,127.0	5,932.4	19.0	37.2	19.2	1,256.0	11,155.1	11.30
2000	1,318.2	7,778.0	16.9	46.9	30.2	1,285.6	12,661.9	10.20
2001	1,387.5	8,152.5	17.0	45.1	28.6	1,229.0	12,905.1	9.50
2002	1,154.7	6,750.0	17.1	36.4	25.9	1,083.4	12,665.0	8.60
2003	1,412.2	8,458.8	16.7	48.2	31.7	1,468.9	13,656.0	10.80
2004	1,285.3	10,214.7	12.6	37.7	41.5	1,439.5	15,015.0	9.60
2005	2,485.3	13,751.0	18.1	62.5	56.5	2,297.8	19,073.5	12.00
2006	2,317.0	17,298.0	13.4	65.5	66.0	2,314.0	18,030.0	12.83
2007	2,803.0	16,647.0	16.8	68.6	72.0	2,273.0	21,023.0	10.81
2008	2,205.0	22,070.0	10.0	56.6	99.6	2,556.0	24,778.0	10.32
Average 1990s	722.8	4,722.1	15.0	32.0	19.5	689.2	7,542.7	9.10
Average 2000–2008	1,818.7	12,346.7	15.4	51.9	50.2	1,771.9	16,645.3	10.50

Source: UNCOMTRADE (various years).

Table 1.15: Intra-CARICOM Trade as a
Percentage of Total Trade for
the Grouping of all CARICOM
Countries

1980	4.37
1981	4.85
1982	4.67
1983	5.35
1984	4.55
1985	5.76
1986	4.24
1987	4.94
1988	5.87
1989	10.43
1990	10.06
1991	9.42
1992	9.38
1993	11.95
1994	11.94
1995	10.86
1996	12.86
1997	11.18
1998	11.56
1999	13.95
2000	12.74
2001	12.43
2002	11.53
2003	13.03
2004	10.80
2005	14.57
2006	13.11
2007	13.48
2008	10.61

Source: www.CARICOMstats.org.

from 28.8% in 1973 to 56.6% in 2008. The average share of total intra-CARICOM exports accounted for by exports of petroleum-based products averaged 32.04% in the 1990s and 51.9% for the first decade of the twenty-first century. This rapid increase in the share of SITC 3 in total intra-CARICOM exports was motivated in part by the rapid increase in oil prices that occurred toward the end of the data period. Specifically, the intra-regional imports of oil increased from US$150.2 million in 1973 to US$2,556 million in 2008, an increase of 1,602%. On average and in nominal dollar terms, the average level of imports in the 1990s was US$689.2 million, compared to US$1,771.9 million for the 2000s thus far. As a proportion of total imports, however, intra-regional imports have not increased considerably, moving from 7.1% in 1973 to 10.3% in 2008. The average value of this variable for the 1990s was 9.1% as compared to 10.2% for the new century thus far.

Overall, the share of CARICOM's intra-regional trade as a proportion of its total trade has not improved as the region would have liked (see table 1.15). In 2008, intra-CARICOM trade accounted for 10.61% of total CARICOM trade compared to 12.74% in 2000, 10.1% in 1990 or 4.37% in 1980.

As participants in the informal sector, ICIs are visible in terms of their involvement in intra-regional trade. A known feature of informal commercial importing is the undervaluation of a significant percentage of the invoices presented to customs across the region. Accordingly, the data in tables 1.17 and 1.18 do not fully capture the value of related activities of the informal sector.

1.12. Trade Intensity Indices for CARICOM Countries[6]

A common theme emanates from the trade intensity indices for the Caribbean countries listed in table 1.16. Basically, the stated economies engage in a high degree of bilateral trade intensity with the other listed CARICOM member states, but in a much lower degree of trade intensity with the United States, Canada and the United Kingdom. The United States' trade intensity is on average in excess of unity with all of the listed CARICOM economies, while the United Kingdom's bilateral trade intensity with the relevant CARICOM member states has been declining over time (see table 1.16).

The intensity of trade, as highlighted in table 1.16, may be assumed to be distributed across both formal and informal lines. As a result, where there is a high degree of trade intensity in formal lines, one can assume it also exists in the informal sector.

Table 1.16: Trade Intensity of Various CARICOM Member States

Barbados with Various Trade Partners

	1975	1980	1985	1990	1995	2000	2005	2006
The Bahamas	0.48	0.58	1.79		20.66	24.90	34.45	28.63
Belize	0.13	2.15	0.80	59.29	104.62	143.33	110.72	77.53
Guyana	37.44	n/a	n/a	n/a	n/a	291.87	230.29	194.70
Jamaica	28.71	52.32	4.41	104.11	128.87	141.19	122.37	112.40
St Lucia	313.02	451.64	135.91	555.08	797.47	957.05	1,308.83	1,027.57
Suriname	n/a	n/a	n/a	1.13	6.89	154.92	91.45	72.30
Trinidad and Tobago	30.80	73.14	14.63	224.25	257.41	256.40	197.22	202.02
United States	1.01	1.36	2.86	0.84	1.01	0.81	0.81	1.24
United Kingdom	4.16	1.13	1.03	2.70	3.05	2.49	1.77	1.46
Canada	1.41	1.40	0.36	0.83	1.57	0.55	0.60	0.60

Trinidad and Tobago with Various Trade Partners

	1975	1980	1985	1990	1995	2000	2005	2006
The Bahamas	0.62	2.04	2.21	n/a	n/a	24.23	40.49	8.34
Barbados	44.77	59.20	86.69	167.80	219.88	267.57	268.07	243.05
Belize	2.26	0.60	3.76	12.50	35.92	21.33	19.69	6.79
Guyana	74.01	n/a	n/a	235.60	231.43	255.01	380.60	320.36
Jamaica	22.33	23.86	28.40	46.58	147.89	157.23	158.50	135.68
St Lucia	61.57	60.80	90.96	155.65	231.46	246.96	185.36	165.44
Suriname	n/a	n/a	n/a	146.30	167.74	309.97	231.69	276.90
United States	3.54	2.89	3.11	3.64	2.72	2.38	3.52	3.60
United Kingdom	0.59	0.24	0.63	0.42	0.46	0.32	0.15	0.16
Canada	0.28	0.22	0.36	0.39	0.56	0.35	0.36	0.42

Jamaica with Various Trade Partners

	1975	1980	1985	1990	1995	2000	2005	2006
The Bahamas	0.40	0.38	8.57	n/a	1.96	5.32	4.03	3.62
Barbados	26.72	35.65	62.96	65.00	41.23	32.94	39.52	39.14
Belize	25.80	21.09	44.41	118.70	65.42	38.79	48.07	34.12
Guyana	23.55	n/a	n/a	n/a	26.74	25.43	22.56	24.97
St Lucia	21.31	31.80	34.88	30.33	41.82	34.60	55.06	37.93
Suriname	n/a	n/a	n/a	18.12	8.65	9.59	6.03	8.76

	1975	1980	1985	1990	1995	2000	2005	2006
Trinidad and Tobago	10.77	20.54	31.98	73.19	40.10	31.84	20.05	16.65
United States	1.43	1.95	1.69	1.91	2.21	2.00	1.54	1.89
United Kingdom	3.53	2.98	2.76	2.24	2.51	2.16	2.16	2.01
Canada	0.86	1.22	3.90	3.22	2.76	2.74	6.45	5.32

St Lucia with Various Trade Partners

	1975	1980	1985	1990	1995	2000	2005	2006
The Bahamas	n/a	n/a	n/a	n/a	n/a	0.1	22.5	1.0
Barbados	302.2	153.7	150.6	143.6	161.7	610.7	624.7	478.9
Belize	0	0	0	13.1	29.8	48.8	63.5	27.3
Guyana	12.1	n/a	n/a	n/a	n/a	88.6	187.8	70.7
Jamaica	70.6	140.9	6.9	42.7	4.5	0.5	1.8	37.8
Suriname	n/a	n/a	n/a	n/a	0.6	24.7	36.1	29.3
Trinidad and Tobago	28.7	35	28.1	44.1	83.7	31.9	410.1	550.7
United States	n/a	n/a	0.7	1.4	1.6	0.9	0.8	1.3
United Kingdom	0.6	0.2	0.6	0.4	0.5	0.3	0.2	0.2
Canada	0.2	0.1	0	0.1	0.3	0.2	0.1	0.0

n/a Not applicable
Source: UNCOMTRADE (various years).

1.13. Specialization Indices for CARICOM Countries

CARICOM economies inherited narrow production structures from their colonial heritage. These economies were captive producers and the production structures of these economies were orchestrated to provide a complementary source of output to the economies of the metropolis. Founded on FDI, production platforms in the Caribbean were engaged for sugar and banana cultivation. At later points in their development, other forms of productive activities like cocoa, oil, bauxite and rice emerged in the Caribbean. In this type of environment, the trading regimes of the Caribbean did not get an appropriate subset of opportunities to diversify (see table 1.17). This no doubt inhibited their capacity to become globally competitive. In addition, this feature of their trading regimes reared its ugly head as various preferential packages on which these economies were built came tumbling down.

The economies of countries like Belize, Suriname, St Lucia, St Vincent and the Grenadines, and Dominica grew in the 1980s from banana exports under the African, Caribbean and Pacific Group of States (ACP), but contracted significantly in the 1990s as a result of a series of World Trade Organization (WTO) decisions that targeted the banana industry in these countries. Production levels in Dominica, for example, fell from some 65,000 tonnes in 1990 to some 16,000 tonnes in 2006, and consequently could no longer support the participation of a significant number of persons in the banana industry. Government revenues fell significantly and so too did the size of trade within the formal sector. Initially, as export levels fell, more fruit became available for export by the informal sector by ICIs. Unfortunately, the limited capacity of ICIs in the area of marketing and shipping constrained their ability to fully take advantage of increased availability of fruit for export. As banana farmers abandoned the industry, the amount of fruit for export by the informal sector fell and the level of profitability of the ICIs also fell, resulting in a reduction in the number of persons involved in the ICI trade.

Table 1.17 shows that in terms of a proportion of total exports, a few commodities account for a significant share of total exports in most Caribbean economies. Yeats (1998) has argued that economies with a heavy degree of export specialization may experience a greater degree of

Table 1.17: Exports of Commodities, 2002–2006 (% of Total Exports)

Country	% of Total Exports
The Bahamas (non-crude oil)	25.7
Barbados (oil, sugar)	30.0
Belize (oil, sugar, banana and plantain)	33.2
Guyana (aluminum ore, sugar, rice)	38.8
Jamaica (non-crude oil, aluminum oxide/hydroxide, aluminum ore, sugar)	75.0
Suriname (oil, aluminum oxide/hydroxide, rice, banana and plantain)	62.1
Trinidad and Tobago (oil)	66.8
Dominica (banana and plantain)	20.7
St Lucia (banana and plantain)	25.4
St Vincent and the Grenadines (banana and plantain)	35.2

Source: UNECLAC (2009).

export revenue volatility, and this could potentially undermine any financial commitments necessary for the functioning of the various preferential trading agreements in which they may participate.

Table 1.18 indicates that the listed CARICOM economies had distinctly higher levels of extra-regional specialization indices when compared to their specialization indices with the internal market.[7] The exception, based on the period averages at the end of table 1.18, are the Bahamas, Belize and Guyana. Intra-regionally, only three economies had export specialization for which the general trend was positive: Dominica, Grenada, and Trinidad and Tobago. Most of the countries listed in the table had extra-regional export specialization patterns that tended to decrease over the listed time period (with the exception of St Kitts, Suriname, and Trinidad and Tobago), indicating the export of a more diversified export portfolio of goods extra regionally.

1.14. CARICOM Bilateral Trade Agreements

In terms of a trade strategy, CARICOM has tried to adopt an approach that involves a series of widening concentric circles to increase the degree of competition to which its membership is exposed. The West Indian Commission articulated this point of view early on as it chose to remain as a separate economic integration entity while it collectively negotiated with large Caribbean and Latin American countries. The opinion at the time was rather than let the bigger Caribbean partners join the regional integration movement as members, they should be engaged via trade and economic cooperation agreements so that the small and fragile economies of the membership would not be overly exposed. Gonzáles(2002) noted that from the perspective of the West Indian Commission, the first concentric circle was CARICOM itself, comprised of the smaller nation states in the Caribbean.

Table 1.19 illustrates the correlation between the intra-CARICOM trading shares of CARICOM economies and their real GDP for the same time period. In none of the listed cases was the correlation very positive, and in several cases it was negative. It is on this type of basis that CARICOM was seen as failing and the thrust toward the CARICOM Single Market and Economy (CSME) was founded. It was also on this basis that a pronounced effort was made for greater trading ties with a variety of extra-regional trading partners.

Over the last two decades in particular, CARICOM trading arrangements have been based on reciprocating terms, the most recent of which

Table 1.18: Specialization Indices of Various CARICOM Member States Intra-Regional Specialization

	ANT	BAH	BRB	BLZ	DOM	GRD	GUY	HTI	JAM	MONT	KNA	LCA	VCT	SUR	TTO
1975	0.93	0.20	0.43						0.18			0.31			0.40
1980		0.50	0.20	0.70	0.36	0.00			0.17			0.17	0.38		0.65
1985		0.70	0.53	0.90	0.45	1.00			0.18			0.31			0.73
1990			0.23	0.80	0.00	0.00		0.00	0.16			0.23		0.90	0.27
1995		0.60	0.21	0.80	0.45	0.00		1.00	0.17		0.39	0.33	0.61	0.80	0.28
2000	0.36	0.40	0.19	1.00	0.91	0.00	0.34		0.22	0.31	0.23	0.53	0.49	0.20	0.42
2001		0.40	0.20	0.50	0.81	0.00	0.47		0.27	0.26	0.32	0.47	0.58	0.20	0.38
2002		0.40	0.21	0.50	0.56	0.00	0.48		0.22	0.45	0.31	0.22	0.56	0.20	0.30
2003		0.30	0.19	0.90	0.69	0.00	0.42		0.25	0.59	0.24	0.23	0.49	0.20	0.43
2004		0.20	0.18	0.90	0.69	0.00	0.57		0.22	0.53	0.33	0.21	0.51	0.20	0.32
2005	0.42	0.80	0.16	0.90	0.53	0.00	0.50		0.21	0.39	0.38	0.23	0.48	0.30	0.57
2006		0.30	0.16	0.90	0.83	0.00	0.45		0.23	0.44	0.48	0.27	0.51		0.61
Avg	0.41	0.40	0.24	0.80	0.57	0.00	0.81	0.00	0.21	0.38	0.35	0.29	0.49	0.40	0.45

Extra-regional Specialization

	ANT	BAH	BRB	BLZ	DOM	GRD	GUY	HTI	JAM	MONT	KNA	LCA	VCT	SUR	TTO
1975	0.86	0.90	0.43	0.50			0.49	0.00	0.36	0.49		0.82			0.82
1980		0.90	0.27	0.50		1.00			0.42			0.28	0.89		0.89
1985		0.80	0.39	0.60	0.74	1.00			0.25			0.57			0.63
1990			0.25	0.70	0.84	1.00		0.00	0.39			0.54		0.60	0.53
1995		0.30	0.19	0.60	0.98	1.00		0.00	0.31		0.40	0.45	0.68	0.50	0.34
2000	0.45	0.20	0.19	0.70	0.35	1.00	0.42		0.40	0.40	0.53	0.53	0.60	0.90	0.49
2001		0.20	0.18	0.50	0.37	0.00	0.35		0.40	0.30	0.51	0.51	0.60	0.90	0.31
2002		0.20	0.15	0.70	0.60	1.00	0.35		0.42	0.36	0.52	0.40	0.79	0.90	0.45
2003		0.20	0.21	0.70	0.45	0.00	0.39		0.45	0.35	0.58	0.33	0.53	0.90	0.44
2004		0.20	0.21	0.70	0.41	1.00	0.33		0.46	0.70	0.52	0.28	0.71	0.90	0.46
2005	0.57	0.40	0.25	0.70	0.48	1.00	0.38		0.46	0.36	0.86	0.36	0.63	0.90	0.53
2006	0.45	0.30	0.22	0.50	0.35	0.00	0.33		0.37	0.36	0.86	0.29	0.63	0.90	0.61
Avg	0.58	0.40	0.24	0.60	0.57	1.00	0.38	0.00	0.39	0.30	0.62	0.45	0.61	0.70	0.54

Note: Corresponding country names are as follows: Antigua, Bahamas, Barbados, Belize, Dominica, Grenada, Guyana, Haiti, Jamaica, Montserrat, St Kitts–Nevis, St Lucia, St Vincent, Suriname, Trinidad and Tobago
Source: Computed from UNCOMTRADE.

was the recently concluded Regional Economic Partnership Agreement. Some of the other bilateral trading agreements that CARICOM as a body has entered into and the associated utilization rates are outlined in figure 1.1. None of these appear particularly welcoming.

Table 1.19: Correlation between the Intra-CARICOM Trade Performance and Real GDP Growth Performance of Various CARICOM Member States, 1990–2008

	Trinidad and Tobago Real GDP Growth %	Trinidad and Tobago Intra-regional Exports as a % of Total Exports	Barbados Real GDP Growth %	Barbados Intra-CARICOM Export as a % of Total Exports	Jamaica Real GDP Growth	Jamaica Intra-CARICOM Export as a % of Total Exports	Real GDP Growth %	Guyana Intra-CARICOM Export as a % of Total Exports	St Lucia Real GDP Growth %	St Lucia Intra-CARICOM Export as a % of Total Exports
1990	1.5	12.7	-4.8	30.7	-4.2	6.1	-2.4	7.3	23.5	17.1
1991	2.7	20.0	-2.9	32.7	-4.8	5.5	5.7	6.3	2.7	17.5
1992	-1.7	13.4	-5.0	34.3	-2.0	5.7	7.5	6.1	7.0	12.6
1993	-1.5	19.8	1.0	38.8	-3.2	5.6	7.8	5.8	2.6	17.4
1994	3.6	19.5	4.0	35.5	-2.7	4.9	8.1	6.3	1.4	15.4
1995	4.0	23.8	1.5	37.4	-4.6	4.1	4.6	7.9	3.3	16.0
1996	3.8	24.4	1.8	35.8	-2.3	3.8	7.5	8.9	1.4	13.4
1997	2.8	25.4	6.4	35.4	0	3.3	5.8	10.6	0.6	16.1
1998	7.8	31.5	4.1	43.3	9.3	3.3	-2.1	10.1	4.7	19.5
1999	4.4	26.3	2.6	46.5	-0.9	3.4	2.5	11.3	2.9	22.0
2000	7.3	22.6	2.3	43.2	-0.8	3.7	-1.8	13.5	0.1	28.0
2001	4.2	23.6	-2.1	41.5	-1.5	4.1	1.8	14.7	-4.3	25.2
2002	7.9	20.7	-2.1	46.2	-1.1	4.4	0.6	20.3	0.4	37.1
2003	14.4	19.4	2.0	40.2	2.3	4.3	-0.7	18.8	3.1	43.6
2004	8.0	13.1	4.8	37.8	1.0	3.7	1.6	20.5	4.5	35.6
2005	5.4	20.6	4.1	38.7	1.4	3.1	-2.0	19.2	3.8	53.3
2006	13.3	14.0	3.9	46.7	2.7	2.0	5.1	15.9	4.0	38.5
2007	5.5	18.4	3.4	42.1	1.4	2.2	5.4	18.1	0.8	47.2
2008	3.5	9.5	2.9	67.7	-1.3	2.0	3.0	18.3	0.5	3.5
Correlation	0.06		0.28		-0.56		-0.48		-0.20	

Source: www.CARICOMstats.org.

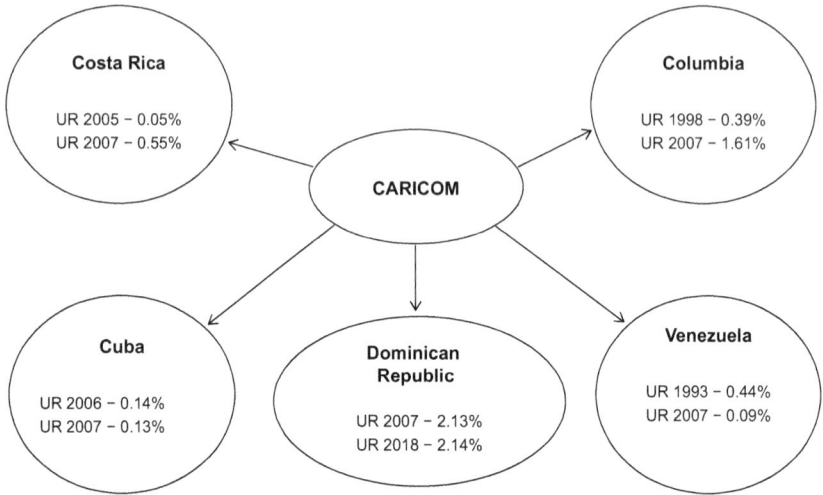

Figure 1.1 The utilization rate (UR) of CARICOM with some of the bilateral trade agreements

The CSME was formally established in 1992 for the integration of all CARICOM member states into a single economic space. The agreement that established the CSME identified it as the predominant vessel for the deepening of the regional integration movement, and sets out the following as its main objectives (CARICOM 2010):

- The free movement of labour – workers move freely from island to island, especially graduates from the University of the West Indies.
- The establishment of a common external tariff – a common rate of duty for goods from countries outside of CARICOM member states.
- The gelling of economic policy, in particular fiscal and monetary policies – coordinating both exchange rates and interest rates within the region and agreeing on targets for budgetary deficits by member states.
- The formation of a common currency – it is hoped that with time, a common Caribbean currency can be established that would facilitate transactions in the region.

The CSME's mandate is to help facilitate the attainment of "sustained economic development, international competitiveness, coordinated economic and foreign policies, functional cooperation and enhanced trade and economic relations with other countries" (CARICOM 2009, 1). Accordingly, the CSME was conceptualized on five key pillars (CARICOM 2010):

1. the provision for the free movement of capital
2. the provision for the free movement of goods, services and people within the CSME
3. the establishment of common trade and economic policies
4. the harmonization of economic, fiscal and monetary policies
5. a common currency

Conceptually, the CSME was designed to operate within the framework of nine protocols, as shown in table 1.20. All nine protocols were incorporated as chapters within the revised treaty. The CSME Unit (2005) lists the proposed benefits of these protocols as follows:

- access to a larger regional market
- expansion of investment opportunities in the region for both regional investors and foreign investors
- creation of the opportunity for some services at the regional level;
- provision of the opportunities to operate and display their services within the region
- provision of the opportunity for graduates of the University of the West Indies to gain employment in any CARICOM member state of their choice
- improvement of the entity's negotiating power

Table 1.20: The Nine Protocols of the CSME

Protocol Number	Aspect(s) addressed by the Protocol
I	The organs, institutions and procedures of the community
II	The right of establishment; the right to provide services and the right to move capital by any CARICOM national in the community, which has been defined to include the single market and economy
III	The community's industrial policy
IV	Trade liberalization
V	The community's agricultural policy
VI	The community's transport policy
VII	Disadvantaged countries, regions and sectors
VIII	Dispute settlement
IX	Rules of competition

Source: CSME Unit (2005).

Three of the five pillars of the CSME deserve further mention in the context of facilitating the informal sector:

1. Free intra-regional movement of capital: This involves the movement of capital from island to island. The free intra-regional movement of capital is to be facilitated through a number of interventions, including the removal of foreign exchange control, intra-CARICOM currency convertibility and over time, the development of a stock exchange.

   As of March 2010, only three member states of CARICOM had not issued common intra-CARICOM passports: Bahamas, Montserrat and Haiti. One of the main benefits of the CARICOM passport is that it sends a strong signaling effect that CARICOM nationals are members not only of a specific country, but also of the community.

2. Free movement of skilled nationals: The free movement of skills entails the removal of the need for work permits and residency. This is explicitly stated in the Revised Treaty of Chaguaramas in article 45, which states: "Member States commit themselves to the goal of free movement of their nationals within the community" (Revised Treaty of Chaguaramas, 30). The Conference of the Heads of Government in the Caribbean agreed to implement the free movement of labour on a phased basis beginning with categories that were granted the right to seek employment or to engage in gainful employment, either as wage earner or non-wage earner. The free movement of labour within the Caribbean is therefore linked to some kind of economic activity.

   The Grand Anse Declaration in 1989 established the Free Movement of Skills initiative. This policy, while originally separate, was also linked to the Protocol II of the revised Treaty of Chaguaramas. The agreed CARICOM policy, called the Caribbean Community (CARICOM) Free Movement of Persons Act, is now enacted as legislation in all CSME member states. This policy currently caters to the free movement of skilled labour, and it is planned that its coverage will be extended to provide for the free movement of all categories of labour.

   In July 1995 at the CARICOM Heads of Government meeting, the agreement was made that CARICOM nationals who were university graduates should be allowed to move freely in the region for work-related purposes without the need for work permits. To operationalize this agreement, several legal requirements were necessary. The secretariat has since tried to improve the facilitation process through the provision of model legislation that could then be adjusted by the member states. Additionally, administrative and other procedural frameworks need to be enacted.

Free movement under the CSME applies only to certain categories of labour.[8] The CARICOM Skills Certificate allows regional citizens to freely live and work throughout CSME. Another name for this certificate is the Certificate of Recognition of CARICOM Skills Qualification. This certificate essentially replaces the work permit and is obtained once all the essential documents/qualifications (which vary with each category of skilled persons) are submitted with an application. The skills certificate can be applied for in either the home or host country.

From the start of the CSME, there have been four categories of skilled workers who can move through the region without the need for work permits: university graduates, managers, technical and supervisory staff attached to a company and self-employed persons/service providers. By July 2006 at the CARICOM summit, given the regional situation regarding nurses and teachers, it was agreed to add these two categories to those who are allowed free movement. The July 2006 summit also expanded the categories of persons who are allowed free movement for work purposes to include artistes, sportspersons, musicians and media workers (CARICOM 2010). Allowance was also made for the free movement of the spouses of these categories of skilled workers and their associated dependents – these people are not required to obtain a work permit.

It was noted that a further group of workers consisting of higglers from the informal sector, artisans, domestic workers and hospitality workers were to be added to the listing of economic agents permitted free inter-regional movement, providing they had appropriate certification (Sheil 2006). In February during the eighteenth Intercessional Meeting of the CARICOM Heads of Government Conference, an agreement was reached whereby Caribbean vocational qualifications based on industrial occupational standards would be awarded to facilitate the free movement of artisans within the CARICOM region.

3. Freer movement of goods: Two important CSME developments pertaining to the free movement of goods are developments with respect to free circulation of goods and the CARICOM Common External Tariff. Free circulation means that taxes levied on extra regional goods imported in the region would be collected at the first point of entry into CSME and then this collected revenue would be shared

among all the CSME members. This process will allow for free movement of extra regional goods within the region.

By June 1998 only two countries had implemented the four phases of the Common External Tariff, although by December 2008 the numbers increased to eleven.[9] As it stands, CARICOM member states are implementing the revised Common External Tariff structure based on the 2002 Harmonized System. Several countries including Barbados, Guyana, Jamaica, Montserrat, and Trinidad and Tobago have already implemented the revised structure. One of the most cogent arguments in favour of a rapid dismantling of the CARICOM Common External Tarriff was articulated by the Nineteenth Meeting of the Conference of Heads of Government of the Caribbean Community. At this meeting, one of the discussion papers noted:

> The idea of keeping some defensible margin of preference for local producers in the form of a tariff is no longer tenable for a small CARICOM market seeking to link trade and production with the rest of the hemisphere and region. While such a policy can still bring creation gains for large schemes such as Mercosur and even reconcile regional trade protection with universal liberalization if it bears a low tariff, it is counterproductive for CARICOM. (Gonzáles 1998, 6)

Overall, while both the formal sector and the informal sector are generally expected to benefit in the future from all five pillars of the CSME, the informal sector should benefit specifically from two of the pillars: the free movement of capital and the free movement of goods, services and people across CARICOM.

1.15. Reciprocity, Trading Agreements, the Global Financial Crisis and the Potential for Greater Informalization of Economic Activity in CARICOM

The Treaty of Rome established the European Economic Community in 1957. During the establishment, it was agreed that this community would provide favourable economic treatment to those African economies that held colonial ties to France. One year later, the first European Development Fund was created with the main purpose of providing assistance to former francophone colonies. As some of these francophone countries gained independence, there were negotiations with the European Economic Community to maintain the continuation of preferential treatment; this is the foundation upon which the European Union–Africa

Partnership was built. The signing of the Yaounde Convention in 1963 formalized the partnership between the European Economic Community and eighteen other colonies, most of which were former French colonies. The Yaounde Convention matured into the Lomé Convention, which eventually evolved into the Regional Economic Partnership Agreement. The Forum of the Caribbean Group of African, Caribbean and Pacific States Economic Partnership Agreement was signed by all partners on 15 October 2008, excluding Haiti which signed on 10 December 2009. The Bahamas signed a services and investment deal with the European Union on 27 January 2010.

The case of preferential treatment for bananas is especially interesting and sparked a five-year trade war between the European Union and the United States. Bananas are grown exclusively in less-developed countries. The trends and the performance of the banana sector during the 1990s are illustrative of some of the problems that characterize a traditional agricultural export sector. At the start of the 1990s, the banana-producing sector contributed 12% to GDP in the Windward Islands.[10] By 1999, however, the contribution of the banana sector to this subregional bloc of countries within CARICOM had fallen to 7%. Moreover, the overall volume of banana exported had contracted by more than 50% between 1993 and 1999, representing a decline from 238,878 tons to 130,419 tons. In addition, the number of banana producers decreased from 24,111 in 1993 to 11,665 in 1999. When banana production was at its peak in the early 1990s, it contributed as much as 20% of GDP to the Windward Islands, although in recent years this has declined considerably. Employment in the industry has also decreased sharply from about twenty-four thousand farmers in 1993 to five thousand in 2005 (IMF 2002).

The cost of producing bananas in the Caribbean sphere is higher than the cost of producing bananas in most other producing countries, although the available data is very limited. One source, Griffith (2002), posted the average cost of producing bananas in Jamaica at approximately US$391 when compared to US$291 in Colombia, US$179 in Costa Rica, and US$161 in Ecuador. With the formation of the European Union, the ACP was concerned that they would lose shares in the European Union to non-ACP more efficient producers. However, the Lomé agreement demonstrated the commitment of the European Union to the continued development of their former colonies by explicitly stating in Protocol 5 of Lomé IV: "In respect of its banana exports to the community markets, no ACP state shall be placed, as regards access to traditional markets and its advantages on those markets in a less favourable situation than in the past or at present" (WTO 1997, 36).

The European Union launched its new banana regime on 1 July 1993. This regime was characterized by the distinguishing feature that it replaced various national banana import regimes with a more common marketing arrangement between the European Union and its former member states.[11] Latin American banana producers as well as the United States strongly opposed this new regime and took their grievances both to the European Court of Justice as well as to the WTO. While the United States does not produce bananas, many of the transnational companies that dominate the Latin American market are owned by US nationals and the United States thus acted on their behalf.[12]

In 1997, the WTO became formally involved in this dispute and issued a statement to the European Union to provide an alternative to its banana arrangement with ACP nations. The European Union responded by issuing a new regulation that gave continued preferential treatment to ACP nations but with the specific form of the arrangement now being a combination of tariffs, quotas and cross-subsidies (through import licences). In April 1999, the WTO ruled that the new preferential arrangement was still very short of its requirements and the WTO in turn made its own suggestions to the European Union. The WTO proposals, while allowing the European Union to facilitate its former colonial dependencies by favourable margins of preference, also argued in favour of a general reduction in tariff rates.[13] The new banana regime consisted of a two-million-ton quota on imports from Latin American and non-industrialized ACP nations. In 2001, at the ministerial conference in Doha, WTO waivers were approved, allowing the European Union countries a temporary bout of tariffs (until 2007) to safeguard their ACP member states.

With this compromise, the European Union agreed that the waiver would be applied only if the new tariff was set at a rate that maintained total market access for all the WTO member suppliers (ECDPM 2003). The reform of the European Union banana regime toward a tariff-only system also adversely affected the preferences of the small OECS economies. In particular, on 1 January 2006 the European Union changed its system of preferences to one based on tariffs only, with a most favoured nation tariff of €176 per tonne for bananas originating out of Latin America and a duty-free quota of 0.775 million-tonne for the ACP states. In January 2008 bananas and all other agricultural exports from the Caribbean were allowed duty-free quota-free access to the European Union market.

The data in table 1.21 show that the various CARICOM member states from the Windward Islands have benefited considerably from implicit transfers associated with European Union Banana Preferences.

Table 1.21: Windward Islands Implicit Assistance from European Union Banana Preferences, 1995–2008, US$m

	1995	1996	1997	1998	1999	2000	2001	2002	2003	2004	2005	2006	2007	2008	Average
Calculations are based on European wholesale and US landed prices															
Dominica	13.6	15.0	15.5	14.4	13.0	7.9	3.4	3.9	4.3	4.7	6.4	2.4	2.5	2.8	7.8
In % of total goods and services	12.6	12.3	11.3	9.5	8.3	5.5	2.8	3.2	3.6	3.6	4.9	1.7	1.7	1.9	5.9
In % of GDP	6.2	6.4	6.4	5.6	4.9	2.9	1.3	1.5	1.6	1.6	2.1	0.8	0.7	0.8	3.1
Grenada	1.9	0.7	0.0	0.0	0.3	0.2	0.1	0.1	0.2	0.1	0.0	0.2	0.5	0.7	0.4
In % of total goods and services	1.5	0.5	0.0	0.0	0.1	0.1	0.1	0.1	0.1	0.1	0.0	0.2	0.3	0.4	0.2
In % of GDP	0.7	0.2	0.0	0.0	0.1	0.0	0.0	0.0	0.0	0.0	0.0	0.0	0.1	0.0	0.1
St Lucia	43.6	39.8	31.8	37.5	31.1	20.4	6.6	11.2	14.1	15.5	8.0	7.3	10.9	13.6	21.5
In % of total goods and services	11.5	11.3	8.9	9.6	8.4	5.4	2.0	3.5	3.6	3.4	35	1.7	2.4	2.5	5.5
In % of GDP	7.9	7.0	5.5	5.7	4.5	2.9	1.0	1.6	1.9	1.9	2.0	0.8	1.1	1.4	3.2
St Vincent	21.0	16.7	13.8	20.5	17.8	12.3	5.9	7.7	9.4	8.3	0.4	3.4	5.1	2.9	11.1
In % of total goods and services	15.4	11.2	9.3	13.0	10.1	6.8	3.3	4.3	5.4	4.5	5.2	1.6	2.4	1.5	6.7
In % of GDP	7.9	5.9	4.7	6.5	5.4	3.7	1.7	2.1	2.5	2.0	2.3	0.7	0.9	0.5	3.3

Source: Mlachila et al. (2010).

Not surprisingly, in the context of the changes in trading conditions of Windward Islands bananas with the European Union, these transfers have declined substantively and by 2008 stood on average at around 1% of GDP as compared to 5.6% in 1995. This erosion of trading preferences has had an adverse impact on the economies of the Windward Islands. The policy challenge in these economies now hovers around how to deal with the fallout from the decline in these implicit transfers. In particular, the income and employment opportunities available to small farmers have been adversely affected. This therefore requires well-designed safety nets and other transition interventions, such as retraining programmes, to be set in motion. Indeed, some of these dislocated farmers would have migrated to the informal sector.

Along this same line but from a broader perspective, Greenaway and Milner (2003) have estimated the welfare impact of the Regional Economic Partnership Agreement on CARICOM economies (see table 1.22). They did this by estimating the losses in customs revenues for certain CARICOM countries.

Any large decrease in fiscal earnings will eventually cause a negative impact on The Forum of the Caribbean Group of African, Caribbean and Pacific States countries as their ability to finance developmental areas like health care, education and poverty will be negatively affected. This, in turn, may cause some economic agents without adequate state-provided safety nets to turn to the informal sector for sustenance.

Even more, the global financial crisis has resulted in the economic growth rate of the global economy being lower than what prevailed in

Table 1.22: Changes in Customs Revenue by Country

Country	Customs Revenue (EC$m)
Barbados	182.4
Belize	52.8
Dominica	21.8
Grenada	31.2
Jamaica	635.1
St Kitts	25.9
St Lucia	60.4
St Vincent	27.3
Trinidad	390.1

Source: Greenaway and Milner (2003).

2007. The United Nations Economic Commission of Latin America and the Caribbean (ECLAC 2010) noted that the recovery of the international marketplace from this crisis will depend heavily on the timing, pace and magnitude of any further stimulus package implemented by the US economy. Even more, the new world economic environment that will emerge after the dust clears from the current financial crisis will no doubt be weaker due to the reduced import capacity of third economies from the United States and China, two main drivers of global economic growth. Much of the strong growth of the CARICOM economies during the new century thus far has depended on the strong growth of extra-regional economies that import products from the region. These economies may not be as strong in the medium term as many will have been weakened by the global financial crisis. These predictions are supported by empirical evidence listed in table 1.23. Indeed, as compared to 2009, China and India are expected to continue their upward growth trajectory, however when compared to 2007, growth in these economies have slowed.

To provide a rough estimate of the impact of the global financial crisis on Caribbean countries, ECLAC (2010) subtracted from the actual value of real GDP the associated trend values generated using a Hodrick Prescott filter. The difference between the actual recorded value and the associated trend values is shown in table 1.24. For CARICOM as a whole in 2009, this amounted to US$1.54 billion. This represents a significant loss of economic activity for the region.

Table 1.23: GDP Annual Growth Rate, 2007–2010

	2007	2008	2009	2010 (f)
World	3.8	1.7	–2.2	2.5
Developed countries	2.5	0.4	–3.6	1.4
United States	2.1	0.4	–2.5	2.0
Euro area	2.7	0.6	–4.0	0.7
Japan	2.3	–0.7	–5.9	1.1
Developing countries	7.5	5.2	1.7	5.3
China	13.0	9.0	8.4	8.7
India	9.3	7.3	5.9	6.5

(f) = forecast
Source: UNECLAC (2009).

Table 1.24: Difference in GDP US$m at 2000 Prices

Country	US$m
Antigua and Barbuda	−70.9
The Bahamas	−322.3
Barbados	−68.4
Belize	−44.4
Dominica	2.0
Grenada	−34.0
Guyana	7.9
Jamaica	−302.4
St Kitts and Nevis	−26.9
St Vincent and the Grenadines	−14.7
St Lucia	−30.9
Suriname	12.4
Trinidad and Tobago	−654.7
Caribbean	−1,547.3

Source: UNECLAC (2010).

Coming on the heels of the erosion of banana preferences and the introduction of the Regional Economic Partnership Agreement with the associated potential welfare losses for CARICOM economies, the global financial crisis has the capacity to intensify the type of environment in which unemployment rates can increase and provide the type of backdrop in which shuttle trading can become more pronounced. The necessity of remaining in the Caribbean and engaging in the shuttle trade or some form of informal commercial importing also derives from diminishing opportunities for migration to the United States, United Kingdom and Canada, consequent on the increased levels of unemployment and the declines in living standards being experienced in those economies as a fall-out of the global financial crisis.

Levitt (1991) posits that under these conditions, the entrepreneurial spirit drives affected members of the population to grasp at opportunities to earn additional income, thereby allowing the struggle of the hustling to thrive. The researcher sums it up this way in the context of Jamaica, but this conclusion can be extended to all countries in CARICOM: "The combination of chronic unemployment, declining living standards, deteriorating real incomes and reduced ability to purchase both necessities and comforts has changed the pattern of behaviour. It is no longer possible for a man or a woman dependent solely on a wage or salary income to hope ever to own a home. Hence the increase in hustling, higgling and reliance on multiple sources of income" (Levitt 1991, 56).

It is under these types of conditions that informality becomes attractive to affected individuals in the region. The attraction is derived from observed characteristics of the informal sector, such as the small scale of operation, opportunities to evade taxation and legal requirements for operating a business, the flexibility of the overarching labour market, the removal of the insistence on formal contracts with suppliers and customers, the lower educational entry requirements and the prospects for independent operation. When these characteristics are superimposed on the platform of high levels of penetration of cellular phones and the Internet across CARICOM countries, several opportunities for trade with individuals and organizations in traditional markets and in developing South–South markets become available to existing and new ICIs. Indeed, this chapter has provided a context within which the Caribbean informal sector can be discussed and evaluated given its increasingly important role in the lives and economies in which the trade is most prominent.

2 THE ORIGINS AND EVOLUTION OF WOMEN IN THE SHUTTLE TRADE IN THE CARIBBEAN

Shuttle trade or suitcase trade is a form of unrecorded international transaction in goods that currently takes place at the edge of formal trade (IMF 1998). The Organisation for Economic Co-operation and Development (2002) defined the shuttle trade as the activity in which individual entrepreneurs buy goods abroad and import them for resale in street markets or small shops. Other researchers such as Sahin et al. (2008) describe the shuttle trade as being part of the survival strategy of many households. It is for the most part characterized by unregistered small-scale traders evading taxes and customs duties (Yuskseker 2004). The IMF (1998) identified that the shuttle trade is typically associated with persons who are travellers. This type of trade, they argue, is opportunistic and depends on rigidities in the economic system being in place and the failure of these systems to react to needs of the market and anomalies in regulations in an economy that gives these forms of trade a distinct advantage.

This type of trade includes individuals who reside in both urban and rural areas, and both the unemployed and the employed who engage in the shuttle trade to supplement their income. While both male and female engage in this suitcase trade, based on a combination of field work, statistical research and scholarly analysis it was estimated that approximately 80% of the participants in the shuttle trade are women (Mukhina 2010).

Within the Caribbean, shuttle traders or ICIs represent the latest phase in an evolutionary pattern of employment of women from the period of slavery through indentureship and apprenticeship up to the present. This chapter investigates the evolution and persistence of ICIs, with some emphasis in the CARICOM sphere. It is organized into six sections. Section 2.1 defines the structure and nature of the shuttle trade outside of the Caribbean. Section 2.2 details the historical roots of the shuttle trade in the Caribbean. The movement from higgler to ICI in the Caribbean is captured in sections 2.3 and 2.4. Section 2.4 examines the link between import substituting industrialization and the suitcase trade in Jamaica, Trinidad and Tobago, and Dominica. Section 2.5 investigates globalization and the increasing informalization of labour markets in the Caribbean, while section 2.6 investigates de-agriculturalization in the Caribbean. Section 2.7 concludes the chapter and allows for comparisons to be made between shuttle traders operating in CARICOM and developed countries, as well as comparisons over time within the CARICOM sphere. It provides a historical account of the importance of the informal sector to the development of the Caribbean economies, and particularly to its women since the early 1970s. Indeed, informalization has been perpetuated in the Caribbean in response to a lack of employment opportunities and absent markets – when there are no markets for certain products, shuttle traders fill market niches.

2.1. Excerpts from the Literature on the Structure and Nature of the Shuttle Trade Outside of the Caribbean Region

The 2005 edition of the *Global Politician* online magazine reported that shuttle traders who crossed borders under the guise of tourists and returned with luggage packed with goods for resale could be found in "Mongolia and Russia, China and Ukraine, Bulgaria and Kosovo, the West Bank and Turkey." It also reported that the entrepreneurs engaged in the shuttle trade fulfilled local demands that were not met by domestic producers or via formal imports. This magazine recognized shuttle traders as contributors to the economies of developing and transition economies employing millions, stimulating transport and infrastructural development and encouraging grassroots capitalism.

The forms of shuttle trade, as the IMF (1998) noted, include trade in which goods are accompanied by the trader and trade that involves the separate transfer of goods via unaccompanied luggage. Where goods are accompanied by the traveller, three variations were observed. Firstly, persons from one country use cash to purchase goods from a foreign country and return to their home country to sell the goods. According to the IMF (1998), this was a common practice by countries that made up the Commonwealth of Independent States. The report noted that a significant amount of the goods sold in these countries were bought in other countries such as the People's Republic of China, Turkey and the United Arab Emirates. On a smaller scale, some of the goods were bought in India, Israel, Pakistan and the Syrian Arab Republic. Secondly, although less common, travellers are also observed to carry goods from their home countries to sell abroad in exchange for cash, which they take back to their home countries. Finally, another variation of the shuttle trade involves goods traded on the border where there are low tax thresholds and relaxed law enforcement by customs officials. Clothing and apparel are the most common goods traded via the shuttle trade; however, agricultural produce and certain vehicles which are driven across borders are also traded. Travellers were also reported to have shipped goods as unaccompanied luggage since the treatment by customs of the former and of accompanied luggage was no different (IMF 1998).

Eder et al. (2003) reviewed the pattern of shuttle trade that existed between Turkish and Russian economies. These authors attempted to identify and classify the shuttle traders and their activities. It was found that in Turkey, the majority of shuttle trade took place in Laleli, Istanbul. Russians visited Turkey to purchase clothing and textiles, light consumer goods and leather garments. This activity is an important source of Turkish exports. Turkish shopkeepers revealed that they engaged in substantial trade, with as much as 81.5% of their goods being sold to foreign markets. Of these foreign markets, Russia was ranked as number one, comprising 91% of the Turkish suitcase trade. Table 2.1 shows the countries and their share of exports as reported by Turkish survey respondents in Eder et al. (2003).

Eder et al. (2003) also found that family members participated in many of the respondents' operations, with 62% of shops having family workers. Some of the shops also employed part-time employees. Regarding Turkish traders, these researchers also noted the following:

- The age of the shopkeepers ranged from twenty-five years to sixty years.
- In Turkey, traders were mostly male and no trader used bank credit. In fact, business was run mainly on a cash basis, with 95% of business done in cash. A minimal number of shops (representing 5%) extended credit, however on a short-term basis (maximum period of one month).
- Mostly foreign female employees were employed by the shops.[1] Shopkeepers were very informal, neglecting to pay full taxes, hiring

Table 2.1: Turkish Exports (Informal) to Various Countries

Country	Number	%
Russia	99	91
Romania	41	38
Bulgaria	33	30
Ukraine	27	25
Poland	24	22
Arabic Countries	22	20
Yugoslavia	18	17
Hungary	15	14
Azerbaijan	14	13
Czech Republic	13	12
Tunisia	9	8
Israel	7	6
Macedonia	7	6
Republic of Turkey	7	6
Moldavia	5	5
Albania	4	4
Serbia	4	4
Croatia	3	3
Georgia	3	3
Armenia	2	2

Note: Figures sum to greater than 100 because of overlap of
    countries trading with shopkeepers.
Source: Eder et al. (2003).

temporary workers (some of whom were illegal) and operating in collaboration with street-side vendors.

- Many admitted to bribing customs officials to obtain preferential treatment.

With regard to Russian traders, Eder et al. (2003) noted the following:

- The shuttle trade comprised mostly women (two thirds), with half of these being highly educated (post-secondary school training).
- The traders ranged in age from twenty-five to forty-five years.
- Most of these (87.5%) regularly visited and received goods from Turkey.

- Many of them entered the shuttle trade since they were unable to obtain employment in line with their training.
- The tourism and cargo industries in these countries have flourished as a result of shuttle trade.

To note some demographic characteristics, Little (1999) observed that women dominated the trader populations (84% in Banjul and 95% in Maputo). However, many of the high-earning activities were dominated by men, for example in the long-distance border trade. Furthermore, twice as many men than women owned shops, although more women were involved in the trade. In terms of education, formal educational background was "extremely low with averages of 1.7 and 1.1 years in formal education in Maputo and Banjul respectively" (Little 1999, 22).

Sadovskaya (2007) reviewed the migration patterns between China and Kazakhstan and identified commercial migrants as one of the main reasons for overall migrations. In fact, the researcher traced the beginning and expansion of Chinese migration to Kazakhstan to the shuttle trade. Given China's status as a fast-growing economy in terms of economic and population growth and the constraints on its labour market, it was estimated that its labour market would not be able to absorb the sharp increases in the number of persons coming of working age; this factor drove migration from China to other parts. It was reported that Chinese shuttle traders operated informally and emerged as a result of the economic crisis. In addition, Chinese commercial migrants specialized in the trading of clothing and footwear made in small artisan shops. Furthermore, shuttle traders identified themselves as tourists or private visitors when crossing the borders between Kazakhstan and China (Sadovskaya 2007).

2.2. The Historical Roots of the Shuttle Trade in the Caribbean

In the first half of the seventeenth century, the British settled in St Christopher, Barbados, Montserrat, Antigua and Jamaica. The British established these colonies with the intent of forming a mercantilist empire. From the very outset, these Caribbean colonies were agriculture based and the rise of sugar in the Caribbean fuelled the demand for slave labour. The system of slavery involved slaves producing the majority of their food on an allocated plot of land, which came to be known as the provision grounds, and the whole system of planting on these provision grounds became known as the provision ground system. These provision grounds were generally located at the periphery of the plantations, and sometimes this was a very far distance from the centre of the plantation itself. Slaves were granted free time to plant on their provision grounds (see Phillips 2002). The slaves mainly planted plantains, coconut, maize, yams, eddoes and cassava. Alongside their endeavours in these provision grounds, the enslaved also planted on house plots. These house plots (referred to as polinks in Jamaica) adjoined the homes of the slaves. The surplus from both the house plot and the plantation grounds were sold in local markets.

The provision ground system was also beneficial to planters as it brought peripheral land into productive life. Significantly, the system helped to cultivate the entrepreneurial skills of the enslaved, their identities and their consciousness (Ulysse 2007). Slave higglers initially entered the market system to sell goods for their masters, however, as Mintz (1974) noted, because slaves were not supervised in the production of their own food, they could do as they pleased and many slaves sold some of their own produce.[2] A substantial number of the slaves who were brought to the Caribbean came from West Africa, where trading played an important role in the lives of women. In this regard, Mintz (1995) is of the opinion that these West African women brought with them the concept of "woman as trader" to the new world; other researchers share a similar sentiment (see, for example, Bolles 1992). Slaves exchanged their surplus with other slaves from within their own plantations and sometimes even with slaves from outside of their own plantations.

The internal marketing system in the Caribbean islands today is no doubt slightly different from what occurred in the pre-emancipation period, but the substance of it remains very much the same. Basically, women have remained the marketers and men the cultivators.[3] As LeFranc et al. (1987, 103) note, "A man may let his produce rot if he has no wife, daughter or other female relative to take it to the market, rather than be seen standing over a basket."

Female dominance of the plantations became common, occurring in some economies as early as 1812 (see table 2.2).[4]

Although the whites created the marketplace for their benefit, it was eventually taken over by the enslaved population and played a pivotal role in the exchange of information. Eventually the white plantation owners introduced rules that prevented slaves helping out each other with their respective plots. Formal legislative measures were also introduced limiting the number of autonomous economic activities in which slaves could be engaged. One example of these restrictions was that slaves could not sell in

Table 2.2: Ratio of Females Slaves to Male Slaves for the Years 1812 to 1825

Year	Male Slaves	Female Slaves	Ratio of Females to Males
1812	14,352	14,439	1.0 to 1
1813	14,026	14,156	1.0 to 1
1814	13,074	14,005	1.1 to 1
1815	13,484	13,766	1.0 to 1
1816	13,450	13,783	1.0 to 1
1817	13,510	14,188	1.1 to 1
1818	13,328	14,087	1.1 to 1
1819	13,155	13,905	1.1 to 1
1820	13,022	13,878	1.1 to 1
1821	12,398	13,269	1.1 to 1
1822	12,355	13,231	1.1 to 1
1823	12,258	13,052	1.1 to 1
1824	12,101	12,871	1.1 to 1
1825	12,057	12,840	1.1 to 1

Source: Kossek (1993).

the marketplace unless they had a permit from their master granting them permission.[5] However, by the mid-1700s, slaves were bartering a wide variety of goods, ranging from fish, poultry and eggs to their ground provisions and plantains. Significantly, not all of these goods were bartered, but some were exchanged for cash.

The slave higglers supplied meats and a wide range of ground provisions in later years to both other slaves and to the planter class, as well as to other free people. Sundays were a big market day in the colonial era and the colonial rulers did not regulate Sunday market activities – in fact, where they tried to regulate activities on a Sunday, they failed. Critically, Momsen (1988) noted that Sunday morning markets grew to such importance that there was a relaxation of some laws to allow slaves to participate. By the eighteenth century, the market became very important and buoyant, and was predominantly run by slaves. Simmonds (1987) identified that the rural higgler grew in economic importance as "they facilitated the distribution of a wide variety of imports, local products and provisions during their time off. The rural female slave higglers provided the chief means by which the rural slave population was able to acquire the necessary and desired supplements to the basics provided by their owners and some urban slaves were able to obtain the entire means for subsistence, independent of their owners" (quoted in Ulysse 2007, 63).

The market afforded slaves a form and avenue to derive material strength, and sometimes they increased prices, much to the displeasure of the elitist white. The market played an important role in the evolution of the enslaved into freed people.[6] It provided a meeting point where they could communicate with family and friends. Indeed, as Ulysse (2007, 63) noted, "It is not surprising that rural dwellers walked as many as twenty-five miles carrying goods on their heads to attend the town's Sunday market."

During emancipation negotiations, the whites used the provision grounds and house plots as bargaining chips to keep slaves working on the plantations. They charged the slaves higher rents as the provision grounds were valuable to them in terms of mature trees and ripening crops, and it also hosted the burial sites of their ancestors (Sheller 1997). As planters brought in indentured labourers from other countries, tension heightened between the freed slaves and the planter class. An important source of this tension was the lack of access by the slaves to land. Many slaves, for a variety of reasons, turned to squatting near their old provision grounds.

Even with the emancipation of slavery, the dominance of women in the marketplace continued as men left the islands in search of better employment opportunities with higher salaries. Particularly in Jamaica, many men migrated to work on the Panama railway where McLean (1988) noted the salaries were three times as high as in Jamaica. This migratory pattern increased the demand for employment by Caribbean women as they headed a significant number of households in various CARICOM territories. In Jamaica, this was as high as 30% (Clarke 1957). Higgling allowed these women to attend to their domestic needs as well as earn a living. Massiah (1989) noted that although there have been variations over time, usually women workers in the informal sector cared for their children as their main responsibility, and so focused their energies less on building up vibrant and very functional enterprises when compared to trying to source an immediate bloc of cash. In support of this argument, Ulysse (2007, 69) noted that "even when men are present in their households, the women still consider the children as their primary responsibility. Those who participate in haggling do so to replace the absent family image of the male breadwinner and to fulfill societal obligations of their gender."

East Indian indentured servants began to arrive in the Caribbean with the termination of slavery and the failure of a variety of immigration schemes out of Africa, China, Europe, Java, Madeira and Portugal. Table 2.3 provides an overview of the number of East Indian immigrants in the Caribbean for the period 1838–1920.

According to Roopnarine (2006), most of the women brought from East India to the Caribbean were single, with a small sector being married who came either with or without their families, and some who even brought their young daughters with them. In this regard, the researcher noted: "it is well known that daughters are regarded by the average Indian family as a doubtful blessing owing to the expenses that have to be incurred in finding husbands for them and the novel prospect of having their girls sought after by eligible young men in the colonies might be an inducement to them to emigrate" (Roopnarine 2006, 96). Another category of migrant women were widows and women abandoning their families from the sprawling metropolis of Calcutta and Madras.

In the mid-nineteenth century there was a rapid increase in the price of agricultural goods, and this forced many women back into agriculture (Roopnarine 2006). The two largest bodies of East Indians in the Caribbean now settle in Trinidad and Tobago and Guyana. With the emergence of economic crises in these various economies, some East Indian women became

Table 2.3: Number of Indentured East Indian Immigrants Introduced to the Caribbean, 1838–1920

British Guiana	238,960
Trinidad	143,939
Dutch Guiana	43,404
Guadeloupe	42,236
Jamaica	37,027
Martinique	25,404
French Guiana	8,500
Grenada	3,200
Belize	3,000
St Vincent	2,472
St Lucia	2,300
St Kitts	361
Nevis	342
Danish St Croix	325

Source: Roopnarine (2006).

ICIs to help supplement their incomes. The various details attached to the emergence of these economic crises are discussed later in the text.

2.3. From Higgler to ICI

ICIs emerged in the Caribbean sphere in the post-emancipation era just after the independence movement for a variety of reasons, including:

- the adoption of import substituting industrialization policies in the Caribbean;
- the globalization and the increasing informalization of labour markets in the Caribbean; and
- de-agriculturalization in the Caribbean.

These are now discussed in turn.

2.4. Import Substituting Industrialization and the Suitcase Trade

Before the 1980s, the trading regimes of the Caribbean sphere were parallel to those of many other developing economies. These economies made considerable use of non-tariff barriers and high tariff levels. In this environment, the effective level of protection in the manufacturing sector was substantially higher than the associated nominal levels. The rest of this section provides some specific details regarding the emergence of ICIs in Jamaica, Guyana, Trinidad and Tobago, and Dominica in the context of import substituting industrialization.

Jamaica

Jamaica was discovered in 1494 by Columbus and was settled by the Spanish in the sixteenth century. The natives of Jamaica were originally Taino Indians. They were eliminated and replaced by slave labour from Africa. The British took over the island from Spain in 1655 and in the process introduced a plantation system of agriculture founded on cocoa, coffee and sugar. For several centuries the Jamaican economy revolved around sugar, but all that changed with the discovery of bauxite in 1942 and the arrival of the aluminum companies. However, economic growth in Jamaica tended to widen income inequality gaps during the period 1945–90. At the start of the 1970s, the economic outlook for the Jamaican economy was not dismal. The growth rate of the economy in the late 1960s had averaged 5% per annum. The main problem was unemployment, which Worrell (1987) cited at 25% after the Second World War and 13.5% in the 1960s. Large-scale emigration during the 1950s only partly ended labour market tension. When this channel was closed, the unemployment level started to climb. In the 1970s, sugar was in trouble and banana was the main export crop. These industries, however, were affected by the migration of workers from the country to the town. Bauxite production started in Jamaica in 1952 with three companies, and a fourth company was established in 1963.[7] The tourism industry was also growing. However, even though the economic outlook of the Jamaican economy in 1970 seemed bright because of the promising outlook for bauxite and tourism, social tension linked to skewed patterns of income was high.

The US dollar crisis of 1971 and the oil price shocks of 1973 helped to catapult the Jamaican economy into a decline, and in 1974 the economy slumped. The inflation rate remained very high for the next decade and the unemployment rate climbed above 20%. Ghettoization also emerged amid increased income inequality (Witter and Kirton 1990). Ghettoization and widening income gaps led to the emergence, in the words of Witter and Kirton (1990) of a type of "hustle economy".[8] The government of 1974 embraced an import substituting industrialization stance which had its genesis in the 1950s and tried to promote indigenous production and at the same time restrict consumption of foreign produced goods. The greater socialist tendencies of the Jamaican government, however, encouraged the flight of the merchant class. With their departure the manufacturing sector in Jamaica plunged and female unemployment increased to 36.9% in 1988.

In the midst of the import substituting industrialization strategy, self-employment in the form of higgling became a viable economic stance. The shortage of key merchandise became obvious everywhere and was heightened as some merchants withheld goods from the marketplace in anticipation of further price increases. A further strategy of "marrying goods" was implemented. This involved a practice where a scarce good could only be obtained if a more abundant and sometimes unpopular good was purchased (Ulysse 2007).

LeFranc and Downes (2001) have provided some evidence that the hustle economy has had a favourable effect on poverty. Specifically, these researchers noted that although Jamaica's economic growth between 1989 and 1999 followed a downward trend, unemployment rates had not shifted out of the 15–17% range. Also noted is the fact that the level of poverty had significantly decreased during the period (1989–1999), although Jamaica experienced declining economic growth during this same period. Table 2.4 shows the poverty level, unemployment and GDP growth in Jamaica for the period 1989–99. Le Franc and Downes (2001) have identified the informal economy and remittances as the reasons for this seemingly peculiar occurrence, unexplained by the formal economy. They also note that an expanding informal economy exists in Jamaica that is concentrated in petty trading and the distributive sectors.[9]

Amid the economic chaos in Jamaica, female traders turned to the Cayman Islands, Miami, Caracas and Panama to provide scarce goods to the Jamaican marketplace.[10] Taylor (1988, 2) noted that "thus began the 'onion runs' as the flights to Cayman were called, because the higglers would import into Jamaica large amounts of this commodity which was scarce in the markets throughout the island". Panama was also a preferred destination because of the ease with which a visa could be obtained and also because Panama had a free zone and offered the best prices to these traders.[11] Reid (1989, as cited in Ulysse 2007) noted that these female ICIs exported goods such as thyme, scallions, June plums and guineps, and purchased food stuff such as cereals and canned food, dry goods and haberdashery. As time passed, these ICIs traded other goods such as Jamaican cheese, reggae music tapes, ackee and Jamaican rum in which Jamaica held

Table 2.4: Poverty and Selected Macroeconomic Indicators for Jamaica, 1989–1999

Year	Population below Poverty Line (%)	Unemployment Rate (%)	Growth Rate (%)
1989	30.5	17.7	6.8
1990	28.4	15.3	5.5
1991	44.6	15.4	0.7
1992	33.9	15.8	1.5
1993	24.4	16.2	1.7
1994	22.8	15.4	1.0
1995	27.5	16.2	0.7
1996	26.1	16.0	–1.4
1997	19.9	16.5	–2.1
1998	15.9	15.5	–0.7
1999	16.9	15.7	–0.4

Source: Le Franc and Downes (2001).

a comparative advantage. The category of goods imported also widened to include small appliances, clothing and footwear. Ulysse (2007, 78) noted that "foreign higgling, like the provision ground system, which provided a temporary truce between slaves and planter during slavery, aided the Government. Suitcase trading, in a sense, replaced the Government's social welfare system at a time of massive economic and social crisis."

Guyana

Guyana was sighted by Christopher Columbus in 1498 and came under Dutch control by the mid-1700s. By 1620, the Dutch West India Company established an armed base and brought in slaves from Africa to work on sugar cane plantations. In 1814, during the Napoleonic wars, Britain took over Guyana. With the abolition of slavery in 1834, indentured workers were brought in from India to work on the sugar plantations in Guyana. This created an ethno-cultural divide, and even today politics in Guyana is very turbulent.

Guyana is a land of abundant natural wealth and opportunity. Merely on the basis of its natural resources, the Guyanese economy offers tremendous potential, but the real challenge resides with converting this opportunity into economic growth. By 1970, Guyana had a strong educational system in place and the Guyanese people were generally literate. Worrell (1987) noted that in 1970, the economic outlook for Guyana was promising. The economy was growing and prospects for its bauxite and sugar sector were bright. There were plans for diversification into timber and fisheries. However, in 1972 and 1973, the production of Guyana's two main export items – bauxite and sugar – fell, and in 1976 there was a decrease in the price of sugar. The bauxite industry in Guyana was characterized by a wide array of problems (see Worrell 1987; Ambursely and Cohen 1983). The decline in its revenue earning capacity, alongside a strategy of import substitution industrialization from 1971 to 1977, led to a plethora of economic problems, including an increase in public debt from US$133.5 million in 1970 to US$521.6 million in 1976.

ECLAC (2006) identifies that in this economic environment, there was a wave of migration of people out of the Guyanese economy. Table 2.5 documents the net migration rate for Guyana from 1960 to 2005. The trends indicate increasing outward migration.

In the swirls of the economic crisis, the Government of Guyana tried a variety of interventions including a process of continued nationalization, fiscal contraction and control over the main credit institutions (Worrell 1985).

Table 2.5: Net Migration for Guyana, 1960–2005

Year	Net Migration
1960	8,687
1965	−6,564
1970	−33,712
1975	−64,618
1980	−56,354
1985	−85,000
1990	−85,000
1995	−50,000
2000	−60,000
2005	−40,000

Source: World Bank, *World Development Indicators* (2010).

The government became involved in the sugar and bauxite industries and in the major financial institutions (ibid.). The government tried to boost domestic industry by squeezing imports of consumer goods through an extensive system of price controls and foreign exchange rationing while facilitating capital goods imports. The consequence of all this was that a wide range of imported consumer goods was removed from the market-place. This, among other measures, motivated an increase in the size of the underground economy. The underground economy in Guyana, according to Worrell (1987), was fuelled by a decline in real wages in the 1980s. In 1986, the Guyanese government, in the aftermath of the death of President Forbes Burnham, re-established ties with the IMF and the World Bank.[12] A plethora of price controls was imposed and many consumers could not get basic goods to which they had become accustomed. It was in this era that ICIs grew in Guyana as many town higglers turned to the Trinidad and Tobago economy to get scarce consumer goods that they could bring to the Guyanese market (Holder 1988).

To circumvent the need for foreign exchange, Guyanese ICIs took out jewellery and other precious goods that they sold in the Trinidad and Tobago market for cash and then purchased consumer goods. This became problematic, and Holder (1988, 30–31) noted that "at the airport, women are 'invited' by a customs officer into a room where they are thoroughly searched. This is a direct result of the high incidence of smuggling of gold and currency out of the country. Government has estimated the loss to the country's economy in smuggling of gold at an annual average of G$17m."

The participation of Guyanese women in the labour force, according to Peake and Trotz (1999), was highest during the first decade of the twentieth century, but by 1970 had declined to 19%. During the era of nationalization, Guyanese women found employment with the government. However, between 1980 and 1992, when the government was forced to downsize its employment from 51% to 26% of total employment, women (who were mainly employed by the state) were acutely affected.

The use of import controls promoted smuggling of consumer goods to which the Guyanese people had grown accustomed, but which were no longer on the shelves. The Guyanese economy was forced into the arms of the multilateral lending agencies in 1989, and the consequent structural adjustment programme[13] favoured some sectors such as construction, commerce and agriculture. These sectors tended to benefit the employment of men more than women. The escalation in prices in the Guyanese economy and the subsequent erosion of real wages forced many women who were employed in the public sector to seek other means of supplementing their income. McFee (2007) notes that "the informal economy by way of domestics, petty traders and traders provided an opportunity for many of these women to extend their income".

Trinidad and Tobago

The island of Trinidad was first encountered by Christopher Columbus on his third voyage to the new world in 1498. In 1532 the island was colonized by Spain and a governor was established to rule the island. In the 1630s the Dutch settled in Tobago and planted sugar cane. Under the Treaty of Amiens, the Spanish ceded Trinidad to the British. The French, who had captured Tobago from the Dutch in 1781, ceded Tobago to the British in 1814. Sugarcane was introduced by Roman Catholic settlers in Trinidad as early as the 1770s, but was adversely affected by the emancipation of slavery in 1834. Slave manpower was replaced after emancipation by the importation of contract labourers from India between 1845 and 1917, and this boosted sugar and cocoa output. Oil was discovered in Trinidad in 1910.

At the dawn of the 1970s, the Trinidad and Tobago economy prospered from an oil boom. This boom emerged in an environment that was sympathetic to change since this country had gained its political independence in 1962. In 1970, there were massive street protests concerning unemployment and growing discontent with regard to the presence of "foreign control over the commanding heights of the economy". A wave of nationalization programmes followed, with the oil boom providing the resources for greater government involvement. Table 2.6 provides some basic trends in crude oil production and prices in Trinidad and Tobago.[14]

The years 1973 and 1974 represented the beginning of a change in the structure of the economy toward a greater dependence on crude oil. In 1972, the Trinidad and Tobago economy produced 140,200 barrels per day of crude oil. Production increased sharply thereafter, and peaked in 1978 at 229,490 barrels per day (63.5% more than in 1972). By 1989, however, crude oil production had fallen sharply to 149,340 barrels per day or 34.9% less than in 1978. The boom in the oil sector was complemented by similar trend movements in the price of oil, which increased from US$2.7 per barrel in 1972 to US$36.7 per barrel in 1980, before falling to US$17.8 per barrel by 1989. The parallel movements in the price and production of crude oil triggered a massive revenue windfall for the Trinidad and Tobago government in the 1970s, and a similarly dramatic fall in oil revenues in the 1980s, when both the price and production of crude oil fell. In particular, oil revenues increased sharply from US$75.6 million in 1972 to US$1,772.1 million in 1981, but thereafter declined to US$471.6 million in 1989. As a proportion of total government revenues, oil revenues increased from 36.8% in 1972 to 71.1% in 1980, a 35% increase. By 1989, however, the share of oil revenues in total government revenues declined to 41%.

In the export sector, oil exports (approximated by the exports of SITC 3) increased from US$145.4 million in 1972 to US$2,474.8 million in 1980, an increase of 1,600%. However, by 1989 it had fallen to US$934.9

Table 2.6: Trends in Oil Production and Oil Prices for Trinidad and Tobago, 1966–2008

	Oil Production '000 Barrels	Crude Oil Prices (WTI US$ barrel)
1966	55,603.0	1.3
1967	64,995.0	1.3
1968	66,904.0	1.3
1969	57,429.0	1.3
1970	51,043.0	1.3
1971	47,144.0	1.7

(*Table 2.6 continues*)

	Oil Production '000 Barrels	Crude Oil Prices (WTI US$ barrel)
1972	51,211.0	1.9
1973	60,670.0	2.7
1974	68,136.0	9.8
1975	78,621.0	10.7
1976	77,673.0	11.5
1977	83,609.0	12.4
1978	83,809.0	12.7
1979	78,209.0	17.3
1980	77,608.0	28.7
1981	69,109.0	32.5
1982	64,621.0	33.5
1983	58,340.0	29.3
1984	61,897.0	28.5
1985	64,361.0	28.0
1986	61,652.0	15.0
1987	56,642.0	17.3
1988	55,208.0	17.0
1989	54,509.0	19.6
1990	55,039.0	24.1
1991	52,423.0	21.6
1992	49,195.0	20.6
1993	44,633.0	18.5
1994	47,235.0	17.1
1995	47,576.0	18.4
1996	47,112.0	20.2
1997	45,166.0	20.4
1998	44,759.0	14.4
1999	45,688.9	19.2
2000	43,680.5	30.2
2001	41,521.3	28.6
2002	47,706.6	25.9
2003	48,981.1	31.7
2004	44,984.7	41.5
2005	52,739.6	56.5
2006	52,104.8	66.0
2007	43,807.0	72.3
2008	41,826.0	99.6

Source: Trinidad and Tobago, *Annual Economic Survey* (various years).

million. As a proportion of total merchandise exports, oil exports increased from 54.5% in 1972 to 90.6% in 1980 as the oil sector clearly became the commanding height of the economy. However, by 1989, as both the price and production of crude oil fell away, the share of oil exports in total exports declined to 60.3%. The boom in the petroleum sector also resulted in a rise in the proportion of petroleum GDP in real GDP from a paltry 8.1% in 1972 to 39.3% in 1980 at the height of the oil boom. After 1980, the proportion of real GDP accounted for by petroleum GDP fell (19.3% in 1989) as the level of economic activity in the oil sector declined. Figure 2.1 shows that trade as a percentage of GDP increased from 77.7% in 1966 to 96% in 1976, and then decreased to 61% in 1985 as the government's import substituting industrialization agenda took root in the economy.

As the oil economy prospered, the spending effect and resource movement effect associated with the Dutch Disease resulted in the crumbling of the agricultural sector.[15] In particular, the agricultural sector, which employed just over 54,000 people in 1973, employed only 26,448 people in 2006. The agricultural sector, being predominantly female, brought

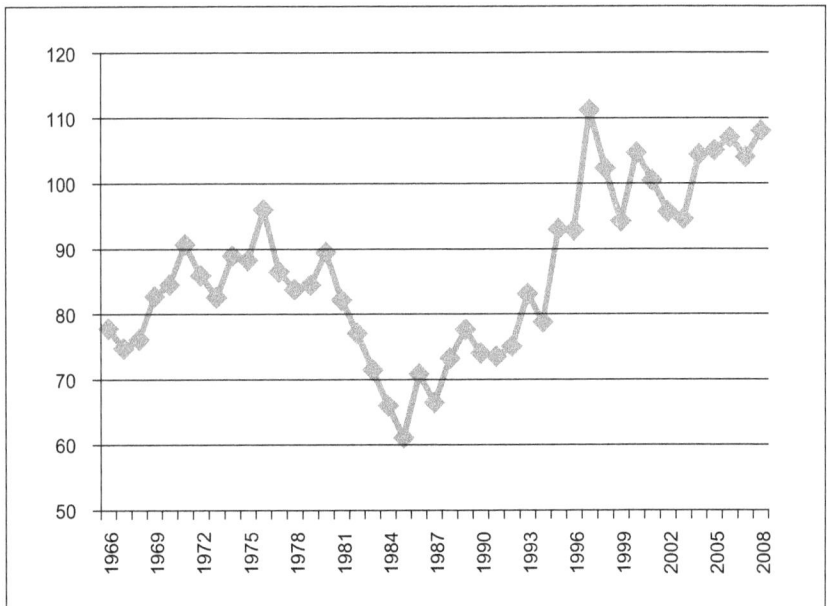

Figure 2.1 Trade as a percentage of GDP for Trinidad and Tobago
Source: World Bank (various years).

a greater number of women into the workplace. Amid rising import protection, particularly during the 1980s, and increasing unemployment, many unemployed women turned to Curaçao and Margarita for clothing and other goods to ply on the local market.

2.5. Globalization and the Informalization of Labour Markets in the Caribbean

Thomas (2002) identified two types of informalization of the labour markets that took place in the urban informal sector of Latin America: the top-down informalization and bottom-up informalization. Top-down informalization occurs when firms are exposed to a greater degree of competition via the general process of liberalization. This prompts a greater degree of flexibility and promotes formal sector firms to cut costs by employing fewer workers or more workers on temporary contracts or more workers without contracts. Bottom-up informalization occurs when the growth of the economically active population exceeds that of the creation of employment opportunities in the urban formal sector. In the context of jobless growth or slow growth, there is unlikely to be a growth in demand for labour.

Globalization is certainly one of the factors influencing the amount of ICI trade in the Caribbean region. It is well understood that the globalization process is linked to a greater degree of competition, and the ILO (2002, 35) noted that competition

> also encourages formal firms to shift formal wage workers to informal employment arrangements without minimum wages, assured work or benefits, and to encourage informal units to switch from semi-permanent contracts with their workers to piece-rate or casual work arrangements – also without assured work, minimum wages or benefits. Globalization also often leads to shifts from secure self-employment to more precarious self-employment, as producers and traders lose their market niche. With these shifts, as more and more men enter the informal economy, women tend to be pushed to the lowest-income end of the informal economy, often as industrial workers or petty traders.

In terms of the Trinidad and Tobago economy, for example, there is a clear positive relationship between the extent of trade liberalization in the economy (measured as trade as a percentage of GDP) and the number of own account workers employed in the economy (the correlation between both variables is 73%), as shown in table 2.7.

Table 2.7: Relationship between Trade Openness and Own Account
Workers Employed in the Trinidad and Tobago Economy,
1991–2008

	Trade (% of GDP)	Own account workers employed
1991	73.5	65,900
1992	75.0	68,400
1993	83.0	70,500
1994	78.7	72,300
1995	93.0	75,700
1996	92.8	76,300
1997	111.2	75,700
1998	102.3	76,100
1999	94.2	81,600
2000	104.6	81,800
2001	100.5	84,700
2002	95.6	83,100
2003	94.5	82,900
2004	104.4	84,400
2005	96.3	84,800
2006	98.2	83,100
2007	98.5	87,500
2008	101.0	87,300
Correlation: 0.73		

Source: World Bank, *World Development Indicators* (2010); data from the
Central Statistical Office of Trinidad and Tobago, Ministry of Planning
and the Economy (various years).

Globalization has helped to promote the disintegration of trade and to
improve the integration of trade to the extent that firms from high cost
labour economies outsource some of their productive activities to economies with a low wage rate. The consequence of this has been the increase
in retrenchment in economies from which the activity was outsourced
(Feenstra and Hanson 1996). In those economies without established
social security systems, these workers are likely to migrate into the informal sector. Nadvi (2004) has noted that the increased degree of pressure
that is applied by global purchasers coerce producers to both improve on
the quality of their products as well as reduce the cost of production.

2.6. De-agriculturalization in the Caribbean

As a consequence of policies adopted in the post-independence period, a perverse kind of development has taken place in CARICOM, which in essential ways has weakened rather than strengthened the economic structure and promoted the decline of the agricultural sector (Guyana is an exception). The agricultural sector is typically labour-intensive, and with its demise comes a fall in employment opportunities. In many CARICOM economies, the agriculture sector has contracted over time as the manufacturing sector and the services sector have expanded (see table 2.8). This helped to precipitate a decline in both agricultural output and employment over time, with some of these displaced unemployed women finding refuge operating as ICIs.[16]

Above all this, ECLAC (2005) points out that in those CARICOM economies where commercial extra-regional agricultural exports exist, they typically use the best agricultural lands and employment patterns are predominated by men. The agricultural sector is typically labour-intensive, hence the stronger inclination of CARICOM economies toward service sector economies (as highlighted in table 2.7) will point to a decrease in the

Table 2.8: Relative Contribution of Causal Variables to the Size of the Informal Economy

Country	Importance of Agriculture (% of GDP)	Size of the Informal Economy from Vuletin (Absolute Value [% of GDP]) Early 2000s
Antigua and Barbuda	6.1	31.2
Barbados	31.2	24.5
Belize	49.3	46.8
Dominica	30.7	34.2
Grenada	40.9	22.5
Guyana	47.6	36.7
Jamaica	17.6	35.0
St Kitts and Nevis	28.1	24.2
St Lucia	48.7	41.5
St Vincent and the Grenadines	41.0	50.6
The Bahamas	42.3	15.9
Trinidad and Tobago	6.5	24.4

Source: Vuletin (2008).

employment capacity of CARICOM economies. The consequence of all this is an increase in the number of workers on-the-job seeking employment, and some of these workers inevitably spill over into the informal sector. These trends are seen markedly in Antigua and Barbuda and Jamaica, as shown in table 2.8.

2.7. Conclusion

This chapter traced the origins and evolution of ICIs in three countries: Jamaica, Guyana, and Trinidad and Tobago. Furthermore, it established the trading ties of ICIs as having inertia tendencies coming out of West Africa. With slavery and subsequent economic crises in the various economies, ICIs provided fertile ground for the shuttle trade to evolve. This chapter also traced the evolution of shuttle trader price discrimination/ market failure, and subsequently the motivation for the informal sector to fill market niches where legitimate markets for some commodities have been largely absent in the Caribbean.

The chapter highlighted that although the region was originally settled to be agriculture-focused in support of its colonizers, as a result of global events and domestic policies post-independence, most of the islands moved away from agriculture. The brunt of this shift away from the agriculture sector was felt mainly by the employment sector, which has forced people in the region to find creative ways of supporting themselves and their families. While the manufacturing and service sectors were able to absorb some of the excess labour, this was more so the consequence of the inclusion of a larger proportion of men to women in the region. Thus, given the fact that the regional economies are characterized by market failure, price discrimination and market niches, there was ample opportunity for the informal sector to fertilize and grow, particularly by women within the region.

3 THE PERSISTENCE OF THE SUITCASE TRADE

The shuttle trade in CARICOM is still very much alive. Women and increasingly men (particularly in the OECS economies) now participate in this trade. Although the parameters and rules of the trade keep changing, price discrimination and market failure are the fundamental reasons for persistence of the trade. This chapter discusses several other reasons that have helped the suitcase trade to persist. These reasons are culled from available literature and from interviews with a multitude of stakeholders.

3.1. Pattern of Economic Growth

The first explanation for the persistence of the suitcase trade pertains to the pattern of economic growth. In some Caribbean economies there has been jobless growth. The best example is perhaps the Trinidad and Tobago economy. As the data in table 3.1 show, economic activity in the Trinidad and Tobago economy increased sharply from TT$31,288 million in 1994 to TT$92,071 million in 2008, an increase of 194% in current prices. In this same interval of time, the share of petroleum GDP in total GDP climbed from 31% in 1994 to 40% in 2008. Significantly, however, employment in this segment of the economy remained fairly constant (3.83% in 1994 to 3.33% in 2008), although the overall national unemployment rate fell. This phenomena of jobless growth in the formal sector of the economy fits in well with one of the most established models of dualistic labour employment, the Lewis model. In Lewis's model, the percentage movement

Table 3.1: Real GDP, Petroleum Share of GDP and Employment for Trinidad and Tobago, 1994–2008

Year	Real GDP	Petroleum Share in GDP (%)	Petroleum Share in Employment (%)
1994	31,288.94	30.92	3.83
1995	34,556.50	28.14	3.73
1996	36,338.50	28.66	3.81
1997	38,836.20	27.29	3.72
1998	41,816.10	27.44	3.66
1999	46,280.00	30.24	3.06
2000	51,370.70	31.29	3.10
2001	53,516.00	31.71	3.02
2002	57,759.20	33.34	3.27
2003	66,084.40	38.29	3.03
2004	71,915.70	38.08	3.28
2005	75,785.60	35.17	3.32
2006	86,028.00	41.97	3.27
2007	90,005.40	40.79	3.64
2008	92,071.50	39.69	3.33

Source: Trinidad and Tobago, *Review of the Economy* (various years).

of workers from the informal sector to the modern industrialist sector is constrained by the number of jobs that the formal sector can provide.

Even more than this, CARICOM economies are characterized by twin deficits, with the exception of Trinidad and Tobago and Suriname. In particular, the current account deficits in both periods in table 3.2 exceed the fiscal deficit by factors of at least 400%.

Carr and Chen (2002, 2) have argued that "during periods of economic adjustment, whether due to economic reforms or economic crisis, the informal economy tends to expand". Amid such expansion, the number of ICIs increases.

3.2. The Tax Morality of Workers

Another reason for the persistence of the suitcase trade is the tax morality of workers. Tax morality has been referred to by Maurin et al. (2006) as the willingness of workers to pay the appropriate amount of taxes at the right

Table 3.2: Triple Deficits, 2005–2009 (percentage of GDP)

Country	2005–2007		2008–2009	
	Fiscal deficit	Current account deficit	Fiscal deficit	Current account deficit
Antigua and Barbuda	7.1	31.7	6.9	34.2
The Bahamas	2.2	15.3	2.5	11.1
Barbados	2.7	8.7	4.6	7.8
Belize	2.5	6.5	–0.8	8.5
Dominica	–1.7	22.4	–1.5	30.1
Grenada	3.1	36.8	6.0	43.7
Guyana	11.4	21.4	7.2	21.1
Jamaica	4.5	11.6	9.2	12.7
St Kitts and Nevis	3.0	18.1	–5.7	25.3
St Vincent and the Grenadines	3.9	26.9	2.2	36.6
St Lucia	4.9	28.0	–0.6	26.7
Suriname	–1.9	–8.0	–0.7	–14.7
Trinidad and Tobago	–4.4	–28.6	–1.3	–28.7
The Caribbean	2.8	14.2	2.2	16.5

Source: ECLAC (various years), on the basis of official figures.

time. For countries like Antigua and Barbuda, Barbados, and Trinidad and Tobago, Vuletin (2008) posits that the main factor influencing the informal economy is the tax burden. Further, Vuletin estimates that the relative contributions of the tax burden to the size of the informal economy range from 60% to 66% in the case of Barbados, Trinidad and Tobago, and Antigua and Barbuda, to as low as 21% in the case of Belize. Researchers are of the view that tax morality and the instruments imposed by government are positively correlated so that the greater the restrictions imposed by government, the greater the tendency to break the rules and become tax immoral. Although most Caribbean economies have significantly lowered restrictions to trade, some still exist, so there remains some margin of economic benefit for a trader to bring in goods via the shuttle trade.

Table 3.3 provides a summary of the most recent data on most-favoured nation tariffs in various CARICOM countries. High most-favoured-nation tariffs provide a strong incentive to employ the shuttle trade relative to formal importation methods. Consistent with an open regionalism stance,

Table 3.3: Summary Analysis of Most-Favoured-Nation Tariffs in Various CARICOM Member States

	Number of Tariff Lines	Current Average (%)	Previous Average (%)	Agricultural Goods (%)	Non-agricultural Goods (%)
Antigua and Barbuda	6,413 (2007)	10.7 (2007)	10.7[a]	–	9.7
Barbados	6,890 (2007)	16.2 (2007)	16.5 (2001)	33.7	12.8
Belize	6,292 (2004)	11.3 (2004)	n/a	17.9	10.1
Dominica	6,479 (2007)	12.2 (2007)	n/a	25.8	9.5
Grenada	6,330 (2007)	11.2 (2007)	n/a	18.2	9.8
Guyana	6,397 (2009)	12.0 (2008)	12.1 (2003)	22.5	10.0
Jamaica	6,439 (2004)	8.6 (2004)	10.9 (1997)	18.1	6.7
St Kitts	6,340 (2007)	10.3 (2007)	n/a	14.2	9.6
St Lucia	6,352 (2007)	10.0 (2007)	n/a	16.7	8.6
St Vincent	6,274 (2007)	10.9 (2007)	n/a	18.0	9.6
Suriname	5,291 (2007)	11.1 (2007)	35.0 (1994)	18.6	9.5
Trinidad and Tobago	6,437 (2005)	9.1 (2005)	9.1(1998)	17.1	7.6

[a]Unchanged since Phase 4 of the Common External Tariff was introduced in 2001.
Source: WTO (various years).

the most-favoured-nation tariffs in CARICOM member states declined in those member states for which data were available. Even so, the average most-favoured-nation tax rates are still non-trivial.

When an economy has a high rate of taxation, firms are more likely to either migrate to the informal sector or purchase goods and services from ICIs and other informal sector enterprises to avoid paying the taxes.

3.3. Female-headed Households Continue to Abound

In the Caribbean, female-headed households continue to be the dominant type of household (see table 3.4). An International Fund for Agricultural Development study undertaken in 2000 estimated that around 45% of households in Grenada are headed by females.

A UNICEF (2000) study found that the majority of Jamaican children are born while their parents are in a common-law relationship. The study also noted that most of these relationships end when the child is between five and six years old. The main implication of this trend is that the children grow up in single-parent female-headed households. De Albuquerque and

Table 3.4: Percentage of Households Headed by Women, by Size of Household, for Selected Caribbean Countries, 1990–1991 and 2008

	% of all households, 1990–1991	% of all households, 2008
Antigua and Barbuda	41	48.05
The Bahamas	35	40.52
Barbados	43	50.66
Belize	22	21.76
Dominica	37	42.88
Grenada	43	50.16
Guyana	28	26.92
Jamaica	40	49.22
Montserrat	40	45.51
St Kitts and Nevis	44	57.85
St Lucia	40	49.04
St Vincent and the Grenadines	39	50.78
Trinidad and Tobago	28	28.83

Source: CARICOM (various years).

McElroy (1999) indicated that female-headed households in the Caribbean are more prevalent than male-headed households. For the Caribbean, there is also an established tendency for the poorest households to be headed by women. Kairi Consultants (2007), using data from the Trinidad and Tobago Survey of Living Conditions 2004, found that 38% of the poorest households were headed by women, whereas the national percentage was 33%. Pearson (1993) asserted that women from female-headed households are more likely to accept low paying jobs in the informal sector if only to provide for the well-being of their children. Females who are heads of such households and value the independence and flexibility offered by the shuttle trade will opt to be ICIs instead.

Furthermore, women also suffer from a type of "time" poverty. Specifically, time poverty refers to a situation in which women have to do so much that they hardly have time to do anything else. In the long run this undermines their capacity to form human capital. The International Fund for Agricultural Development (2000) noted that female-headed households in the Caribbean experience greater difficulties escaping poverty than their male counterparts. Female-headed households fall into two categories: (1) young female head of households with young children supported by inter- mittent partners, and (2) older female head of households, with adult chil- dren, who may not have the help of a male. Specifically, for the first group, pregnancy represents the end of schooling for the young mothers-to-be and the beginning of their financial responsibilities. Child caring duties hinder these young mothers from accessing business opportunities, obtain- ing a job and continuing their education. Older female head of households escape the time poverty trap. Practically, these women have more time to become involved in income-generating activities such as the shuttle trade.

3.4. The Changing Structure of CARICOM Economies

Changes in the structure of the agricultural sector of CARICOM econo- mies, among other factors, have typically absorbed the majority of female workers. However, as table 3.5 illustrates, the structure of CARICOM economies has been changing, with an overall decline in the size of the agricultural sector. Consider the situation in Jamaica and St Lucia, for example. The share of women employed in the agricultural sector fell from 15.9% in Jamaica in 1992 to 8.8% in 2004 and for St Lucia from 14.9% in 1993 to 8.6% in 2003.

Table 3.5: Female Agricultural Employees as
Percentage of Female Employment for
Jamaica and St Lucia

	Jamaica	St Lucia
1991	–	–
1992	15.9	–
1993	12.0	14.9
1994	12.1	17.7
1995	11.7	17.7
1996	11.3	18.8
1997	10.1	13.8
1998	9.9	16.5
1999	8.9	15.9
2000	9.2	14.3
2001	9.6	–
2002	9.9	8.7
2003	8.8	8.5
2004	8.8	9.8
2005	8.5	–
2006	8.3	–
2007	–	–

Source: World Bank, *World Development Indicators* (2010)

Given the typically labour-intensive mode of employment of the agricultural sector, one would expect a general increase in the number of unskilled women looking for employment. The shuttle trade provides one avenue for such employment.

3.5. Institutional Weakness Continues to Plague Caribbean Economies

Weak institutions also play a role in promoting the development of the informal economy, including the shuttle trade. For example, if there is not the strictest of regulation at points of entry by customs officials, then antibiotics and other medications can enter an economy unscreened, via the shuttle trade, with questionable distribution.

Formal and informal sector firms are characterized by different sets of constraints. Suitcase traders (and participants in the informal sector in general) obviously avoid a number of regulatory costs that firms in the formal sector cannot avoid. These regulatory costs, especially for starting up, can be quite high. Djankov et al. (2002) found that for a sample of eighty-five countries, entry costs vary from 2.63% of per capita GDP in Canada to 463% of per capita GDP in the Dominican Republic.[1]

To conduct business in the formal sector, a number of costs have to be incurred. In the Caribbean context this generally includes:

- the cost of a licence, as may be relevant for some types of business;
- the cost of leasing or acquiring the business premises;
- hiring employees according to the minimum wages established by the state;
- knowing the various relevant government laws and regulations and adhering to them;
- obtaining pertinent information about the goods on the market, about prices and about the quality and quantity of the good or service the market requires;
- buying supplies for the enterprise; and

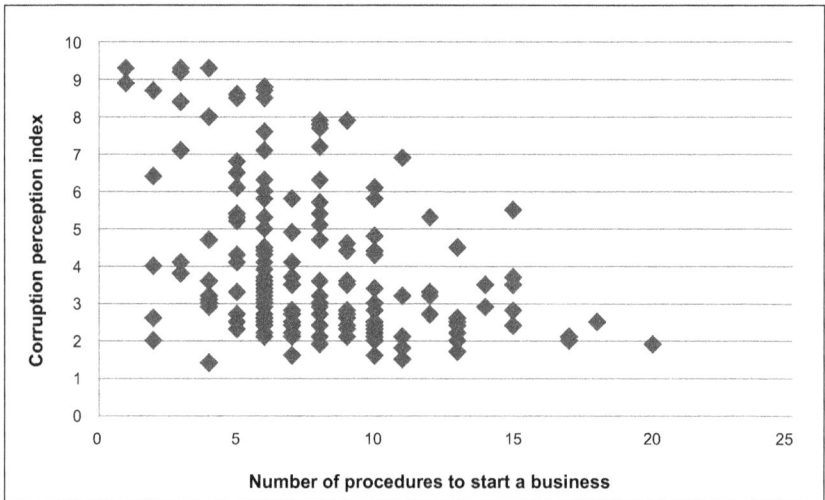

Figure 3.1 Scatterplot of corruption perception index and the number of procedures
Source: World Bank (2010).

- establishing the various utility connections, such as electricity, water, telephone, and so on.

One school of thought (the tollbooth view) hypothesizes that the level of corruption is higher in countries in which there is a greater element of regulation (Treisman 1998; Alesina and Angeletos 2005).

In countries with a low Corruption Perception Index score, it takes more time to formally import. This being the case, it follows that traders may choose to bring in some of their merchandise via the suitcase trade to improve the conversion rate of their investment in stocks into an income stream. Figures 3.1 and 3.2 show an increase in the number of procedures required to start a business and longer time to import, respectively. These have the effect of creating unwarranted bottlenecks that weaken the administrative process.

Table 3.6 abstracts from the two scatterplots in figures 3.1 and 3.2 and provides a CARICOM-specific focus. The data in table 3.6 highlight that it is relatively tedious and expensive to import goods into the Caribbean in relation to other economies, and as a consequence some entrepreneurs tend to go to the foreign market themselves and informally import. The data indicate that as the time taken to import increases or the number of

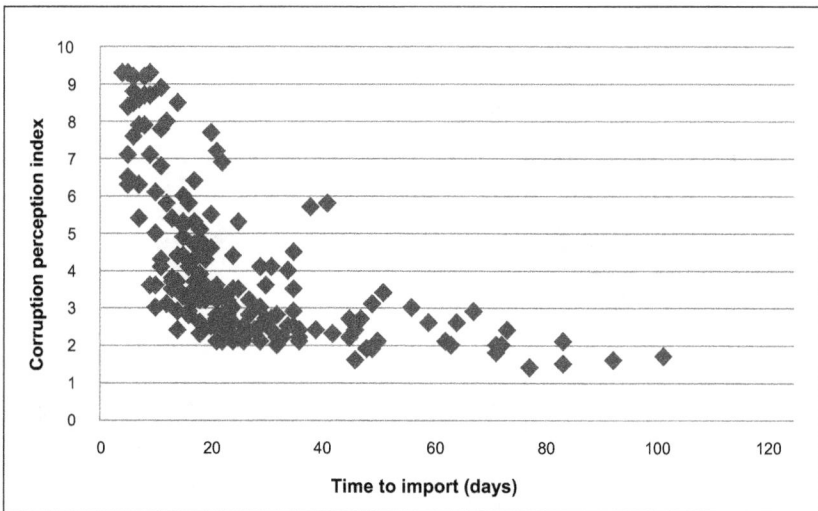

Figure 3.2 Scatterplot of time to import and corruption perception index
Source: World Bank (2010).

Table 3.6: Trading Across Borders, Metrics for CARICOM Economies, 2009, and the Size of the Informal Sector

	Documents to Export (Number)	Time to Export (Days)	Cost of Exporting (US$ per Container)	Documents to Import (Number)	Time to Import (Days)	Cost of Importing (US$ per Container)	Informal Economy in % of GNP 1999–2000
Antigua and Barbuda	5	15	1,133	5	15	1,633	31.2
The Bahamas	5	16	930	5	13	1,380	15.9
Belize	7	21	1,710	6	21	1,870	46.8
Dominica	7	13	1,297	8	15	1,310	34.2
Grenada	6	14	1,226	5	19	2,479	22.5
Guyana	7	20	730	8	24	730	36.7
Jamaica	6	21	1,750	6	22	1,420	35.0
St Kitts and Nevis	6	12	850	6	13	2,138	24.2
St Lucia	5	14	1,600	8	18	2,645	41.5
Trinidad and Tobago	5	14	866	6	26	1,100	24.4
Singapore	4	5	456	4	3	439	

Source: World Bank (2010).

documents to import increases or the cost of importing increases, so too do the sizes of informal commercial importing and the larger informal economy in total economic activity in the CARICOM sphere.

3.6. Relatively High Levels of Female Unemployment Continue to Persist

In CARICOM, women have traditionally been engaged in the shuttle trade. This trend partly prevails because of the continued relatively high female unemployment rates when compared to male unemployment rates in CARICOM, as demonstrated in table 3.7, which shows a sampling of countries.

In this type of setting, alongside the lure of travelling and seeing new places and meeting new people, informal commercial importing will certainly remain an option for unemployed women.

Table 3.7: Male and Female Unemployment Rates (%) for Various CARICOM Economies, 1980–2007

	Jamaica		Guyana		Trinidad and Tobago		St Lucia	
	Female	Male	Female	Male	Female	Male	Female	Male
1980	40	16	–	–	14	8	–	–
1985	36	16	–	–	17	15	–	–
1990	23	9	–	–	24	18	–	–
1995	23	11	–	–	21	15	21	12
2000	22	10	–	–	15	10	21	13
2001	21	10	14	6	14	9	–	–
2002	21	11	15	10	14	8	18	12
2003	17	8	–	–	14	8	28	17
2004	16	8	–	–	11	6	25	17
2005	15	7	–	–	11	6	–	–
2006	13	7	–	–	7	3	–	–
2007	14	5	–	–	10	4	–	–

Source: World Bank, *World Development Indicators* (2010).

3.7. Globalization and the Employment of Women

With globalization, the Caribbean continues to experience cross border mergers and the closure of regional and multinational companies. More recently, these economies have been subjected to high oil prices in the period 2006–8 and the external shock from the global financial crisis from 2008 to present. Intra-Caribbean trade is down; so too is the number of international tourist visitors to the region. These combined shocks have resulted in increased levels of job layoffs across most Caribbean economies. One report noted that "In several countries in the OECS unemployment is now estimated to be around 20%; the rate is around 10% in Barbados and Jamaica and around 5% in Trinidad and Tobago. Widespread layoffs associated with weak tourism performance continue. Around 30,000 Jamaicans (or 2.5% of the workforce) have lost their jobs since September 2008. Additional layoffs are expected during the peak winter tourism season" (EIU 2009). This report also noted that hotel bookings remain weak and discounts are large, leading to reductions in profitability for many firms. In response to the slow collapse in tourist arrivals since the middle of 2008, many popular destinations have been cutting their prices. In the Caribbean specifically, the IMF noted that by the end of 2008 there was around a 7% decline in hotel rates, which was cut even further in 2009. This trend is worrisome as it has the potential to cause sharp cuts in revenues and in turn declines in foreign exchange earnings in 2010.

The decline of the tourist sector is also compounded by tourists themselves cutting back on the amount that they spend while on holiday. Businesses that support the tourist sector are negatively impacted by this reduction in spending. There is also a change in how tourists spend their holidays, meaning that instead of flying to the destination and staying for a length of time, many are opting for cruises over beach holidays since cruises are relatively cheap and all-inclusive. However, cruise holidays also contribute far less to host economies when compared to stopover tourists. According to the latest statistics from the Barbados-based Caribbean Tourism Organization, most countries that rely heavily on tourism have seen double-digit year-on-year declines in stopover arrivals in 2009.

Jamaica is one country that has bucked this trend, as stopover arrivals to the island were 3.4% higher year-on-year in the first half of 2009. This aberration experienced by Jamaica was mainly due to two factors: a 25% increase in Canadian tourists during the period, and an increase in budget all-inclusive resorts. Even with this aberration, overall tourist expenditures in Jamaica remained low and workers within the sector continued to be laid off.

Given the fact that many countries rely heavily on the tourism sector to spur economic growth (for many countries, tourism accounts for over half of their economic input), the shaky consumer demand from the United States and United Kingdom in particular has had a profound effect on their economies. Looking at the case of Barbados, the adverse impact of the decline in the tourism sector on GDP can be highlighted. In 2009, the tourism value-added slumped by 9.8% in the first nine months for the country, representing the sector's largest nine-month decline in nearly twenty years. In turn, this led to a contraction in real GDP of 4.4%.

Even if the US recession ended, this will not result in an end to the recession being experienced by most of the English-speaking Caribbean islands. This is because the tourism sector and remittance flows follow the trend of the unemployment rate in the United States, which happens to be a lagging indicator. Thus, until US unemployment improves, these two important sectors will not improve.

Given the significant number of female-headed households within the socioeconomic profile of the tourism sector, it is not unreasonable to conclude that the majority of the persons displaced are female. One option available to displaced female workers is informal commercial importing, in particular higgling and huckstering. Mulakala (1991) identified two motivators for persons to become hucksters: financial return and the level of independence that the trade offers. These motivators remain relevant in today's globalized environment. Lagro (1988) posits that for many women the decision to become a huckster stems from the need to provide for large households that are surviving on limited or strained financial resources. This too remains relevant in the current globalized environment.

Babb et al. (2004) observed that the shuttle trade has been less visible with the advance of trade liberalization in the Caribbean region. The prolonged rollout of the CSME across the region will bring with it new challenges and new opportunities for these traders. Undoubtedly, shuttle traders must adjust their trade as they respond to the CSME. The adjustments that they make to their trade will determine to a significant degree their continued survival and growth in the new trading environment.

3.8. Conclusion

This chapter reviewed several factors that may be responsible for the persistence of the shuttle trade in the Caribbean and that complement the perpetuity of price discrimination and market failure. Indeed, as the informal economy expands, more space is created for ICI activity. In particular, this chapter examined factors such as the prevalence of female-headed households and the changing structure of Caribbean economies, in particular the declining size of their agricultural sector, high levels of female unemployment, the high regulatory cost of starting a business and lastly (but by no means least) the impact of globalization.

The chapter noted that for many islands within the region, the economic growth experienced in the most recent times can be classified as jobless growth, and women are more negatively affected by this than men. The change experienced by almost all the islands from an agriculture-based economy to a more service-driven economy has resulted in decreased employment levels, as the former sector is more labour intensive than the latter. This economic pattern, combined with the institutional weakness that is pervasive throughout the region, has led to the persistence of the shuttle trade.

The chapter noted that the informal sector in the Caribbean is dominated by women, and given the fact that Caribbean households are mainly female driven, this is not surprising. Female-driven households in the Caribbean have been a fact from the days of slavery and have persisted over time. This fact is also compounded by the negative effects of globalization on Caribbean economies, in particular the tourism sector. The chapter notes that as this sector shrinks due to the global recession,women have been more negatively impacted, thus forcing them to enter the informal sector to provide for the households that they lead. On this basis, the next three chapters of this study provide empirical analyses of the shuttle trade as it exists in Trinidad and Tobago, Guyana, Dominica, and Jamaica.

4 INTRA-CARICOM INFORMAL COMMERCIAL IMPORTERS: EVIDENCE FROM TRINIDAD AND TOBAGO AND GUYANA

This chapter assesses the size and nature of the suitcase trade between Trinidad and Tobago and Guyana and is organized into six sections. Section 4.1 gives a brief overview of the Guyanese and Trinidadian economies. This is followed by an inquisition into Trinidad and Tobago's revealed comparative advantage with Guyana in section 4.2. Section 4.3 provides an empirical overview of intra-industry trade between Guyana and Trinidad and Tobago. Section 4.4 discusses weight as a conditioning factor for travel and trade, with the following section providing a review of previous research on the shuttle trade between Trinidad and Tobago and Guyana. The empirical analysis is undertaken in section 4.6. The chapter conclusion includes some relevant options that should be considered by policymakers, particularly the various facilities and systems that could aid in the formalization process in Trinidad and Tobago and Guyana.

4.1. Preliminary Overview of the Economies of Guyana and Trinidad and Tobago

The Guyanese economy was adversely affected by economic mismanagement in the 1970s, the consequence of which was a decline in real GDP by 3% per annum during the 1980s. In 1988, an economic recovery programme was initiated and although this helped to halt the extent of economic decline, it was only in 2001 that the output levels of 1976 were re-attained. During the period 1991–97, GDP growth accelerated to about 7% per annum, motivated principally by inflows of FDI, as well as the market reform exercise. By 1998, however, on account of a wave of civil disturbances within the economy, there was a 1.7% contraction in the economy.[1] Since 1998, growth has been mild and averaged a mere 0.3% in the period 2001–5.[2] After a flood-related contraction of the economy in 2005, the Guyanese economy showed stronger signs of growth, triggered mainly by enhanced inflows of remittances and FDI. As a result of the global economic recession, the Guyanese economy contracted in 2009, although growth is expected to resume in 2010 (CIA *WorldFactbook*).

Table 4.1 shows the trend in the GDP of Guyana and Guyana's GDP expressed as a percentage of GDP in Trinidad and Tobago. The GDP of Guyana was US$603.2 million in 1980, but thereafter plummeted by 44.18% to US$336.71 million in 1991. The economy has since realized something of a revival and by 2008, Guyana's GDP stood at US$1,155.3 million. As a percentage of Trinidad and Tobago's GDP, Guyana's GDP has lost considerable margin, decreasing from 9.67% in 1980 to around 4.46% in 2008.

Table 4.2 presents information on the evolving production structures of the Guyanese and Trinidad and Tobago economies. Note the differences in the relative size of the agricultural sector and mining sectors between the two economies. The difference between the agriculture, mining and quarrying and manufacturing sectors (excluding rice and sugar) is such that it lends itself easier to Heckscher Ohlin[3] type trade when compared to intra-industry type trade.

The Economic Intelligence Unit (2009) cited the 1999 Household Income and Expenditure Survey in Guyana as listing the unemployment rate as 9%. Notwithstanding, the unit argues that approximately one half of the working age population is underemployed. The Economic Intelligence Unit also highlights the low wages in Guyana, with starting salaries in the public sector at US$145 a month when compared to US$260 in Trinidad and Tobago.

In terms of exports and imports between the two trading nations, Trinidad and Tobago has always been a net exporter to the Guyanese economy, as indicated in table 4.3. Observe that after 1987, there has been a widening of the gap between the exports and imports of Trinidad and Tobago and Guyana.

Guyana's imports from Trinidad and Tobago have become increasingly concentrated in the oil sector. Oil exports can be proxied by SITC 3. The share of oil exports as a fraction of total imports by Guyana from Trinidad and Tobago increased to 73.6% in 2005, compared to 23.4% in 1998.[4] This is a significant increase. Note that whereas the import expenditure

Table 4.1: GDP for Guyana and Trinidad and Tobago, 1980–2008
(current US$m)

	Guyana	Trinidad and Tobago	Trinidad and Tobago/Guyana (%)
1980	603.20	6,235.87	9.67
1981	570.36	6,849.17	8.33
1982	482.00	7,989.79	6.03
1983	489.33	7,799.75	6.27
1984	437.63	7,756.17	5.64
1985	453.49	7,376.00	6.15
1986	504.65	4,794.36	10.53
1987	354.59	4,797.75	7.39
1988	413.80	4,496.81	9.20
1989	379.78	4,323.04	8.79
1990	396.58	5,068.07	7.83
1991	336.71	5,362.82	6.28
1992	368.28	5,532.12	6.66
1993	442.27	4,584.65	9.65
1994	540.87	4,947.21	10.93
1995	621.63	5,329.21	11.66
1996	705.41	5,759.54	12.25
1997	749.14	5,737.75	13.06
1998	717.53	6,043.71	11.87
1999	694.75	6,808.98	10.20
2000	712.67	8,154.32	8.74
2001	696.28	8,824.87	7.89
2002	722.46	9,008.27	8.02
2003	741.93	11,235.96	6.60
2004	785.92	12,884.71	6.10
2005	824.88	15,982.28	5.16
2006	914.56	18,369.06	4.98
2007	1,075.14	20,904.05	5.14
2008	1,159.24	25,968.28	4.46

Source: World Bank (various years).

by Guyana on Trinidad and Tobago's goods increased 238% in the indicated time period, the import expenditure on crude oil increased even more dramatically by 931%.[5] Table 4.4, specifically panels (a) and (b), shows

Table 4.2: Sectoral (%) Value-Added, Guyana and Trinidad and Tobago

Guyana

	Agriculture	Mining and Quarrying	Manufacturing Excluding Rice and Sugar	Services
1994	45.0	21.5	3.6	29.9
2005	34.7	10.5	3.6	51.2
2005–2009	30.1	6.8	6.1	55.2

Trinidad and Tobago

	Agriculture	Mining and Quarrying	Manufacturing Excluding Rice and Sugar	Services
1994	2.2	29.2	7.8	60.8
2005	1.3	34.1	7.1	57.5
2005–2009	0.5	40.5	8.1	51.1

Source: World Bank (various years).

that the main imports and exports by Guyana from Trinidad and Tobago are lodged in different sections of the international trade classification. Even more, this tendency has become more pronounced with time. This partly provides some basic indication that the Trinidad and Tobago economy and the Guyanese economy are engaging in Heckscher Ohlin–type trade with each other.

4.2. Revealed Comparative Advantage of Trinidad and Tobago's Exports with Guyana

Balassa (1965), in an evaluation of the factors that determine the comparative advantage of an economy, noted that comparative advantage is attributed to several factors, some quantitative and some qualitative. The convention, however, is that measuring the comparative advantage of an economy begins with its trade performance. On this basis, Balassa promoted the line of enquiry focusing on post-trade equilibrium rather than pre-trade equilibrium. Concerning post trade equilibrium, Balassa highlights that it "reflects relative costs as well as differences in non-price factors".

Table 4.3: Trinidad and Tobago Exports to and Imports from Guyana in US$m, 1973–2009

	Export	Import
1973	24.98	5.65
1974	48.6	10.98
1975	54.99	16.48
1976	69.34	18.29
1977	62.33	16.40
1978	55.47	17.24
1979	72.36	21.14
1980	90.84	23.92
1981	108.86	31.65
1982	110.45	32.55
1983	66.67	26.05
1984	72.85	22.03
1985	66.33	17.75
1986	19.70	4.34
1987	6.82	2.78
1988	9.96	4.40
1989	24.39	2.54
1990	27.26	3.57
1991	30.40	6.00
1992	41.38	6.98
1993	58.52	6.35
1994	59.77	7.07
1995	80.61	9.96
1996	90.11	12.45
1997	110.20	13.63
1998	83.86	10.58
1999	76.23	11.90
2000	97.43	14.79
2001	95.90	16.33
2002	82.49	15.74
2003	150.87	22.57
2004	121.83	25.92
2005	274.33	21.86
2006	338.32	18.62
2007	241.11	25.45
2008	319.10	31.53
2009p	169.86	25.80

Source: UNCOMTRADE (various years).

Table 4.4: Guyana Imports and Exports from Trinidad and Tobago, 1998–2009

Imports US$m

	0	1	2	3	4	5	6	7	8	9
1998	13.43	6.34	1.00	17.99	0.32	11.2	20.18	1.99	4.34	–
1999	9.16	5.06	0.31	17.66	0.06	9.01	16.50	2.07	4.61	–
2000	8.76	5.66	1.20	28.89	0.03	11.65	19.15	1.96	5.81	0.02
2001	10.08	10.16	1.03	29.28	0.06	12.28	18.41	2.40	5.05	0.01
2002	9.99	8.14	2.04	30.28	0.08	11.72	18.74	2.90	4.78	0.01
2003	10.50	8.51	3.57	91.90	0.10	11.29	16.21	2.32	4.21	0.00
2004	10.73	8.17	4.04	102.86	0.02	14.14	20.57	2.23	6.58	–
2005	12.57	12.00	2.34	190.85	0.13	12.17	17.21	3.43	8.25	0.23
2006	12.94	11.39	1.20	222.76	0.05	18.64	21.84	3.67	7.37	0.08
2007	16.56	12.89	1.58	172.59	0.07	21.13	20.06	4.14	9.25	–
2008	26.11	15.15	2.26	187.89	0.00	26.07	26.18	5.37	8.07	–

Exports US$m

	0	1	2	3	4	5	6	7	8	9
1998	4.55	0.19	1.17	0.21	0.08	1.08	2.47	0.09	0.41	–
1999	5.90	0.12	1.00	0.02	0.30	1.07	2.60	0.14	0.17	–
2000	6.06	0.34	2.58	–	0.57	1.36	3.89	7.60	0.20	0.01
2001	8.30	0.53	1.82	0.03	0.17	0.83	3.19	0.17	0.10	0.02
2002	11.26	0.78	1.29	–	0.52	1.37	2.08	4.73	0.22	0.04
2003	17.97	0.75	1.42	0.02	0.19	0.97	3.06	3.22	0.30	0.39
2004	26.98	0.91	2.50	0.01	0.36	0.88	3.36	0.77	0.20	1.46
2005	19.75	0.97	1.35	0.00	0.57	0.89	2.00	3.15	0.73	0.32
2006	18.92	1.20	1.58	0.01	1.14	0.70	2.83	8.72	0.22	0.10
2007	28.56	1.76	1.97	0.01	1.29	1.17	1.84	1.32	2.91	–
2008	23.25	1.31	2.34	0.01	0.82	1.30	2.27	0.54	0.59	0.00
2009	21.69	1.26	2.51	0.00	0.48	1.42	1.97	0.46	0.27	–

Source: UNCOMTRADE (various years).

Balassa (1965) revealed comparative advantage index can be expressed as follows:

$$B = [X_{ij} / X_{it}] / [X_{nj} / X_{nt}]$$

where X represents exports; i represents a country; j represents a commodity; t represents a set of commodities; and n represents a set of countries.

Table 4.5 shows the revealed comparative advantage between the Trinidad and Tobago economy and Guyanese economy. Observe also that the

Table 4.5: Trinidad and Tobago Revealed Comparative Advantage with Various CARICOM Trade Partners

Trinidad and Tobago RCA with the World						Trinidad and Tobago RCA with Guyana					
2000		2005		2008		2000		2005		2008	
SITC Commodity Code	RCA	SITC Commodity Code	RCA	SITC Commodity Code	RCA	SITC Commodity Codes	RCA	SITC Commodity Codes	RCA	SITC Commodity Codes	RCA
98	1.04	46	1.09	46	1.501	17	1.72	17	1.52	1	2.01
46	1.87	48	1.81	48	1.149	34	2.03	44	2.61	17	1.09
48	3.35	59	1.93	59	1.118	35	3.21	48	1.69	35	1.25
58	1.52	61	1.64	111	3.134	48	2.65	58	1.60	46	2.38
59	1.39	91	1.59	122	2.051	58	1.93	59	1.13	48	1.92
61	5.55	111	6.02	223	1.081	59	2.62	81	1.74	58	1.23
62	2.30	122	1.43	281	6.038	62	1.85	111	1.87	59	2.13
72	1.04	333	2.46	333	1.769	73	2.02	122	2.38	62	1.50
91	4.16	334	8.62	334	5.984	81	1.09	251	2.61	81	1.07
111	12.01	342	12.32	342	17.939	91	1.00	278	1.42	91	1.43
112	1.72	343	15.62	343	15.897	111	2.89	334	2.48	111	1.50
333	2.38	344	5.72	344	16.743	112	2.06	335	1.55	112	1.06
334	15.23	512	26.78	512	23.969	122	4.25	342	2.61	122	3.64
342	14.14	522	33.05	522	25.200	266	2.16	344	2.60	223	3.57
343	8.14	554	1.03	562	4.320	278	2.14	554	1.42	264	3.80

(*Table 4.5 continues*)

Table 4.5: Trinidad and Tobago Revealed Comparative Advantage with Various CARICOM Trade Partners (*continued*)

	Trinidad and Tobago RCA with the World						Trinidad and Tobago RCA with Guyana					
	2000		2005		2008		2000		2005		2008	
	SITC Commodity Code	RCA	SITC Commodity Code	RCA	SITC Commodity Code	RCA	SITC Commodity Codes	RCA	SITC Commodity Codes	RCA	SITC Commodity Codes	RCA
	344	33.05	562	6.55	671	5.325	291	2.41	562	2.49	273	1.87
	512	28.46	642	1.47	672	1.159	334	3.86	642	1.73	278	3.15
	522	32.59	671	4.48	676	2.020	335	1.22	676	1.85	322	1.69
	554	2.48	672	1.43	723	1.004	342	4.27	689	2.30	334	2.78
	562	7.33	676	3.53			344	4.27	892	1.33	335	1.05
	635	1.06					511	3.20	899	1.15	342	3.80
	642	2.80					516	1.45			344	3.76
	661	2.30					524	4.27			512	2.40
	665	1.45					533	1.59			533	1.56
	671	12.00					554	2.44			554	1.67
	676	10.74					562	2.64			562	2.48
							575	2.15			572	3.80
							582	1.01			575	1.14

592	2.22		582	1.41
598	1.63		593	3.8
642	3.22		642	2.43
653	1.15		654	3.13
656	1.63		672	1.71
657	1.02		676	2.83
658	1.45		692	1.5
661	3.01		778	1.17
665	2.32		892	1.39
675	1.10			
676	2.37			
692	1.71			
733	4.27			
778	1.51			
812	2.21			
813	1.77			
892	1.70			
893	1.10			
897	1.48			
899	1.71			

Source: UNCOMTRADE (2010) and own computations.

range of commodities in which the Trinidad and Tobago economy has a revealed comparative advantage is much wider with Guyana alone, than the range of commodities in which Trinidad and Tobago has a revealed comparative advantage with the world as a whole. This is partly reflective of the relatively underdeveloped state of the Guyanese economy.

4.3. Intra-Industry Trade between Guyana and Trinidad and Tobago

The Grubel-Lloyd (1975) index is by far the most widely used measure of intra-industry trade. At the time of its introduction, the Grubel-Lloyd index represented the most rigorous attempt to quantify intra-industry trade, and even today it is still widely deployed by many researchers. On a multilateral basis, the Grubel-Lloyd (1975) index measures the extent of the absolute amount of commodity exports in a particular industry or commodity grouping which is offset by imports in the same grouping, and expresses this intra-industry trade as a proportion of the total trade in this commodity.

Its value is measured by:

$$G_j = 1 - \frac{\left|X_i - M_i\right|}{\left(X_i + M_i\right)} (3)$$

where G_j is the value of intra-industry trade; and X_i and M_i are the values of exports and imports of industry i, or a given country for a given period.

The clear indication from figure 4.1 is that there is a very close degree of co-movement between the shares of Guyana's GDP as a proportion of Trinidad and Tobago's total GDP and the extent of intra-industry trade between Trinidad and Tobago and Guyana. The correlation between both variables is 0.64. This is not surprising as the literature infers a lower degree of intra-industry trade will take place between countries with dissimilar levels of per capita income. As figure 4.1 illustrates, the share of Guyanese GDP in total GDP, although increasing marginally from 6.3% in 1991 to 13% in 1997, declined to 5.2% in 2005. As the income per capita gap between Trinidad and Tobago and Guyana widened, the extent of intra-industry trade, not surprisingly and consistent with theoretical inference, declined.

A seminal research paper by Maurice Schiff and Won Chang investigated the criteria for determining whether any set of economies entering a preferred trading agreement are "natural trading partners". The natural trading partner hypothesis as defined by Schiff and Chang (2001)

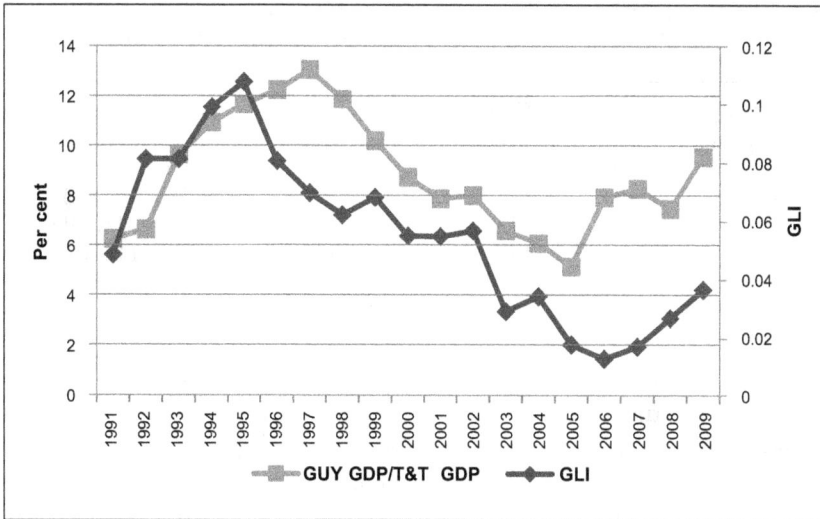

Figure 4.1 Intra-industry trade between Guyana and Trinidad and Tobago, and
        Guyana GDP as a percentage of Trinidad and Tobago GDP, 1991–2009
Source: World Bank (various years); own calculations using data from
        UNCOMTRADE (various years).

establishes that trading partners are natural if their trading situation is
characterized by complementarity in their respective trading structure.
The measurement of trade complementarity between trading partners or
prospective trading partners can be undertaken by employing the trade
complementarity index developed by Drysdale (1967).[6] This trade complementarity index was deployed to investigate whether Trinidad and
Tobago and Guyana are real natural trading partners, the results of which
are presented in table 4.6. The results indicate that there exists an intense
trading relationship between Trinidad and Tobago and Guyana. This
intense trade relationship is due to a low degree of trade complementarity
and an associated high degree of trade bias between Trinidad and Tobago
and Guyana for 2000, 2005 and 2008.

4.4. Weight as a Conditioning Factor

Luggage weight restrictions are globally applied to persons travelling by
air. The Caribbean is no exception. The weight requirements for travelling
with one of the region's foremost airlines, Caribbean Airlines (formerly British West Indian Airlines), distinguish between intra- and extra-Caribbean

Table 4.6: Trade Intensity Index ( ), Trade Complementarity Index [ ] and Trade Bias Index for Trinidad and Tobago and Guyana (2000, 2005 and 2008)

Exports to Exports from	Guyana (2000)	Guyana (2005)	Guyana (2008)
Trinidad and Tobago	(344.85) [2.33] 148.00	(404.15) [2.90] 139.36	(213.47) [1.83] 116.65

Source: UNCOMTRADE (2010) and own calculations.

travel. Specifically, for intra-Caribbean routes, except that of St Maarten and Kingston, the maximum luggage weight is stipulated at 20 kilograms or 44 pounds. For extra-Caribbean destinations, luggage restrictions are based on class of flight and destination. For example, business class passengers travelling to Europe are allowed a maximum of three pieces of luggage, each weighing no more than 23 kilograms or 50 pounds. In economy class, passengers travelling to the same destination are allowed a maximum of only two pieces of luggage, each with the same weight restriction as that of business class. These restrictions are influenced by the significant difference in the cargo capacities of the fleet used by Caribbean Airlines on its extra-Caribbean network and that used by the intra-Caribbean operating airlines.

In addition, at peak travel periods of the year, such as during Carnival, summer and Christmas, it is not unusual for airlines like Caribbean Airlines to apply a baggage embargo in which all luggage restrictions are strictly enforced. These restrictions constrain the level of trade done by ICIs between Trinidad and Tobago and Guyana during peak travel periods.

4.5. Previous Research on Suitcase Trade between Trinidad and Tobago and Guyana

To the best of the authors' knowledge, the first study on the suitcase trade between Trinidad and Tobago and Guyana was completed by Daphne Phillips in 1985. This study was part of a larger ECLAC study on women in trade within the Caribbean. The research was conducted in Trinidad and Tobago in 1984. The study had as its objectives an understanding of the geographical movement of women who trade in Trinidad and Tobago, an identification of the female traders in the Trinidad and Tobago economy, and an identification of problems encountered by female traders while plying their trade. Phillips interviewed 97 women traders and found that the Trinidad and Tobago economy formed a nucleus around which traders in the Caribbean operated. This study was based on information from 97 women, 45 of whom were from Trinidad and Tobago, 20 from Guyana, 20 from St Vincent, and 12 from Grenada.

The main findings of this study were as follows:

- The mean age of the traders was 36.6 years, with the typical Trinidad and Tobago trader being 30.2 years old and those from Guyana, Grenada and St Vincent, 28 years, 38.3 years and 45.5 years old respectively.
- The younger Trinidad and Tobago and Guyanese women engaged trade in manufactured goods, while the older women from St Vincent and Grenada traded in agricultural goods.
- All of the traders were exposed to some degree of education, mainly primary school or incomplete secondary school education. Older women from St Vincent and Grenada generally had a lower level of education than younger women from Trinidad or Guyana.
- Forty per cent of the Guyanese women were married. The corresponding figure from Trinidad, Tobago, Grenada and St Vincent were 20%, 30%, 50% and 20% respectively.
- The Guyanese traders travelled twice a week by air, while the Tobago traders travelled once per week by boat. Traders from St Vincent and Grenada travelled once a week during the relevant season. Significantly, the Trinidadian traders captured in this study travelled only twice a year.
- The Guyanese traders mainly brought clothing, gold, baskets, toothpaste and Ferrol to trade in Trinidad. The Grenadians and Vincentians brought fruits, plantains, ground provisions and lambie. Many of the Trinidadians did not carry goods abroad to sell since they were Type 1 traders.
- Guyanese traders purchased food, drugs, school items and general luxury goods from the Trinidad market for sale in their home economy. The Grenadians and Vincentians took back hardware, lumber, building materials, steel and miscellaneous manufactured goods, such as mattresses, from Trinidad.
- Gross weekly income ranged from GUY$600 to TT$1,000 and an average of EC$850 for Vincentians and Grenadians. More importantly, net incomes after deductions for the cost of the goods, travel

and related expenses of the trade were a mere GUY$200, TT$600 and an average of EC$300 for Vincentians and Grenadians.

In a similar study, Holder (1988) investigated female traders in Guyana. This study focused on 123 female traders from three different geographic blocs within Guyana. Holder found that the trading activities provided opportunities for women who previously could not travel. The main results obtained by Holder regarding these women traders from Guyana were as follows:

- The majority (60%) of women were in the age group of 16–32 years.
- Forty-seven per cent were single while 40% were married.
- Eighty per cent of the women interviewed were the sole supporter of their families.
- The majority of traders had only a primary school education.
- Only 44% of the traders had a full time occupation. The majority of the traders were employed part-time.
- Surprisingly, 30.1% of the traders who engaged in trading as a part-time job were nurses.
- The women had worked anywhere between two weeks and twenty-four years as traders.
- Traders experienced the most difficulty with ground transportation, and 20% had overweight baggage problems.
- Sixty per cent of traders lamented that they experienced problems with the police and customs officials.
- Fifty-five per cent of traders identified that they collected orders from customers before they left their country.

Holder (1998) questioned the traders on areas in which they may need assistance. The top three responses were as folllows:

- assistance in obtaining credit facilities: 13%
- identification of investment opportunities: 32%
- improvement of management skills: 40%

Lagro (1988) cited the findings of studies done by ECLAC in the 1980s that credited the continued domination of the trade by females to be the result of a narrow scope of employment opportunities for women and the withdrawal of males from the trade. This chapter seeks to update these results by providing the findings of a micro survey of traders operating between Guyana and Trinidad and Tobago. In particular, the survey aims to update the demographic and sociological profile of ICIs operating between these two economies.

4.6. Empirical Analysis

Given the date of the last study of ICIs in Guyana, several changes in the economic landscape of Guyana in the 1990s and the 2000s, as discussed earlier in chapter 2, combined with the persistence of these traders, the authors sought to update the demographic and sociological profile of suitcase traders operating between Guyana and Trinidad and Tobago.

Methodology

Reliable documentation constituting the sampling frame of ICI trading between Trinidad and Guyana was unavailable to this study. In the absence of this information, key informant interviews were held with members of the group of ICIs in Guyana. The researchers used a purposive sampling design and the survey took place in Guyana where the traders all reside. A structured questionnaire was developed to capture data on the demographics of ICIs, details of their trade, problems encountered in their trade and suggestions from ICIs for improving their trade. The questionnaire was administered face-to-face. To avoid duplication, a certificate of participation was given to all higglers who were interviewed. As the survey progressed, ICIs were screened to ensure that they were not in possession of such a certificate.

Fieldwork was undertaken in the months of July and August 2007. The sample size was 62, which in the view of the key informants, represents more than 50% of the population of ICIs trading between Guyana and Trinidad and Tobago.

4.7. Summary of Survey Data

Age and Sex

As table 4.7 shows, all age groups from 21 years to 60 years are represented among ICIs in the sample, with the majority of the sample falling in the 21–40 years age group.

The data corroborated the notion that ICIs were typically women, indicating that 73% of the sample was female. Male ICIs were typically younger than female ICIs. Male ICIs were typically 21–30 years, while female ICIs were typically 31–40 years.

Table 4.7: Age Distribution of Trinidad and Tobago and Guyana ICIs by Sex

	Less than 21	21–30	31–40	41–50	51–60	Row total	Row %
Male	1	11	5	0	0	17	27.4
Female	2	12	15	11	5	45	72.6
Column total	3	23	20	11	5	62	100
Column %	4.8	37.1	32.3	17.7	8.1	100	

Education

The data suggests that the majority of ICIs left formal education in fifth form at the secondary level. At this level, they would normally have pursued studies leading up to the Caribbean Examination Council certification. As table 4.8 shows, secondary education to fifth form was consistently the typical highest level of education across all age groups. Further, the suitcase trade between Guyana and Trinidad and Tobago also appeals to some graduates of tertiary education. In the sample, 11% pursued tertiary education.

Marital Status and Dependents

The data suggest that ICIs were most likely to be married. The sample showed 57% were married, 32% were single, 7% were common-law,

Table 4.8: Distribution of Highest Level of Education of Trinidad and Tobago and Guyana ICIs by Age

	Age Group of Respondent						
Highest Level	Less than 21	21–30	31–40	41–50	51–60	Row total	Row %
Primary	0	0	2	2	1	5	8.1
Secondary (up to Form 3)	0	0	4	2	0	6	9.7
Secondary (up to Form 5)	3	19	9	6	2	39	62.9
Secondary (up to Form 6)	0	0	1	1	0	2	3.2
Technical/Vocational	0	1	2	0	0	3	4.8
Tertiary	0	3	2	0	2	7	11.3
Column total	3	23	20	11	5	62	100
Column %	4.8	37.1	32.3	17.7	8.1	100	

and 5% were either divorced or widowed. The data also suggest that the importance of the suitcase trade from both social and economic standpoints is underscored by the significant number of dependents whose lives are linked to the trade, and to a lesser extent by the level of indirect employment. ICIs in the sample tended to have up to five children, with the average number of children being two. As much as 85% of the sample operated as sole traders, 10% employed one worker and the remaining 5% employed two, three or ten workers.

Assets

The data show that the shuttle trade offered ICIs some benefits. One such benefit is the ability to acquire assets. The top three assets owned by ICIs in the sample were a savings account, a vehicle and a house, in that order. Figure 4.2 highlights the ownership profile. The fact that an indigenous asset like credit union shares attracted only 2% of the sample requires further investigation.

ICIs in the sample typically owned two assets. Additionally, 24% and 21% owned three assets and four assets respectively; 10% owned five or six assets; and 2% owned no assets.

Previous Employment

ICIs tend to enter the trade without supervisory or managerial experience. In the sample, a mere 12% of the respondents held supervisory

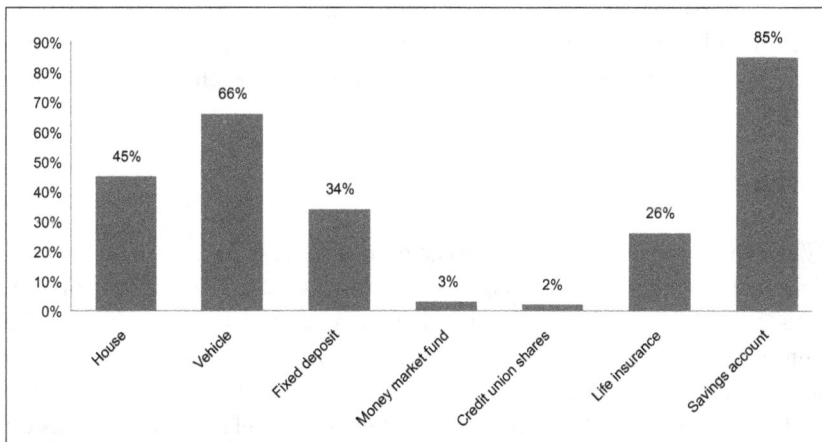

Figure 4.2 Ownership of assets by Trinidad and Tobago, and Guyana ICIs

or managerial positions prior to joining the suitcase trade. Overall, more than 50% of those sampled were employed prior to becoming an ICI. Of this subset, 62.5% were employed in the private sector (with 37.5% in the public sector), with clerical workers (41.2 %) and domestic workers and service sector workers (15% each) being the dominant occupations.

Years in the Suitcase Trade

The number of years in the suitcase trade ranged from one year to twenty-five years, with an average of eleven years. Half of the sample had been in the trade for eight years.

Countries in Which the Trade is Conducted

All persons interviewed conducted their trade in Trinidad and Guyana. The data also corroborated the notion that the predominant type of shuttle trade pursued by ICIs between Trinidad and Tobago and Guyana is more in alignment with Type 2 practice. An overwhelming 90.3% of the sample was Type 2. In addition, 14.8% also traded in Suriname, 11.5% in Barbados and 1.6% each in St Lucia and Curaçao.

Number of Trading Months per Year

Over half (57%) of the sample traded all twelve months of the year. The overall average was ten months per year. Female traders in the 21–30 age group seemed more likely to trade in excess of ten months in the year. Peak periods for carrying out their trade coincided with the pre-Christmas season and Carnival. December was the peak month for 56% of the sample; this was followed by February and November, each cited by 21% of sample.

Profile of Trips Made

While the number of trips made per month by ICIs between Guyana and Trinidad ranged from one to eight, ICIs typically make two trips per month. This exceeds the twenty trips per annum recorded in the literature. The number of days spent per trip ranged from one to fourteen, with a mean of five days. Over half (53%) spent between four and seven days per trip.

Just over half (52%) of the sample stayed with relatives and friends on these trips, while a further 34% stayed in guest houses. A mere 8% used the services of local bed and breakfast, while 7% rented an apartment. This reflects the cost curtailment measures used by ICIs.

The dominant mode of transport on these trips was by air. Generally, the goods purchased accompanied ICIs as checked baggage. Contrary to earlier studies, only 10% of the sample shipped their purchases as unaccompanied baggage or cargo once or twice per month.

The Trade

The data corroborate the view expressed in earlier studies that ICIs sell a range of goods and very often meet the demands of domestic consumers not necessarily met by local distributors. In addition, ICIs typically purchased their goods for the trade from ten suppliers.

Dominant goods purchased in Trinidad for trade were condiments/confectionery (43%), manufactured goods (17%) and garments (10%). The remaining 30% comprised of appliances, cosmetics, haberdashery, novelty goods, fashion accessories, pharmaceuticals and seafood. The dominant goods purchased in Guyana for trade were jewellery (25%), seafood (25%) and haberdashery (21%). The remaining 29% comprised manufactured goods, garments, stationery and pharmaceuticals.

Whereas the literature suggests that ICIs sell their wares from their homes or on the streets, the data offer some qualification to this notion. The dominant customer groups in the sample for ICIs in Trinidad and in Guyana were the general public, street vendors and small shops. Table 4.9 shows the ordering of these groups.

Table 4.9: Comparative Customer Shares for ICIs in Trinidad and Guyana

Purchaser	In Trinidad (%)	In Guyana (%)
Hotels	0.0	1.9
Restaurants	6.5	0.0
Supermarkets	3.2	1.9
Small shops	24.2	18.9
Street vendors	25.8	35.8
General public	35.5	34.0
Stores	1.6	5.7
Wholesalers	1.6	1.7
Pharmacies	1.6	1.9
Total	100	100

Items traded were most often supplied on order, and usually all were sold between trips. The data show that a mere 2% of the sample reported holding unsold goods for personal use. Record systems were for the most part manual. Only one ICI in the sample had a written contract with some suppliers. Generally, all business was transacted on mutual trust with few problems.

Expenses per Trip

Figure 4.3 clearly shows that expenses per trip were for the most part in the range of US$251 to US$500. The average trip expense was estimated at US$502.88.

Profits Per Week

Figure 4.4 highlights that 64% of the sample assessed their profit at less than US$250 per week. The mean weekly profit was estimated at US$256.63.

Other Sources of Income

Just over one-third of the sample (38%) had an additional source of income. A majority (86%) of these were either self-employed or worked in a family business.

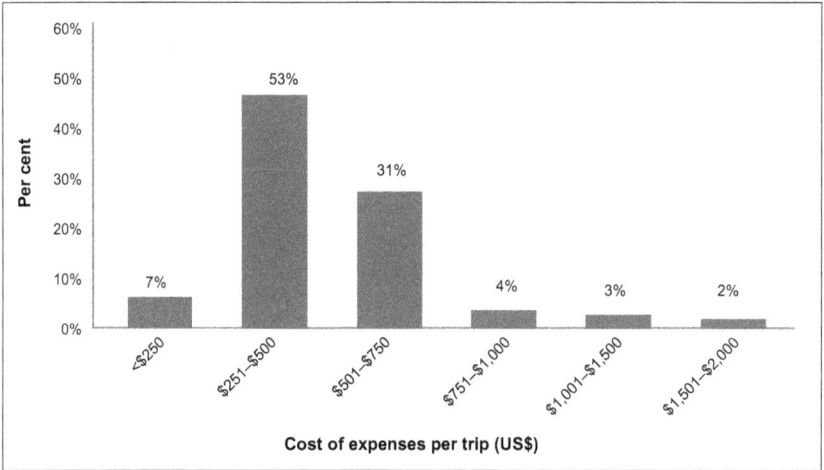

Figure 4.3 Distribution of expenses per trip (US$)

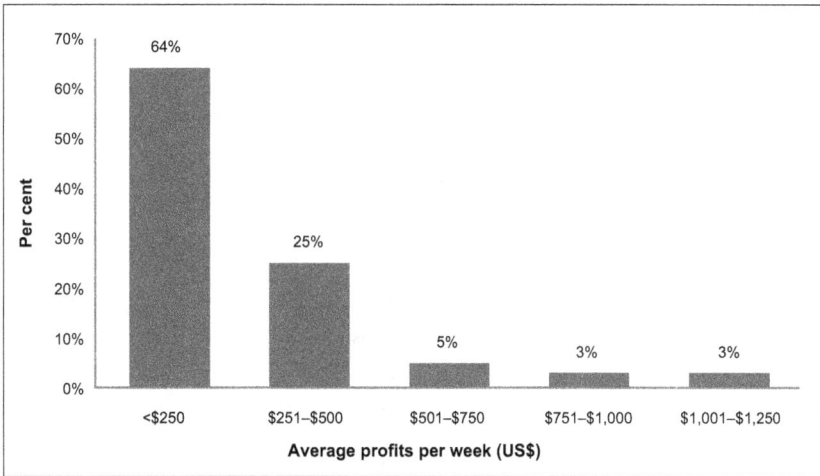

Figure 4.4 Profit per week for Trinidad and Tobago, and Guyana ICIs

Financial Assistance

ICIs tend not to seek financial assistance from the financial sector. In the sample, only 17% of the sample reported seeking such assistance. Some 64% of these were successful. Three-quarters (75%) of those who were refused financial assistance were turned down on the basis of insufficient collateral.

Problems Encountered

A total of 56.5% of the sample reported no problems or difficulties in conducting their trade. The remainder, 43.5%, experienced both occasional and persistent problems in the pursuit of their trade. Of the persistent and recurring problems, those specific to customs and immigration officers were the most common; 24.2% and 21% respectively of the ICIs interviewed reported problems with these two groups. Similarly, for the occasional problems, 22.6% and 25.8% of ICIs cited customs and immigration officers as sources of these problems. However, the most commonly reported occasional problem related to airline airport staff, with 29% of the respondents experiencing this problem.

Table 4.10 provides a summary of the attributes of ICIs who were part of the survey sample compared to the findings from previous research studies.

Table 4.10: Summary Attributes of ICIs Plying their Trade between Trinidad and Tobago and Guyana

73% were females	Previous sample was purposively all female
Most were from Guyana; as per previous study	Same
62% of ICIs had a highest level of education up to Form 5	27% in previous study
57% of ICIs were married and 32% were single	43% married and 47% single in previous study
66% had two children	ICIs had six children on average in previous study
85% operated as sole traders	80% in previous study
62% did not have any other source of income	56% were part-time traders in the previous study
66% had a vehicle and 86% a savings account	16% had savings accounts in previous study
50% of traders had been in the business for eight years	50% had been in the trade for two years in the previous study
90% of traders both buy and sell in a foreign country and their home country	75% in the previous study
An average trip cost approximately US$500	
64% of ICIs generated profits of less than US$250 per week	
38% of traders had an alternative source of income	60% in the previous study
57% of ICIs had no problems in conducting their trade	

Suggestions for Improving the Trade

In terms of other suggestions for improving the trade, by far the most common response was an increase in baggage allowances from the airlines; this suggestion accounted for 38% of all responses. The second most popular response was lower airfares, comprising 24.8% of all responses. Only 10.3% of all responses focused on better treatment from or training for airport staff, while 8.5% focused on the initiation of a traders' association and 4.3% focused on general government assistance. Other less popular suggestions were Guyana specific, including lower rates of customs duties, more space to sell goods, better sea transport and better infrastructure.

No trader association exists. Some ICIs advocated for its formation while others (the majority) suggested that they do not feel that it is necessary. Notwithstanding, ICIs need to lobby for an effective liaison with customs and excise officials at the airports and more attractive airfares and excess baggage charges, as well as an improved level of counter service from airlines.

4.8. Conclusion

The findings of the survey suggest the following:

- A larger proportion of traders were in the 31–50 age group, with a decline in the less than 30 years age group.
- The trade seems to be attracting a greater number of persons with secondary education up to fifth form.
- The proportion of traders who were married increased over the period between the two studies.
- On average, traders had fewer children than in the previous study.
- A vast majority (80%) operated as sole traders.
- On average, traders tended to stay longer in the trade.
- There is a reduced likelihood of traders having access to an additional source of income.
- There appears to be little change in the cohort of traders who experienced problems in conducting their trade.
- A significantly greater percentage of traders had a savings account.
- The percentage of traders seeking credit facilities from commercial financial institutions remained unchanged.
- Traders seem to have greater interest in owning their own home than was evident from the previous study; 9% of respondents in the 1988 study indicated an interest in doing so, compared to 45% of respondents reporting actually owning a home in 2007.
- Traders were more willing to provide quantitative data on their expenses and profits; responses on profitability in the 1988 study were categorical in nature.

Estimating the Size of the ICI Trade between Guyana and Trinidad and Tobago

Based on the profit data provided in figure 4.4, we estimate profit per trader per month at US$1,026.52 (assuming a conversion of four weeks per month). Using the earlier finding of an average of two trips per month and the data from figure 4.3 on expenses per trip, we estimate the expenses per month at US$1,005.76 for each trader. Accordingly, the revenue per trader per month is estimated at US$2,032.28. On average, this equates to US$20,322.80 per trader per annum, since each trader operates for an average of ten months in a calendar year, and is equivalent to 13.5 times the GNI per capita of US$1,502.30 for 2008. The absence of reliable data on the size of the population of ICIs in Guyana makes it impossible to estimate the gross annual revenue of the trade.

Addressing the Barriers for ICIs

Informal commercial importing remains a particularly attractive business opportunity to traders, particularly women, for several reasons. One is the level of profit derived from the trade; other reasons are the relative absence of barriers to entry, especially with regard to the official travel restrictions, the flexibility of engaging in more than one type of business opportunity as well as the relatively low standard of education needed. Further, as a form of suitcase trade, it allows women to manage their roles as both mother and provider for their children.

A number of functional and implementable strategies are associated with the formalization process of ICIs in Trinidad and Tobago and Guyana. For example, governments could facilitate an effective liaison between ICIs and customs and excise officials at the airports. Generally, ICIs perceive customs and excise officials as hostile and an impediment to their trade; they hold the view that governments should intervene on their behalf to smooth out their interaction with this agency. At the least, a help-desk facility could be set up to address ICIs' concerns.

ICIs face high airfares, regulatory weight restrictions and excessive excess baggage charges that severely restrict the volume of trade. Individually, they have admittedly devised crude methods to deal with those issues, but would prefer to have them addressed in a formal way, preferably through an organization of their own. A significant number of the ICIs surveyed, particularly from Guyana, proposed the setting up of a desk to provide advice and information that they need from time to time, such as documentation, duty payable on specific commodities, and so on. Airlines, on the other hand, are known to offer single passenger fares and group fares, with the group fares providing customers with some level of savings. Thus, ICIs could be encouraged to negotiate travel packages with airlines as a group, focusing on more attractive airfares and excess baggage allowances and charges, as well as an improved level of counter service. Savings from travel packages can only enhance the profitability of their trip.

ICIs typically trade in goods that are usually underinvoiced, undervalued and underdeclared. The true extent of the trade is unknown. As another strategy associated with the formalization process of ICIs, a methodology could be employed to capture the nature and extent of this trade. However, this may require a number of measures to be in place. Firstly, ICIs could be encouraged to register as small traders (so each gets a trader's licence); secondly, strict compliance with the regulations governing trade (imports and exports) could be encouraged; thirdly, where possible, the authority could revise the laws and regulations for this type of trade; and finally, stricter surveillance and enforcement should be consistently maintained at the ports of exit and entry. These could help to track ICIs' activities and could also serve as an ideal launching pad to bring ICIs into the formal sector.

An attempt could be made to progressively remove barriers that encourage ICIs to stay out of the formal economy. In doing so, ICIs' contributions to the economy can be determined in measurable ways in terms of the extent of the number and size of loans approved, tax contributions and profits generated from their trade. This would include amending laws and regulations so that they are not burdened with paperwork, sophisticated legal jargon, high processing costs, red tape and the like. It would also entail that a formal credit institution similar to the National Entrepreneurship Development Company Limited in Trinidad and Tobago be established in Guyana to provide easy access to cheap credit. Very often ICIs re-invest their meagre savings in their trade and have little or no hope of accessing bank credit, thereby limiting their entrepreneurial drive. A window should be opened for this group to have easy and unencumbered access to cheap and easy credit.

Consistent with the integration of ICIs into the formal economy is an initiative to bring about an attitudinal change in all agencies that interact with ICIs. Expectedly, resistance will come from ICIs themselves, while the interacting agencies may not be too comfortable dealing with a group of small traders "on a hustle". However, frequent dialogues by all stakeholders could eventually break the barrier during the transition stage and lead to a harmonious working relationship.

Usually ICIs trade in quantities that are not subject to tariffs, duties or taxes because of product mix in light of demand conditions. While that should be encouraged, systems should also be put in place by the authorities to capture their trading activities. In addition, ICIs are not usually subjected to quality controls, health and safety measures. The door is therefore open for trade in counterfeit and substandard goods, especially medical products, clothing, toys and electrical goods, other drugs (narcotics) and even weapons. The health and other risks involved are a good enough reason to begin regulating their activities.

ICIs, mainly self-employed women, enjoy little or no social welfare protection and benefits. This exposes their vulnerability. The authority could devise plans aimed at reducing the level of risk these traders can face, such as encouraging them to join national social welfare schemes. In addition, governments could design and implement initiatives (with the appropriate incentives) that are geared toward encouraging ICIs to participate in lifelong learning in areas such as procurement, demand forecasting, marketing and accounting.

Finally, governments and ICIs could jointly own, design and operate facilities (such as a bazaar or mini mall) where ICIs can ply their trade in benefiting CARICOM economies. Such facilities will replace the roadside markets (flea market style) that often block parts of the roadways, block entrances to legitimate businesses and present an unsightly condition at the end of the day's sales (usually at a great concern for the municipal authorities).

5 ICIs OPERATING BETWEEN CARICOM AND THE WIDER CARIBBEAN

This chapter builds on the discussion of the previous chapter by looking at the trade of hucksters in Dominica. Hucksters are traditionally referred to as people (mainly women) who go abroad and sell agricultural products, while ICIs generally resell more durable goods. Given their longstanding and significant presence in the region, it is especially important to understand the impact and dynamics of the trade and trading patterns of hucksters from an economic standpoint. Section 5.1 provides a review of past studies on the Dominican huckster. This section is followed by discussion of the Dominica Hucksters' Association (DHA) and the various contributions it has made to the huckster trade. Section 5.3 provides an analysis of the empirical data, after which a chapter conclusion is provided.

Because of the fierce resistance of the Caribs, Dominica was one of the last Caribbean islands that the Europeans were able to colonize. In 1763, France, who initially controlled the island, ceded to Britain. The British colonized the island in 1805 and introduced sugar, limes and bananas to the island. Dominica's economy thrived during the 1950s and continued to do so up to the mid-1990s on the back of banana production, which was done mainly by small-scale farmers, each working a few acres of privately owned land. Bananas were sold through a National Banana Corporation exclusively to British consumers (Trouillot 1988).

Dominica gained its independence on 3 November 1978. Between 1980 and 1989, revenues from banana exports, the main agricultural product, grew fivefold and represented 64% of the country's exports in 1987.[1] Concurrently, economic growth averaged 4.4% in the period

1981–88. This growth was a reflection of the impact of external funds invested in rebuilding the country's infrastructure and agriculture sector after the severe hurricanes of 1979 and 1980. In the 1980–84 period alone, external aid represented almost 24% of GDP; these funds financed all public investment and helped reverse the chronic trade deficit (World Bank 1990).

Dominica, like the other banana-producing economies of the ACP states, became the object of intense scrutiny by the WTO during the globalized environment of the 1990s. Mantz (2007) posits that the production costs in Dominica were approximately twice that of the world's top three multinational banana producers, Dole, Del Monte and Chiquita, due to the country's terrain and its inability to benefit from economies of scale. Banana export figures, which dominated agricultural exports in the latter half of 1980s and early 1990s, fell in response to a series of WTO decisions that devastated the country's banana industry. Figure 5.1 shows the trend in Dominica's production of bananas.[2]

Accordingly, the agriculture sector that once contributed in excess of 20% of GDP, and by extension a good proportion of Dominica's export revenues, experienced major challenges since the 1990s. The growth of non-banana agricultural exports, however, remained fairly static over that period. Another contraction in domestic growth was recorded in 2001 and 2002 due to the global slowdown after 11 September 2001.[3]

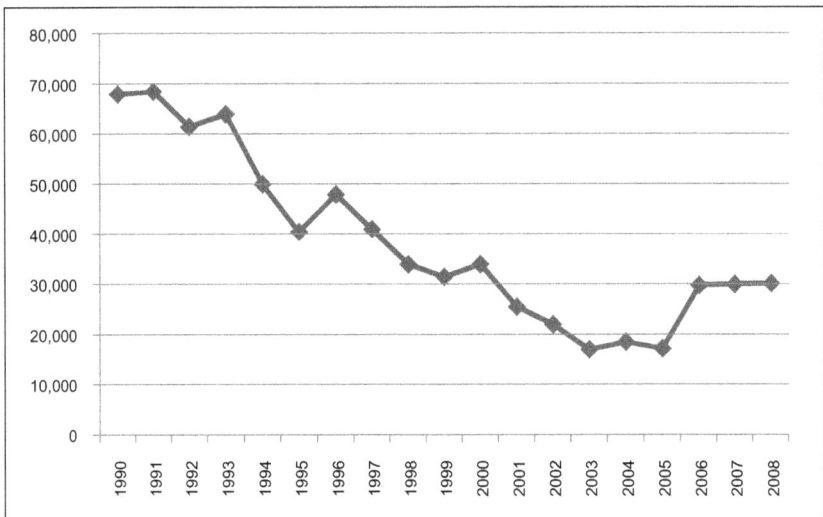

Figure 5.1 Dominica's banana production (tonnes)
Source: Food and Agriculture Organization database.

Mantz (2007) has argued that it is against this type of backdrop that an increased role of the huckster as part of a survival strategy became entrenched. Mantz (2003) noted that agricultural produce that was of a commercial quality but was not sold domestically was absorbed by hucksters for their trade. The huckster commandeers markets externally bananas that the Banana Exporting Company rejects or does not have the capacity to absorb, to produce such as yams and citrus with no major distributor (Mantz 2003). With nearby sources for regional trade, governmental assistance and an association (the DHA) in their favour, hucksterism helped to compensate for the losses to the economy brought about by the WTO rulings. Mantz (2003) points out that the trade routes over which the hucksters were the principal exporters accounted for the second largest contribution to foreign exchange earnings in Dominica in 2000.

In the post-war period, social pressures in Dominica, like the rest of the Caribbean, pushed women in the background of the formal trading environment, and their displacement was compounded by the regional industrialization movement during the 1960s. Two quotes from Mantz (2003) bear this out:

> In the 1930s, urban merchants from elite families drew on the political power and relations with colonial authority they had cultivated in the nineteenth century and entered into regional and international trading. (p. 31)

> By the 1950s and 1960s, customs and importing restrictions favourable to the larger urban elite businesses are gradually attenuating the hucksters' control on local food markets. That antagonism stems from these historically formalized class/color positions particularly as decolonization vested urban merchants with the use of the new state apparatus to enforce these entitlements. (p. 32)

These trends continued through to independence. With independence, the opportunities for women in the formal sector remained limited. In addition, the political heritage, the proximity of Guadeloupe with its high standard of living and a comparatively large population, the proximity of the Eastern Caribbean islands (such as Antigua, St Kitts, St Martin and the Virgin Islands) and the socioeconomic tradition of marketing within the Caribbean combined to produce a conducive atmosphere for huckstering to flourish among women of the English-speaking Caribbean (Mantz 2003). In addition, Mantz (2003, 4) also notes that "huckstering generates its livelihood principally from revenues gained overseas through agricultural exporting". The exporting aspect of hucksters' practices differentiates them from market women, who sell goods at a centralized market location.

A typical week can be hectic for hucksters, and may be cast as follows. On Monday, hucksters organize the necessary paperwork required to travel to Guadeloupe and to Martinique. They travel to these economies and sell their produce to the wholesale market that caters to the cruise ship visitors and some of the hotels. The hucksters return on Thursday or Friday, and some of them bring with them goods from Guadeloupe that generally are not available in Dominica, such as white potatoes, onions, vehicle parts and clothing. These goods are sold in Dominica on Saturday and then the cycle of recollecting produce for the foreign market restarts (WEIGO 2001).

Heeks (1999) developed a systematic view (see figure 5.2) of small and medium enterprises (SMEs) as units operating within an environment that comprises input supply, output demand and other institutions/factors. Conceptually, hucksters can be viewed as SMEs, as outlined by Heeks, as they use finance, their skills, market information, their own premises, packaging methods, their own social infrastructure, public transportation infrastructure and agricultural produce purchased to provide a service (the supply of produce) to both the local and foreign markets to generate earnings. Further, these earnings contribute to development which, in turn, facilitates poverty reduction.

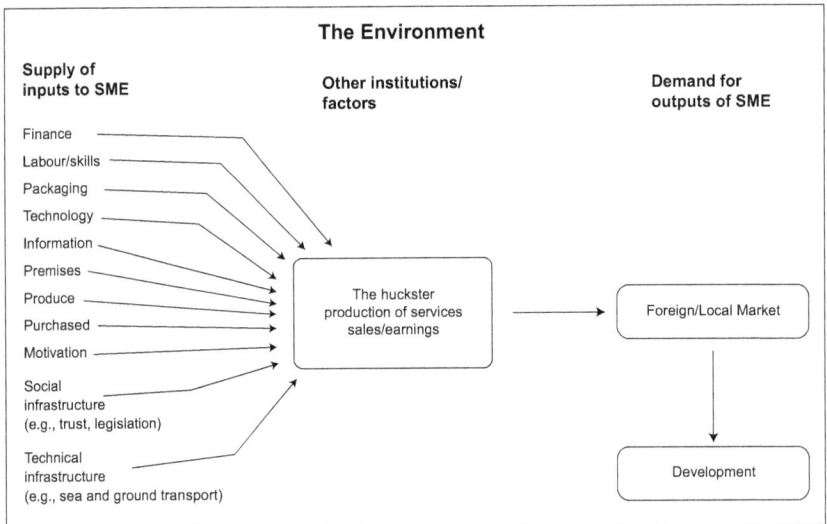

Figure 5.2 A systematic view of the huckster as a small and medium enterprise
Source: Adapted from Heeks (1999, 5).

Hucksters face formidable contemporary challenges. The most prominent of these are regional restrictions and environmental conditions. As a result of dependence on a few trading partners, hucksters find themselves easily susceptible to the policy changes among these partners. For example, in 2007, hucksters doing business in St Martin were told that failure to conform to the standards and quality controls regulating the trade in fresh produce in St Martin would result in them being denied access to that market.[4] Specifically, according to the commissioner of market affairs, permits and authorization in St Martin, "those who fail to satisfy minimum quality requirements will either have their vessels intercepted and turned back at sea or have their produce confiscated without compensation". Although word of such measures has been given since 2001, the indication that they would be rigorously enforced came six days before the 1 March 2007 implementation.

Another major challenge came in 2007, when the requirement for visas to French territories was abolished, and visitors were given up to fifteen days in these territories without the need for a visa. With Martinique and Guadeloupe being the hucksters' major sources of import and export respectively, the face value of this development seemed to be positive. However, with added clauses including mandatory insurance coverage of EC$150,000 and a confirmation from a hotel or a *d'attestation d'acqueil*, the reality was quite different. Lobby by the Government of Dominica and the DHA brought resolution in favour of the hucksters.

Natural disasters also significantly affect the agricultural goods traded by hucksters, in particular hurricanes, flooding and soil erosion. Given the craggy terrain of Dominica, soil erosion is worsened with hurricanes. Dominica's location as the most northerly of the Windward Islands places it well within the Atlantic hurricane belt. Table 5.1 shows that since 1981, Dominica has been affected by seven tropical storms at a total cost of US$237 million.

Table 5.1: Summary Table of Natural Disasters in Dominica, 1981–2010

		Number of Events	Number of Fatalities	Total Affected	Damage (000 US$)
Storm	Tropical cyclone	7	9	24,131	2,37,000
	Average per event		1.3	3,447.3	33,857.1

Source: EM-DAT, International Disaster Database, www.emdat.be/database.

5.1. Review of Past Studies on the Dominican Huckster

Hucksters have also been the subject of the study in the literature by research-ers such as Homiak (1986), Lagro (1988, 1990), ECLAC (1988, 1989), Lagro and Plotkin (1990) and Mulakala (1991). Lagro (1988) revealed that 45.3% of Windward Island female traders were single and the remaining 54.7% lived in partnership arrangements such as married, common-law or a visiting union. Lagro and Plotkin (1990, 18) concluded the following:

- All female traders in the Windward Islands, regardless of marital status, had children.
- The older traders (over 40 years of age) had an average of seven children.
- Most traders came from a background of poverty and were deter-mined to raise their children under more comfortable and privileged circumstances.
- Many of the older women who were hucksters were children in the 1930s and 1940s and hence were subject to the discriminatory edu-cation practices that favoured males over females for higher level education. Accordingly, only 14.2% of traders had some exposure to secondary level schooling.
- Most female hucksters were domestics or engaged in self-employment like petty trading or sewing prior to becoming hucksters.

Mulakala (1991) identified two motivating factors for persons to become hucksters: financial return and the level of independence that the trade offered. Lagro (1988) posited that for many women the decision to become a huckster stemmed from the need to provide for large house-holds that are surviving on limited or strained financial resources. ECLAC (1989) categorized the commodities traded from Dominica by hucksters into staple foods, fruits, vegetables and spices.

Mulakala (1991) specified the qualifications and skills of a huckster as follows:

- ability to endure the stress, strain, hassles and hustling involved in inter-island trade
- ability to manage the financial risks involved in the trade
- ability to survive in a competitive environment
- physical strength
- ability to talk and deal with other people
- well-mannered, patient, courageous, persistent and intelligent

- ability to handle money
- skills in pricing, buying, organizing, marketing and diplomacy
- ability to balance and integrate many activities and responsibilities into their lives

Lagro (1990) noted that there were 1,378 licensed hucksters in 1984; this number had decreased to 467 in 1986. Lagro (1988) quoted the membership at 360. Mulakala (1991) noted that at least 80% of the membership is female. Homiak (1986) characterized the activity cycle of the huckster as shown in figure 5.3.

Mulakala (1991) also identified that traders made significant investment in vehicles[5] that greatly assisted them in purchasing, collecting and

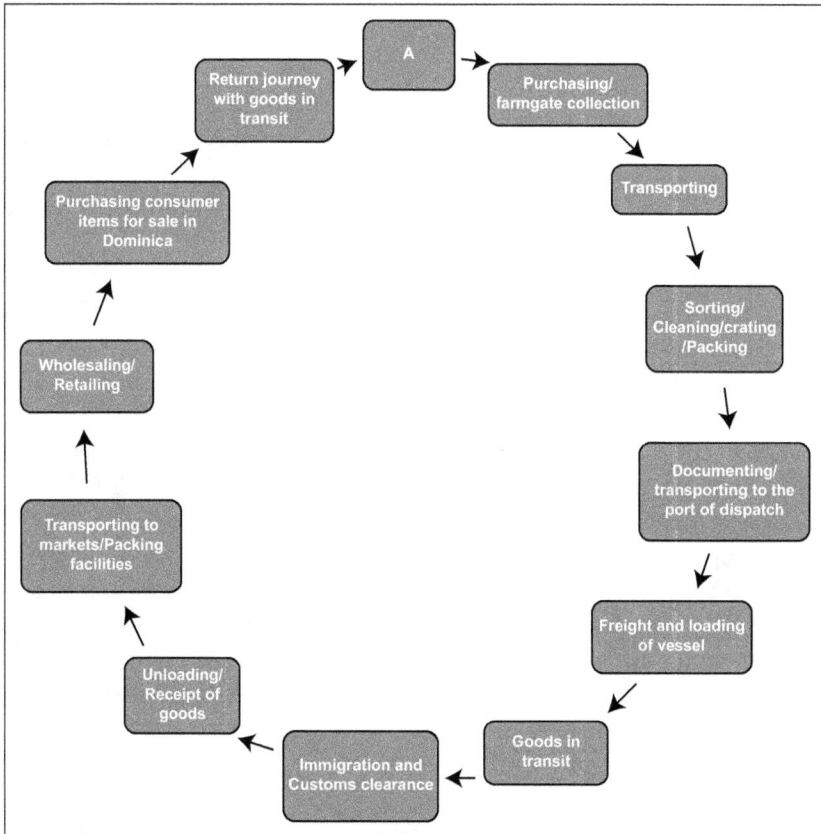

Figure 5.3 Activity cycle of a huckster
Source: Homiak (1986).

transporting their produce. Further, most female traders invested in small businesses at home, such as small shops[6] and boutiques; built homes; and secured education for their children. As far back as 1991, Mulakala cautioned that younger traders were finding it more difficult to make ends meet since windfall profits were not as evident as in the past. As a consequence, many of the traders relied on a variety of income earning strategies to survive.

Lagro (1988) observed that many long-time traders, having made their money, tended to travel less frequently for purposes of the trade. Lagro estimated that 45% of the hucksters in 1989 engaged in reverse or two-way trade to buy onions, potatoes and red beans from Guadeloupe and clothing, cosmetics, ornaments and footwear from St Martin. Some hucksters opened up small shops from which they sold this merchandise. Lagro (1988) estimated that most hucksters imported between EC$267 and EC$4,762 on a trading trip. Homiak (1986) estimated the earnings from the huckster trade to be at least EC$3 million per year.

The only evidence in the literature of formal organizations of traffickers in the Eastern and Southern Caribbean can be found in Mulakala (1991), which cites the formation of the Traffickers' Small Business Association of St Vincent and the Grenadines (Lagro 1988) and the formation of the DHA (Homiak 1986).

In the 1980s, some work on women traders in the Caribbean was undertaken by ECLAC under the theme "Women in Development and Trade in the Caribbean". This project was targeted at providing some base data against which an assessment of women's contribution to the economic development process in the region could be predicated. As relates to the OECS economies, Lagro (1988) undertook a study of women traders in St Vincent and the Grenadines. After the study by Lagro, ECLAC commissioned a survey on the inter-island traders of the Caribbean. ECLAC's work emphasized two core areas: (1) suitcase trade in non-agricultural goods (mainly clothing and light apparel), and (2) the inter-island trade in agricultural produce. When ECLAC did their study, a great part of the inter-island trade in agricultural goods was carried out by the informal sector. ECLAC's work during this period of time showed that small amounts of a variety of different agricultural products were exchanged by hundreds of persons.

Based on their study of women traders in the Eastern Caribbean, Babb et al. (2004) summarized the problems of hucksters into three categories: personal, organizational and national policy. Within the personal category, the researchers cited the high degree of spoilage of produce due to boats and markets not having adequate refrigeration facilities; non-payment on sales on the part of agents who periodically manage the receiving of goods in destination countries; difficulty in achieving economies of scale; inability to find guarantors for their loan applications; and a lack of enthusiasm for adopting the business management approach advocated by the DHA. At the time of its study, the organizational problems cited by Babb et al. related to the DHA. These involved the weakening of the DHA as a result of hucksters moving away from the advisory services and standards of the DHA; the dearth of capacity within the DHA for research, oversight at destination countries, market penetration and expansion; and resource limitations within the DHA that impacted negatively on the timely production of reports on its operating performance. Under the category of national policy, Babb et al. cited the lack of access to non-contributory social security for hucksters; the absence of an updated database of hucksters within either the Ministry of Agriculture or Ministry of Trade or both; and the absence of a legal framework for the oversight of the operations of the inter-island vessels used for the transport of produce between Dominica and its markets.

5.2. The Dominica Hucksters' Association

According to the ILO (2010), the oldest trading organization in the Caribbean is the DHA, which by 1990 was representing approximately 60% of all Dominicans who traded in agricultural products. It was formed by a small group of concerned traders in July 1981 following the devastation caused by hurricanes David and Allen in 1979. It later evolved to a friendly society in 1984 and then by 1995 it evolved further, becoming a non-profit company, limited by guarantee without share capital. According to Homiak (1986) the DHA is the first independent and voluntary organization of its kind in the Caribbean. The association has two offices, one located in the capital of the country, Roseau, and the other in the town of Portsmouth. All services provided to its members, such as sale, assembly, distribution and storage of packaging materials, are done within these offices, which employ five full-time employees. Office space at the two locations is, however, small and as such not all of the members of the association are able to get their needs met, requiring some to do their handling and packing in what they term "their own" facilities.

The French government's decision to impose an entry restriction on all non-domestic traders is one of the main reasons for the creation of the association. The Government of Dominica intervened and negotiated with the French government a requirement for hucksters to apply collectively for visas to the French territories of Guadeloupe, St Martin and Martinique. Thus the need for an association became obvious.

The main focus of the DHA at the beginning was providing credit and administrative services to hucksters. According to the ILO, this was done by creating a revolving loan fund through the use of a donor grant that was used to provide its members with small loans (ILO 2010). This loan facility was based on the peer system – each applicant had to be supported by another huckster (a co-signer), who would also become responsible for the repayment of the loan. In 2004, the DHA gave start-up loans of EC$3,000. Larger loans provided by financial and developmental institutions, such as the credit union, the Agricultural Development Bank, the Dominican Rural Enterprise Programme (a poverty alleviation initiative) and National Development Foundation Micro Business Fund are accessed by the association on behalf of its members. According to Babb et al. (2004), the National Development Foundation Micro Business Fund had already given out EC$320,705 to thirty-four hucksters by 19 August 2004.

Later on in the DHA's existence, it began to purchase packaging materials wholesale for resale to hucksters, thereby allowing them the benefit of economies of scale, increased ability to meet international standards and elimination of the need to source their own material. According to Babb et al. (2004), the DHA evolved into an organization which, in addition to those services previously mentioned,

- provided information about the association and its services to potential members;
- provided training in all aspects of being a business owner, such as record keeping, paclaging and pricing;
- negotiated with overseas government officials on behalf of members and non-members;
- negotiated shipping rates with operators for members;
- collaborated with local and foreign agencies, including the Dominica Export and Import Agency (DEXIA), Bureau of Standards, Produce Chemist Laboratory, Division of Agriculture, Caribbean Agriculture Research and Development Institute, and the Port Authority;

- assisted members in obtaining trade visas for travel to Guadeloupe and Martinique;
- provided support to members in applying for services that fall out of the business sphere but are still essential; and
- represented hucksters in negotiations with the Dominican government and with the agencies of other regional governments.

The DHA was also charged in the post-2004 period with the responsibility of assisting hucksters in their applications for Dominican passports and visas for travel to the United States.[7] Training is available to its members from agencies that collaborate with the DHA, and the association also provides a six-week orientation session for all potential hucksters. DEXIA and technical staff from the Ministry of Agriculture take part in conducting these sessions. The orientation sessions cover a wide variety of topics that are important to the hucksters' success, ranging from plant quarantine requirements to produce quality and packaging standards, as well as documentation required for marketing. Procedures for loan application and management, risk assessment and business decision making are also included. The orientation gives potential hucksters a vivid picture of the trade and all of the activities involved in it and as such, approximately 25% of those who do the orientation (eighteen persons on average) enter the trade. After one year, 10% usually remain in the trade (Babb et al. 2004).

The DHA, DEXIA and the Ministry of Agriculture train active hucksters in how to accurately package their products and how to meet required standards set by various other markets. The Dominica Rural Enterprise Project has been a source of funding to the DHA, enabling them to find and sell packaging materials to hucksters. The proceeds support a revolving fund for acquiring new packaging materials. All assistance with packaging has proved to be of great importance in recent times, as countries have become more rigid in their fresh produce importation standards. In St Maarten, Dominican hucksters were told that failure to conform to the longstanding but newly enforced standards and quality controls regulating the trade in fresh produce meant that they would be denied access to that market.

The relationship with DEXIA has proven to be vital for the DHA in its aim to assist hucksters. Discussions with DEXIA have brought about the availability of their Citrus Packing Plant for hucksters to wash and package produce, as well as for the hot-water treatment of mangoes to guard against the mango seed weevil. Another important area of assistance provided by DEXIA is in employing a representative to stay in Guade-loupe and assist the hucksters with any issues that may arise in dealing with immigration, customs and the market. The customs department offers training and assistance in compliance with any new procedures that are introduced and in the correct completion of trade documents, such as the Customs Declaration and Certificate of Origin.

Concentrating on income-generating activities (while simultaneously providing the aforementioned services), and prudent management of its loan portfolio, the DHA became self-sustaining within seven years (ILO 2010a). The management of DHA has attributed this achievement to the following:

- A clear focus – from the beginning, the main goal was to ensure long-term sustainability with regard to income generation. To ensure this, most services provided required some financial contribution to cover any costs that the association incurred.
- A proactive approach – after a period of financial difficulties, the association reacted positively and searched for different ways to raise income, while at the same time addressing its objectives. This proactive approach by the management is a clear indicator of the sharp vision and sound business management used to create new income-generating services, while at the same time addressing the needs of the association beneficiaries.
- A continuous quest for improvement – this is done to be on top of any new threats from the increasing forces of global competition to protect the niche market in which the organization is operating.

In terms of sustainability, the single factor contributing to the revenue and upkeep of the DHA Secretariat is listed in the DHA's 2007 annual report as the sale of packaging materials. The report highlights that the DHA has not been able to set aside sums of money as retained earnings simply because the operating margins have been too small. Operating per-formance for the years 2005–2007 are shown in table 5.2.

5.3. Empirical Analysis

All hucksters in Dominica are required to register with the DHA. Annual membership dues were collected by the DHA at the same time that mem-bers accessed visa services from the DHA. However, with the abolition of

Table 5.2: Operating Performance for the DHA, 2005–2007

	2005 (EC$)	2006 (EC$)	2007 (EC$)
Purchases	582,025	576,602	589,162
Sales	704,200	714,808	717,070
Gross profit	121,175	139,206	127,908
Other incomes	37,737	43,689	34,472
Total revenue	158,912	182,895	162,380
Administrative and general expenses	177,666	166,842	180,568
Profit (Loss)	–18,754	16,053	–18,188

Source: DHA (2007).

visas for the French territories in May 2007, some hucksters elected to not pay their annual membership dues. Accordingly, the association's records as of August 2008 showed a population of 200 hucksters, down from 360 reported in 1987 (ECLAC 1988) and 500 in the mid-1990s. This pattern correlates strongly with the decrease in the number of farmers in Dominica after the WTO Ruling of 1992 – the number of farmers fell from ten thousand in the pre-1992 period to fifteen hundred in 2008.[8]

This section summarizes the findings of a survey of hucksters undertaken in Dominica in the third quarter of 2008.

Methodology

The methodology adopted reflects a mix of qualitative and quantitative approaches. The qualitative approach took the form of key informant interviews with the general manager of the DHA and a small sample of members of the DHA. The information gathered was used to finalize the survey instrument. The quantitative approach took the form of a survey that used a purposive sampling design and was undertaken among hucksters at the DHA facilities in both Roseau and Portsmouth. The structured questionnaire was developed to capture data on the demographics of hucksters, details of their trade, problems encountered in their trade and their suggestions for improving the trade. This questionnaire was administered face-to-face. Fieldwork was undertaken in September 2008. The achieved sample size was 48, with 96% of the sample being active members of the DHA.

5.4. Summary of Survey Data

Age and Sex

The sample of hucksters was 52% female and 48% male. As table 5.3 shows, all age groups from 21 years to 60 years were represented in the sample, with the majority of the sample falling in the 41–60 years age group. Among the males, the modal age group in the sample was 51–60 years, while for the females it was younger, in the 41–50 years age group.

The data are consistent with Mulaka's (1991) findings that female hucksters constitute the majority of the huckster population. Demographic studies revealed that more women than men take the lead in higgling activity (Ellis 1986; Lagro 1990). However, the literature is divergent in terms of the proportion.

Education

The data suggest that the majority of hucksters in the sample left formal education at the primary school level. As table 5.4 shows, primary education was consistently the highest level of education across all age groups. Furthermore, the huckster trade is also appealing to some graduates of tertiary education. In the sample, 8% pursued tertiary education.

From a gender perspective, the sample results showed equal proportions of males and females with highest qualification at the primary, secondary (up to fifth form) and tertiary levels. Females in the sample exceeded the males with highest qualification at the secondary (up to third form) and technical/vocational levels. These results support Lagro and Plotkin's (1990) findings that younger traders in the Windward Islands tended to have more formal education than older ones.

Table 5.3: Age Distribution of Hucksters by Sex

Age Group	Less than 21	21–30	31–40	41–50	51–60	Over 60	Total	Percentage frequency
Male	0	1	6	3	8	5	23	47.9
Female	0	0	2	13	9	2	25	52.1
Frequency	0	1	8	16	16	7	48	100
Percentage frequency	0	2.1	16.7	33.3	33.3	14.6	100	

Table 5.4: Distribution of Highest Level of Education of Hucksters by Age

Highest level	Age Group of Respondents					Row total	Row %
	21–30	31–40	41–50	51–60	60+		
Primary	0	3	9	15	5	32	66.7
Secondary (up to Form 3)	0	1	0	0	0	1	2.1
Secondary (up to Form 5)	0	2	3	0	1	6	12.5
Secondary (up to Form 6)	0	0	0	0	0	0	0
Technical/ vocational	0	2	2	1	0	5	10.4
Tertiary	1	0	2	0	1	4	8.3
Column total	1	8	16	16	7	48	100
Column %	2.1	16.7	33.3	33.3	14.6	100	

Marital Status and Dependents

The data indicate that hucksters were more likely to be married. The sample was 52% married, 35% single and 4% each common-law, divorced and widowed. From a gender perspective, the males in the sample were more likely to be married, in common-law relationships or widowed; they were as likely as the females to be divorced, but less likely than the females to be single.

In terms of age, the 41–50 age group was more likely to be married; common-law relationships were as likely among hucksters from the 31–40 and 51–60 age groups; the 51–60 age group dominated the divorced cohort; the 41–60 age group dominated the single cohort; and the over 60 age group dominated the widowed cohort.

The data also suggest that the importance of the huckster trade from both the social and economic standpoints is underscored by the significant number of dependents whose lives are linked to the trade and to a lesser extent by the level of indirect employment. Hucksters in the sample had as many as eleven children, with four as both the average and modal number of children; 50% of the sample had as many as four children. A total of 85% of the sample had boys, while 79% had girls. Those hucksters who were parents of male children had on average two boys, while those who were parents of female children had on average two girls.

With respect to indirect employment, hucksters in the sample employed up to seven workers, with two as both the average and modal number of workers employed. Some 17% of the hucksters employed one worker, 43% employed two workers, 23% employed three workers and the remaining 18% employed four to seven workers. These findings underscore the importance of hucksterism to the Dominican economy.

Assets

The data support the observation that the shuttle trade offers hucksters some benefits. One such benefit is the ability to acquire assets. Hucksters in the sample were most likely to own a house and a vehicle. Figure 5.4 shows that on average 68% of the sample owned both these assets; ownership reduced to 33% for shares in a local credit union and 15% each for fixed deposits and life insurance policies.

Previous Employment

Over three-quarters (79%) of the sample were employed prior to joining the huckster trade. This employment was more likely to be in the private sector, given that 81% of these respondents worked in the private sector prior to joining the huckster trade. Hucksters tend to enter the trade without supervisory or managerial experience. In the sample, a mere 6% held

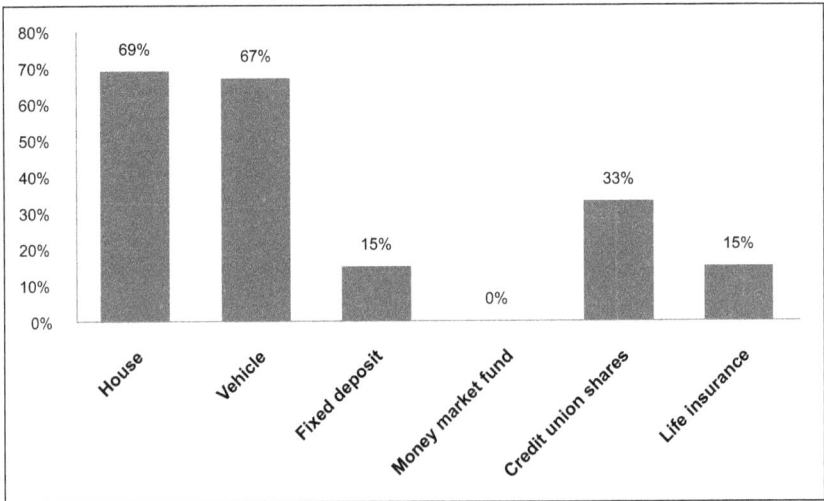

Figure 5.4 Ownership of assets by hucksters in Dominica

supervisory or managerial positions prior to joining the huckster trade. The top three prior occupations among hucksters in the sample were clerk, labourer/other elementary occupation and agricultural worker, in that order; together these accounted for 60% of the sample. These data suggest that hucksterism is a lucrative option.

Years in the Suitcase Trade

The number of years in the huckster trade ranged from one year to thirty years in the sample, with an average of fifteen years. Half of the sample had been in the trade for fifteen years or less. The males in the sample tended to have been in the trade for fifteen years or less, while the females tended to have been in the trade for more than fifteen years. The age group 31–60 accounted for 91% of the hucksters with fifteen years or less in the trade; the greater than 40-years age group accounted for 96% of the hucksters with more than fifteen years in the trade. The majority of the hucksters who were educated to only primary level in the sample tended to have spent more than fifteen years in the trade. The majority of all other education cohorts, except for the secondary level (up to sixth form), had spent no more than fifteen years in the trade. The majority of the hucksters with fifteen years or less experience in the trade tended to be married, while the majority of those with more than fifteen years of experience tended to be either married or single.

Countries in Which the Trade Is Conducted

According to the DHA, the trade out of Dominica is predominantly in agricultural produce; fresh cut flowers and handicraft make up the remainder of the commodities traded. The survey data suggest that each huckster purchases such produce from up to forty local farmers, with a mode of six farmers; an average of eleven farmers supply produce to a huckster. Written agreements do not exist between hucksters and farmers.

Just over half (52%) of the hucksters interviewed conducted their trade in Martinique and Guadeloupe; Antigua and St Martin were the other large markets for the huckster trade, as shown in figure 5.5. This finding shows little change from the list of markets included in the Hucksters Trade Development Report of 1985.[9] The data also corroborate the notion that the predominant type of shuttle trade pursued by hucksters from Dominica is more in alignment with Type 2 practice in shuttle trade.[10] An overwhelming 90.3% of the sample was engaged in Type 2 practice.

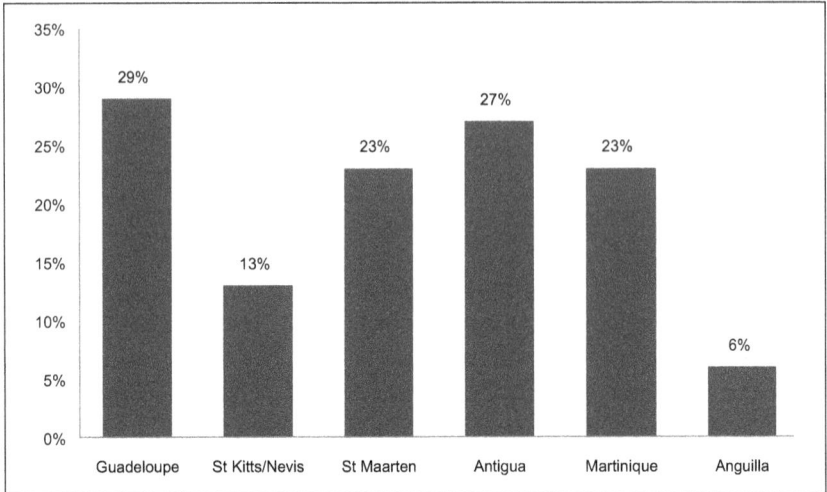

Figure 5.5 Markets in which hucksters conduct their trade

Number of Trading Months per Year

The number of trading months ranged from four to twelve within the year, with 88% of the sample trading for twelve months in a year. The peak period for carrying out the trade coincided with the fourth quarter of the year for respondents in the sample. The dominant trading months from the sample were November, December, October and January, in that order.

Profile of Trips Made

While the number of trips made per month by hucksters ranged from two to five, the modal frequency was four trips per month, and the average was 3.5 per month. This sample clearly exceeds the twenty trips per annum recorded in the literature. The dominant mode of transport on these trips was by sea. A ferry service operating between Dominica, Martinique and Guadeloupe facilitates this mode of transport. The entire sample travelled by sea for their trips. However, 2% of the sample also travelled by air on some trips.

The number of days spent per trip ranged from one to seven, with a mode of four days and a mean of 4.4 days. A mere 7% of the sample used the services of a guest house on these trips, while 13% stayed with relatives and 33% stayed with friends. The remaining 43% made other arrangements, including staying in their own homes. This reflects the cost curtailment measures used by the hucksters.

Generally, the goods purchased accompanied the hucksters as checked baggage. Consistent with earlier studies, 46% of the sample shipped their purchases as unaccompanied baggage or cargo at least once per month, while 64% shipped their purchases as unaccompanied cargo four times per month.

The Trade

The sample data corroborates the view expressed in earlier studies that hucksters sell a range of goods and very often meet the demands of domestic consumers not necessarily met by local distributors. The dominant goods traded by the hucksters are agricultural goods. One hundred percent of the sample traded in agricultural goods. A minority of hucksters in the sample traded in condiments/confectionery (8%), toys (2%), novelty goods (2%), fresh cut flowers (2%), garments (2%) and footwear (2%). This finding is consistent with Lagro's (1998) finding that most women who started off as traders of agricultural produce end up peddling other goods.

Whereas the literature suggests that ICIs sell their wares from their homes or on the streets, the dataset offers some qualification to this notion. The dominant locations in the sample are the market (46%) and the street (30%). Other less common locations are supermarkets, importers/wholesalers, small shops/retailers, restaurants and processing plants. The dominant customer groups in the sample were the general public, street vendors and supermarkets, in that order. Table 5.5 shows the ordering of these groups.

Table 5.5: Comparative Customer Shares for
Hucksters from Dominica

Customer	Frequency (%)
Hotels	8
Restaurants	15
Supermarkets	30
Small shops	15
Street vendors	40
General public	52
Importers/wholesalers	4
Processors	2

Note: Base = 48

Though items traded were most often supplied on order, 60% of the sample reported that they were faced with unsold goods on some trips. The data show that unsold goods are usually given away to friends, dumped, consumed or held over for a week (in cases of non-perishables), in that order.

All hucksters in the sample kept manual records of the trade; only 2% of the sample maintained a parallel computerized records system. Only one huckster in the sample had a written contract with some suppliers. Generally, all business is transacted on mutual trust with few problems.

Expenses per Trip

Figure 5.6 clearly shows that expenses per trip were for the most part in the range of EC$1,501 to EC$4,000. The average trip expense was estimated at EC$1,903.

Profits Per Week

Figure 5.7 highlights that 58% of the sample assessed their profit at approximately EC$2,000 per week. The mean weekly profit was estimated at EC$2,140.

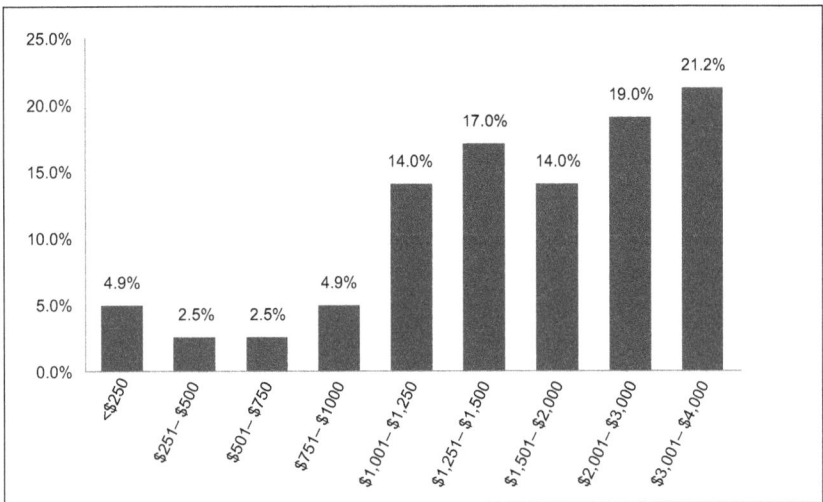

Figure 5.6 Distribution of expenses per trip (EC$)

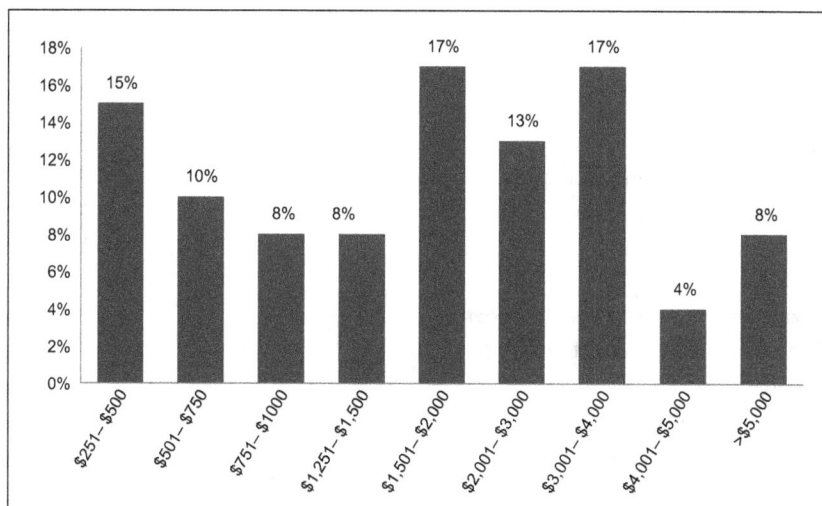

Figure 5.7 Profit per week for hucksters (EC$)

Other Sources of Income

A total of 60% of the sample had an additional source of income. The dominant sources of income within the sample were farming and the sale of dry goods and clothes (see table 5.6 for details).

Financial Assistance

Commercial banks are currently the main providers of loans to hucksters, according to the DHA. The DHA, which was the sole lending agency to hucksters in the 1980s and 1990s, currently acts as a clearing house for hucksters who cannot satisfy the credit requirements of the commercial banks. In the sample, 41% of the hucksters reported seeking loans from financial institutions, and 92% of these were successful.

Problems Encountered

Just over half (52%) of the sample reported having encountered problems or difficulties in conducting their trade. The recurrent problems areas were competition among traders, immigration officers, damage to cargo, airline reservations and space on cargo vessels, in that order. Completion of

Table 5.6: Additional Sources of Income for Hucksters

Additional Source of Income	Frequency
Farming	10
Sale of dry goods and clothes/owns boutique	9
Grocery/small retail shop	4
Ownership of a bar	1
Bus service	1
Ownership of a cargo vessel or boat	2
Roadside vending/market vending	3
Construction	1
Social security/pension	1
Government employment	1

Note: Base = 29

documents does not pose a problem for hucksters as the DHA is author-ized by Government of Dominica to facilitate the preparation of these documents. Problems were encountered to a lesser degree with family members, ground transportation, theft and production inconsistencies among farmers and market authorities. Occasionally, problems were encountered by respondents in the sample with customers, truckers and customs officers.

Generally, these problems concur with those identified in Mulakala (1991): high overheads, excessive competition among hucksters, spoil-age, inadequate security for goods being traded, strained relations with farmers and the lack of streamlined and standardized documentation procedures.

5.5. Conclusion

Based on the data provided on number of months of trading by traders, we estimate that each trader works an average of 10.65 months per year. Using the data provided earlier on the number of trips per month per trader, we estimate an average of 3.5 trips per month per trader. Com-bining the average expenses of EC$1,903 per trip and the average profit of EC$2,140 per month, we estimate the revenue per trader per month at EC$15,220.50. On average, this is equivalent to 1.15 times the GNI Per

Capita of US$4,906.90 for 2008. Using 1500 as the size of the population of hucksters in Dominica, we estimate the gross annual revenue of the trade to be EC$243m or US$90m.

Hucksterism in Dominica provides some insight into the added value of an umbrella association of higglers. The DHA has effectively lobbied on behalf of the hucksters at the level of the Government of Dominica and the financial sector within Dominica. It is accredited as an umbrella organization for hucksters by the governments of the French colonies of Guadeloupe and Martinique. It has disbursed loans to hucksters and provided training for the development of hucksters. Furthermore, it facilitates the visa application process as well as the packaging process adopted by hucksters.

The DHA is, however, challenged with reducing membership. Notably, respondents in the survey (4%) cited the lack of visibility of the benefits of membership in the association as the reason for not belonging to the association. In addition, the DHA must be seen to be addressing the concerns expressed by the sample of hucksters who participated in the key informant interviews, including

- declining profits for hucksters;
- the need to reduce the cost of production as well as increase production of agricultural produce;
- the adoption of measures to reduce spoilage;
- the redesign of the process for the renewal of visas for hucksters;
- the apparent inability to attract young people to the trade;
- lower telephone and Internet costs for hucksters; and
- the imperative to integrate technology with agricultural production.

These concerns are not all new, as some were identified by Mulakala (1991).[11]

In moving forward, the DHA should examine the several suggestions advanced by hucksters in the sample survey and key informant interviews for improving the trade. Any improvement in the trade will redound to the benefit of the hucksters. The more popular suggestions include (1) an increase in financial assistance for hucksters; (2) lobbying for improved market and storage facilities for produce and an improved shipping service in and out of Dominica; (3) providing further training in record keeping and business management; (4) reducing the cost of packaging material; and (5) lobbying for wider market access for produce in the context of the CSME.

Less popular suggestions focused on the DHA facilitating improved relations/communication among hucksters and lobbying for (1) better air services for hucksters to service an expanded market with their produce; (2) increased production and quality of export commodities from farmers; (3) the creation of a marketing board in Dominica for the benefit of both hucksters and farmers; (4) improved port facilities; and (5) improved relations with government agencies.

The content of this list of suggestions makes it necessary for the DHA to critically revisit its mission with a view to regaining its position as the focal organization for the hucksters. The revised mission must take into consideration the changes in the economic and political landscape as evidenced by the CSME, the imperative for CARICOM governments to reduce their food import bill, Dominica's reputation as an eco-tourism destination, the prospects of agro-tourism arising out of the harnessing of eco-tourism and agriculture, increased security restrictions for inter-island travel, planned improvements in intra-regional transportation, proposed political integration of countries within the Southern Caribbean, current and proposed information and communication technologies infrastructure in the Caribbean and the initiatives by regional and extra-regional governments to develop small and medium enterprises (SMEs) within the Caribbean.

The amended vision should take hucksterism to the next level, which should include a vertically integrated business entity in which hucksters cost-effectively manage all aspects of the trade, possess negotiating power in the context of accessing increased funding and contracts with third parties, exploit ICTs to disseminate market and other related information among members, network with other higglers and higgler associations and actively pursue their development as SMEs.

The revised mission for the DHA will not materialize if the organization is not adequately resourced to undertake research; penetrate new markets; expand existing markets; provide oversight on the trade as conducted in destination countries; produce operating reports on a timely basis; facilitate the creation and ongoing maintenance of a hucksters database; and develop and enforce standards of produce quality and packaging.

6 Informal Commercial Importing in Jamaica

In the Jamaican context, shuttle traders arose in response to the economic crises in the 1970s and 1980s (Witter and Anderson 1991). In many regards, the shuttle trade was a reaction to the limited opportunities for employment, as well as low expectations of short-run economic improvement. These shuttle traders can be seen as a group of individuals who engaged in the trading of goods across borders to make a profitable living amid a weak economic environment.

This chapter seeks to update some of the findings in the work of Le Franc et al. (1985), Taylor (1988) and Witter and Kirton (1990) on the shuttle trade in Jamaica. This work is of particular interest in the context of the post-global economic meltdown and in terms of the observation in Witter and Kirton (1990) that engaging in the shuttle trade is one of the reactions to economic crisis situations, like that experienced in Jamaica in the 1970s and 1980s. Furthermore, strategies are offered at the end of this chapter that are particularly targeted at policy cohorts who may be motivated to explore formalization options. This chapter is organized as follows: the findings of previously undertaken studies on the shuttle trade in Jamaica are discussed in section 6.1, followed by the empirical updates in section 6.2, and a conclusion.

6.1. Findings of Previous Empirical Studies of the Shuttle Trade in Jamaica

Empirical studies of the shuttle trade in Jamaica have been reported in Smikle and Taylor (1978), Taylor (1988), Le Franc et al. (1985) and Witter and Kirton (1990). Taylor and Witter and Kirton reported that women dominated the sector, many of whom had a number of dependents for whom they were the main support system. Taylor summarized that the majority of traders in the sample were between the ages of 20 and 39 years and reported having between one and four children. Witter and Kirton (1990) summarized that higglers originated mostly in rural districts and many of them (almost 60%) were over 45 years of age. Witter and Kirton also suggested that higgling was a way for higglers to elevate themselves into an improved economic condition. Further, higglers generally worked without hired help and with little help from family members. Both studies indicated that many traders preferred if their children did not get involved in the trade.

The decision to enter the trade was a personal one for most of the respondents in Taylor (1988). However, a significant number were encouraged by friends or relatives to enter the trade. Many respondents in the survey reported in Witter and Kirton (1990) entered the trade to avoid being unemployed or because they were forced to due to business failure, illness of a partner, being too old or not qualified to do anything else or the dislike for domestic work. Some traders indicated that independence was a reason for engaging in higgling. In the Taylor (1988) survey, the main reasons proffered for entering the trade were "unemployment, the need to assist in family expenses, for gain, or because they had no other form of training". Although it was noted that higgling was an alternative to unemployment, it was not an option that had long-term preference. Taylor (1988) reported that traders were equally divided between remaining in the trade and preferring another job. Witter and Kirton, on the other hand, found that traders opted to get out of the trade as soon as they could.

Higglers sell a narrow range of goods and usually operate from one location. Initial financing either came from own savings (both formal and informal) or money borrowed from family and friends, according to the findings of both Witter and Kirton (1990) and Taylor (1988). Witter and Kirton (1990, 13) noted that many informal sector workers operated from streets and sidewalks in Jamaica, engaging in various types of trade from the "traditional food trade by higglers on the kerb-sides of parochial markets and the trade in imported and locally manufactured consumer goods". As noted by Witter and Kirton, the shuttle trade sprung up in a major way during the late 1970s and further developed into the early 1980s. The development and prevalence of these traders were so pronounced that in

1983 and 1986, special markets called arcades were constructed to house vendors (Taylor 1988).

Witter and Kirton (1990) reported that "47% of higglers in the Smikle and Taylor (1978) survey sample earned less than the minimum wage of $20 per week and 93% earned less than $50". Although it was noted that many of the survey respondents either underreported incomes or were ignorant of the amount that they earned, it was generally accepted that almost half of higglers earned low incomes. The findings of the survey conducted in 1984 and published by Le Franc et al. (1985) also confirmed that higgling was a low-income activity. It is interesting to note that when the surveys were conducted, the economy was in a crisis state. Therefore, although many higglers may have earned less than the minimum wage, these low incomes may have been a reasonable alternative when compared to no income, if jobs could not be obtained.

Formal unemployment increased to great proportions up to 1983 and was followed by an increase in informal employment (Witter and Anderson 1991). These researchers noted that "self-employment has long played and continues to play a critical role in the economic activity of both rural and urban Jamaicans" (p. 26).

6.2. Updating the Profile of the Shuttle Trader in Jamaica: An Empirical Study

The authors undertook an empirical study of shuttle traders in Jamaica in an effort to update the sociological and demographic profile of the shuttle trader.

Methodology

The methodology adopted for the study reflects a mix of qualitative and quantitative approaches. The qualitative approach took the form of key informant interviews with a sample of shuttle traders in Kingston, Jamaica. The information gathered was used to finalize the form of the survey instrument. The quantitative approach took the form of a survey of shuttle traders that used a purposive and convenient sampling design and was undertaken in Kingston, Jamaica. The structured questionnaire was developed to capture data on the demographics of shuttle traders, details of their trade, problems encountered in their trade and various suggestions for improving the trade. This questionnaire was administered face-to-face. Fieldwork was undertaken in September 2008. The achieved sample size was 62.

6.3. Summary of Survey Data

Age and Sex

The sample of shuttle traders was 90% female and 10% male. As table 6.1 shows, all age groups from 21 years to 60 years were represented in the sample, with the majority of the sample falling in the 31–60 years age group. The modal age group for the males as well as the females was 41 to 50 years; accordingly, the modal age for the sample was 41 to 50 years. The average age of respondents in the sample was estimated to be 42 years.

The data on age and gender are consistent with the findings in demographic studies (such as Taylor 1988; Witter and Kirton 1990) that significantly more women than men participate in shuttle trade. The data are also consistent with the findings of Lagro (1990), Ellis (1986) and Girault (1984) for gender and age of higglers. However, the literature is divergent in terms of the proportions.

Education

The sample data suggest that the majority of shuttle traders in the sample either had no formal education or left formal education either at the primary school level or third form at the secondary level. However, the modal status for the sample was technical or vocational. As table 6.2 shows, no formal education was the dominant highest level for the age groups less than 21 years, 51–60 years and over 60 years; secondary education (to third form) was the dominant highest level for the 21–30 age group; technical or vocational education was the dominant highest level for the 31–40 age group; and the subsample of shuttle traders who attained a mix of secondary education (to fifth form) and technical or vocational education

Table 6.1: Age Distribution of the Sample

Age group (years)	<21	21–30	31–40	41–50	51–60	>60	Total
Percentage of sample	3.2	22.6	16.1	32.3	16.1	9.7	100

fell in the 41–50 age group. Further, the shuttle trade does not appear to appeal to graduates of tertiary education.

Marital Status and Dependents

The data in table 6.3 suggest that shuttle traders were more likely to be common-law or married, with the modal status being common-law. From an age perspective, shuttle traders in the less than 21 years age group were more likely to be single; those in the 21–40 age group were more likely

Table 6.2: Highest Education Level Attained by Age

Highest Level Attained	Age						
Education	<21	21–30	31–40	41–50	51–60	>60	Total
No formal education	2	2	0	4	4	4	16
Primary	0	2	2	4	0	0	8
Secondary (to Form 3)	0	8	0	0	2	0	10
Secondary (to Form 5)	0	0	2	4	2	0	8
Secondary (to Form 6)	0	2	0	0	0	2	4
Technical/vocational	0	0	6	4	2	0	12
Tertiary	0	0	0	0	0	0	0
Secondary (to Form 5) and technical/vocational	0	0	0	4	0	0	4
All Levels	2	14	10	20	10	6	62

Table 6.3: Marital Status of Shuttle Traders by Age

	Marital Status					
Age	Married	Common-law	Divorced	Single	Widowed	Total
<21	0	0	0	2	0	2
21–30	0	10	0	2	2	14
31–40	0	10	0	0	0	10
41–50	6	6	0	6	2	20
51–60	4	2	2	0	2	10
Over 60	2	2	0	0	2	6
All ages	12	30	2	10	8	62
%	19.4	48.4	3.2	16.1	12.9	100

to be in a common-law relationship; those in the 41–50 age group were equally likely to be single, married or in common-law relationships; those in the over 60 age group were more likely to be married.

The data also suggest that the importance of the shuttle trade from both the social and economic standpoints is underscored by the significant number of dependents whose lives are linked to the trade and to a lesser extent by the level of indirect employment. Shuttle traders in the sample had as many as twelve children, with both the average and median number of children being four; the sample was multi-modal, as the actual modes were two, three and four children.

Almost half (48%) of the sample had as many as three children, another 36% had between four and six children inclusive, while the remaining 12% had between seven and twelve children inclusive (see table 6.4). This finding is consistent with that of Taylor (1988) and Witter and Kirton (1990) who observed that women in the shuttle trade had a number of dependents for whom they were the main support system. In the case of Taylor (1988), 67% of the sample had between one and four children inclusive.

Shuttle traders with no formal education were more likely to have up to three children; those with primary education were more likely to have four to six children; those with secondary education (up to third form and fifth form) were more likely to have up to three children; those with secondary education (up to sixth form) were equally likely to have up to three children and between four and six children; and those with technical or vocational training were more likely to have between four and six children. However, shuttle traders who had completed secondary education (up to fifth form) and technical or vocational education were equally likely to have up to three children and between four and six children (see table 6.5).

Table 6.4: Number of Children of Shuttle Traders

No. of Children	%
0–3	48.4
4–6	35.5
7–9	6.5
10–12	9.7
	100.0

Table 6.5: Number of Children by Highest Education Level Attained

	Number of Children			
Highest education level attained	0–3	4–6	7–9	10–12
No formal education	8	2	0	6
Primary	2	4	2	0
Secondary (to Form 3)	8	2	0	0
Secondary (to Form 5)	8	0	0	0
Secondary (to Form 6)	2	2	0	0
Technical/vocational	0	10	2	0
Tertiary	0	0	0	0
Secondary (to Form 5) and technical/vocational	2	2	0	0
All Levels	30	22	4	6

With respect to indirect employment, shuttle traders in the sample employed up to four workers, with the modal employment level being zero workers. Some 71% of the sample employed zero workers, 19% employed two workers and 3% each employed one worker, three workers and four workers. This high proportion of traders with no support workers is consistent with the finding of Witter and Kirton (1990) that higglers used very little hired help.

Assets

The sample data support the observation that the shuttle trade offers traders some benefits; one such benefit is the ability to acquire assets. Shuttle traders in the sample were more likely to own a house and a vehicle as well as invest in fixed deposit instruments. Figure 6.1 shows that while on average 68% of the sample owned a house and a vehicle, ownership reduced to 52% for fixed deposits and 10% and 6.5% shares in life insurance policies and local credit unions respectively. No investment in money market funds was recorded.

Previous Employment

A total of 32% of the sample was employed prior to joining the shuttle trade. This employment was more likely to be in the private sector, given that 67% of these respondents worked in the private sector prior to joining

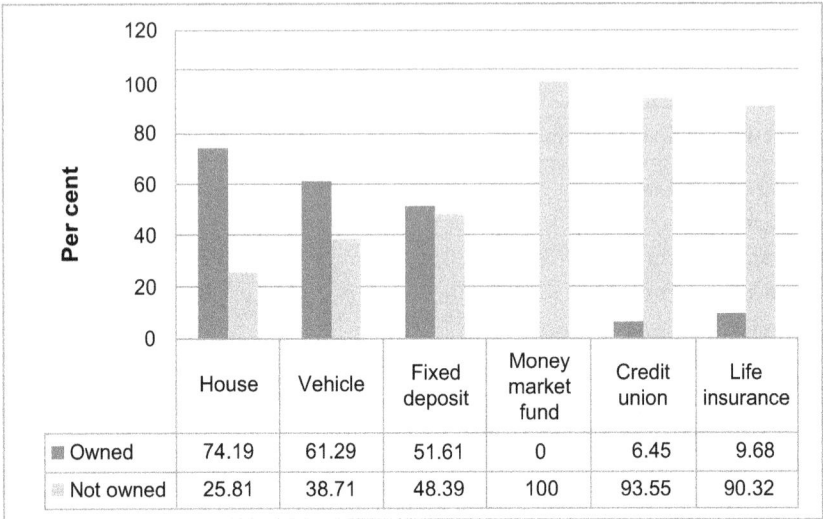

	House	Vehicle	Fixed deposit	Money market fund	Credit union	Life insurance
■ Owned	74.19	61.29	51.61	0	6.45	9.68
▨ Not owned	25.81	38.71	48.39	100	93.55	90.32

Figure 6.1 Ownership of assets by shuttle traders in Jamaica

the shuttle trade. Figure 6.2 highlights that shuttle traders with secondary education to at least fifth form were more likely to have been employed prior to joining the trade.

Shuttle traders tended to enter the trade without supervisory or managerial experience. Only three prior occupations were recorded in the sample: domestics (44%), labourer or other elementary occupations (22%) and service sector occupations (33%). The finding from this sample for the percentage of traders who were previously employed is consistent with a similar finding in Witter and Kirton (1990). In addition, the finding from this sample for the percentage of traders who were previously unemployed is consistent with a similar finding in Taylor (1988).

Years in the Suitcase Trade

The number of years spent in the shuttle trade ranged from one year to forty-eight years in the sample, with an average of 16.5 years. The modal time engaged in the trade was two years; this does not appear to be inconsistent with the finding of Taylor (1988) that traders were equally divided between remaining in the trade or preferring another job. Interestingly, 50% of the sample had been in the trade for fifteen years or less. A possible explanation for such length of time in the trade is the finding by Witter and Kirton (1990) that the shuttle trade provided a sense of independence for traders. The average time in the trade was greatest for shuttle traders with

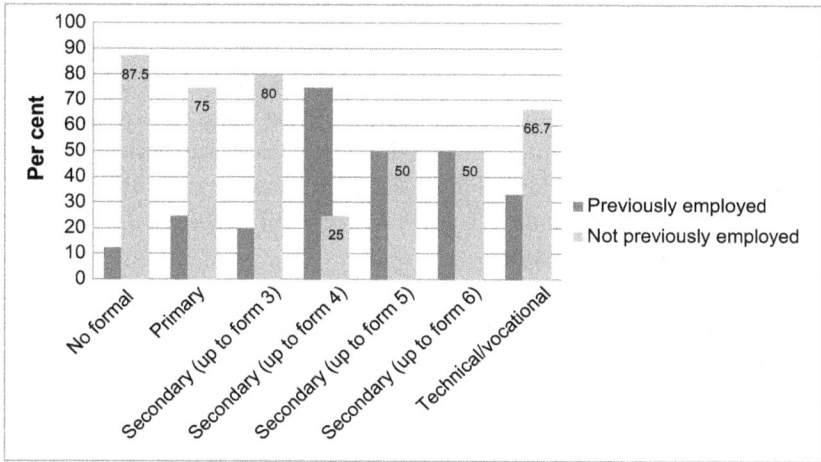

Figure 6.2 Previous employment of shuttle traders by highest education level

either no formal education or secondary education (to sixth form). The technical or vocational subsample was in the trade for an average of eighteen years; those in the secondary (to fifth form) subsample, fourteen years; those in the primary subsample, thirteen years; and those in the secondary (to third form) subsample, seven years.

The majority of the shuttle traders with fifteen years or less experience in the trade from the sample tended to be in common-law relationships, while the majority of those with more than fifteen years in the trade were equally likely to be married or in a common-law relationship. In addition, the entire sample traded their goods in Jamaica only.

Number of Trading Months per Year

The number of trading months ranges from ten to twelve within the year, with 90% of the sample trading for twelve months in a year. The peak period for carrying out the trade varied within the sample; for 26% of the sample it was the summer vacation period, while for another 29% it was the Christmas season.

Profile of Trips Made

While the number of trips made per year by shuttle traders in the sample typically ranged from one to two, the average number of trips per year was 2.6. A minority of respondents indicated that procurement of goods for their trade was done by relatives abroad. The entire sample travelled by air for their trips. Time spent on trips ranged from three days to twenty-eight days, with an average stay of seven days. A total of 29% of the sample used the services of a hotel while on these trips, 32% each stayed with relatives and friends and the remaining 39% used the services of guest houses or bed and breakfasts. Figure 6.3 highlights the curtailment measures employed by the shuttle traders in terms of accommodation costs while on trips out of Jamaica.

Typically, shuttle traders preferred to transport their purchases as checked baggage on airlines. Consistent with earlier studies, 39% of the sample shipped their purchases as unaccompanied baggage or cargo at least once per month.

The Trade

The sample data corroborate the view expressed in earlier studies that shuttle traders sell a range of goods, and very often meet the demands of domestic consumers not necessarily met by local distributors. The dominant goods traded by the shuttle traders were garments (42%), haberdashery (17%), jewellery (13%), appliances (8%), shoes or footwear (8%), accessories (8%) and manufactured goods (4%). This finding reflects an expansion in the list of items identified in Witter and Kirton (1990).

Whereas the literature suggests that ICIs sell their wares from their homes or on the streets, the dataset offers some qualification to this notion.

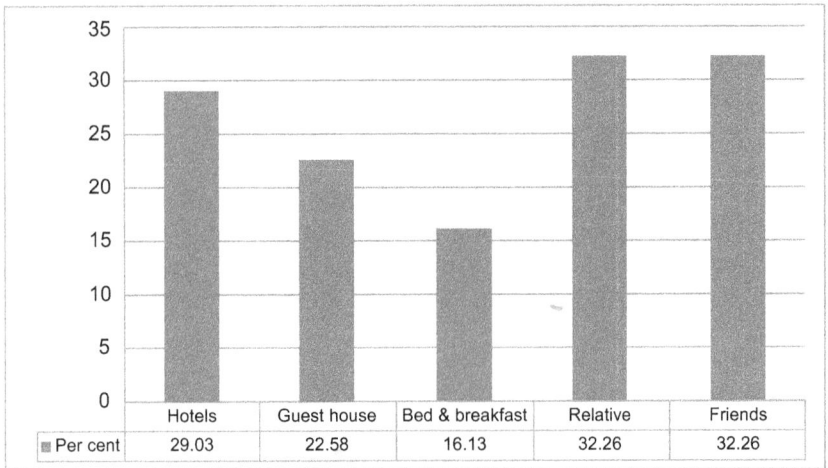

	Hotels	Guest house	Bed & breakfast	Relative	Friends
Per cent	29.03	22.58	16.13	32.26	32.26

Figure 6.3 Types of accommodation used by shuttle traders on trips

A vast majority (97%) of the sample reported the dominant market for their goods was the general public in Jamaica. The sample data suggests that shuttle traders use a mix of sales outlets, namely sidewalk vendors (48%), malls (32%), stores (6.5%) and small shops (13%).

Manual records of the trade were kept by 68% of the sample, while the remaining 32% of the sample maintained computerized records. Only 13% of the sample had a written contract with suppliers. Furthermore, only 6% of the sample held membership in an association that caters to the trade.

Expenses per Trip

Figure 6.4 clearly shows that expenses for airfare, accommodation, food, freight charges, ground transportation, and telephone calls and incidentals per trip were in the range of US$251 to US$4,000, with a median of US$1,125. The average trip expense was estimated at US$1,520.

Profits Per Week

Figure 6.5 highlights that 53% of the sample assessed their profit to be at most US$500 per week. Profits per week for the sample reflected a range of US$1,250, with a median in the US$251–$500 interval. The mean weekly profit was estimated at US$550.

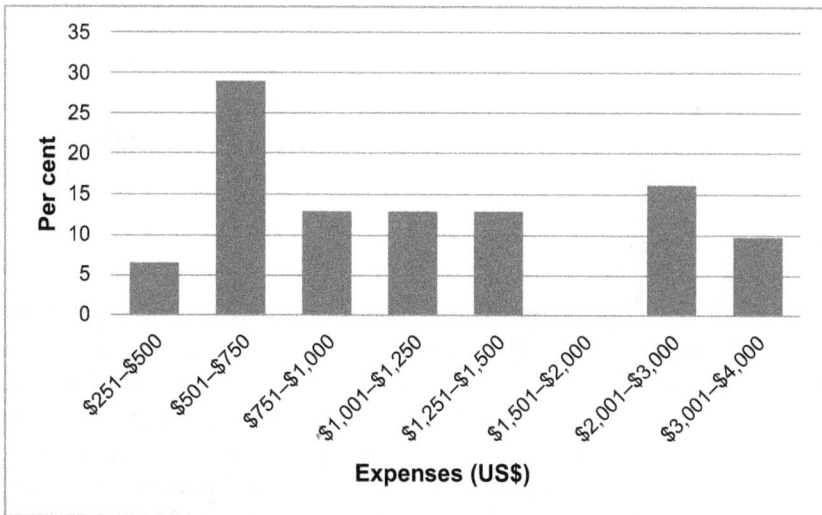

Figure 6.4 Distribution of expenses per trip

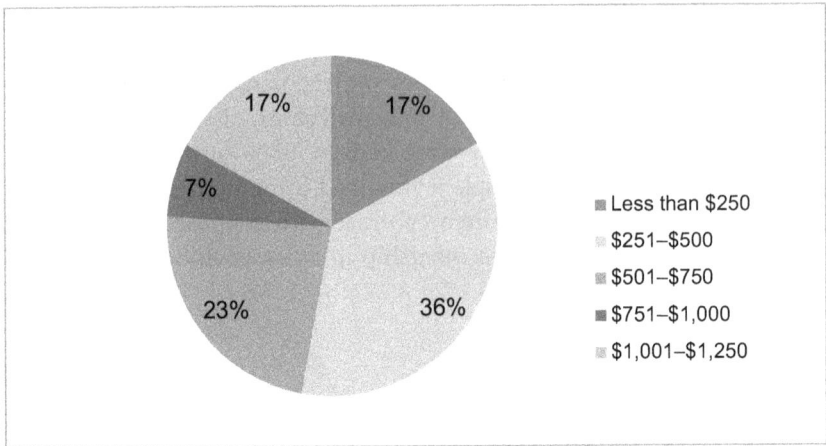

Figure 6.5 Profit per week for the shuttle traders in US$

On the basis of the data for the expenses per trip and profits per week, weekly gross revenue from each shuttle trader is estimated to range from US$251 to US$5,250, with a mean of US$2,070 and a median in the interval of US$1,376–$1,625. This data is consistent with the findings in Taylor (1988) that most traders agreed that they could earn a living from the trade. However, the data do not support the finding of Le Franc et al. (1985) that higgling and shuttle trading are low-income activities.

Other Sources of Income

Only 16% of the sample reported having an additional source of income within their household. The reported sources of income within the sample were rent from leased property and the operation of a taxi.

Financial Assistance

In the sample, 19% of the shuttle traders reported seeking loans from financial institutions to assist with developing their trade, while 42% of these were successful. These findings may not be significantly different from the finding of Witter and Kirton (1990) that financing came either from savings or money borrowed from family and friends. Another source of financing is that of a Rotating Savings and Credit Association (RoSCA) arrangement. A RoSCA is a form of informal banking where a group of individuals meet and make fixed monetary contributions on a regular interval. Following each meeting, the money or pot is then lent to one member of the group who is selected randomly, via a binding RoSCA, based on seniority or on concurrence by the members (Varadharajan 2004). RoSCAs are typically found in developing countries and are for the most part formed by low-income households. Handa and Kirton (1999) conducted an econometric study of the Jamaican RoSCA or partner using logit regression analysis and a data set of one thousand partner members from four of the major parishes of Jamaica where persons are predominantly involved in small-scale non-agricultural activities. Approximately 75% of the partners in the sample were women.

In Jamaica, each contribution is termed a *hand*, which is *thrown* into the *draw* at each prescribed interval, usually determined by the leader of the RoSCA or *banker*. Handa and Kirton (1999) focused on the operational aspect of the RoSCA and its resultant success. A non-linear, inverse relationship was found between the RoSCA size and each partner's contribution. Moreover, even the upper-class in Jamaica participates in RoSCAs. The banker was found to be instrumental to the success of the arrangement; the banker maintains timely and flexible payments that reduce the probability of default. Further, two-thirds of the sample indicated that RoSCA funds were used for the purchase of durable commodities, while 14% opted for precautionary savings.

Problems Encountered

Almost three-quarters (71%) of the sample reported having encountered problems or difficulties in conducting their trade. A vast majority (91%) of these respondents listed customs officers as providing the most problems for the trade; the remaining 9% listed Trade Ministry regulations. All of the respondents also had occasional problems with competition among traders, immigration officers, customers, officers of the Trade Ministry and suppliers.

Suggestions for Improving the Trade

A total of 92% of the sample offered suggestions for improving the trade. The most dominant suggestion (46%) was to standardize shipping and customs procedures, making them easier and less cumbersome for small traders. The next most-popular suggestion (18%) was to provide suitable facilities for the conduct of the trade. The training of customs officers and police officers assigned to ports and airports in terms of interfacing with small traders was next, suggested by 12% of the sample. Other suggestions were as follows: make information and related training on finding suppliers more accessible to traders (9%), disseminate information to persons who want to join the trade (8%), provide small loans and better credit facilities to traders (6%), and form an association to seek their interests.

6.4. Conclusion

The relative size of the informal sector of Jamaica is smaller than that of Guyana, St Lucia, the Dominican Republic, Belize, and St Vincent and the Grenadines, according to the findings of Vuletin (2008). Further, the tax burden and labour rigidity are the more dominant factors determining the size of the country's informal sector, as opposed to inflation and the importance of agriculture (Vuletin 2008). The shuttle trade in Jamaica, which had its origins in the economic crises of the 1970s and 1980s, remains an integral part of the informal economy in Jamaica, given that it provides an avenue of opportunity for those who cannot be absorbed into the formal economy (Witter and Kirton 1990). Earlier empirical studies suggest that the existence of this trade has contributed to the economic livelihood of many persons in the Jamaican economy, as evidenced by the growing size of the sector as a proportion of total employment.

According to the empirical study summarized in this chapter, the typical shuttle trader is female, between 41 and 50 years old, with no formal education and no previous formal employment, who has three children or fewer and who lives in a common-law relationship. The typical trader owns a house and a vehicle, trades twelve months per year in garments and haberdashery that are sold to the public on the sidewalk, has no other source of income and does not access loans from financial institutions. On average, a shuttle trader has been in the trade for 16.5 years.

Witter and Kirton (1990) found that unemployment, limited education or skills, market failure, illness of a partner, old age and the attraction of independence were the reasons for persons joining the trade. The observations that (a) 68% of the sample was unemployed prior to joining the trade and (b) 55% of the sample had either no formal education or were educated to third form suggest that unemployment, followed by limited education and skills, remain dominant reasons for persons joining the shuttle trade in Jamaica.

This study indicates that 32% of traders are neither married nor living in a common-law relationship, 52% of traders have more than three children and 74% of the children of traders were attending primary, secondary or technical or vocational schools, which raises concern for the holistic development of children of traders. It is advisable that every effort should be made to provide for the holistic development of children of traders. This recommendation takes on even greater relevance when we reflect on the findings of the Taylor (1988) survey that some 70% of that sample did not perceive the trade as a good occupation for their children. Support services must be provided at the level of the community. These services must be geared toward assisting children to excel within the education system, crossing the digital divide, ensuring that they have an appreciation for the entrepreneurial spirit of their parent(s) and introducing them to the basics of entrepreneurship and innovation. These services can be delivered via mentorship programmes and homework centres.

Given that the average length of time spent in the trade is 16.5 years and the observation that a shuttle trader can spend as much as 48 years in the trade, consideration should be given to assisting shuttle traders in providing for their retirement. One such approach is the introduction of an Individual Retirement Annuity (IRA) for contribution by the traders. This measure also has the capacity to enhance savings and credit rating among traders.

Another possible recommendation is that shuttle traders gravitate to an association of their own that will advance their trade. Such an association can lobby for improved relations with the officers of the customs departments in Jamaica, the building and upgrading of facilities for traders to sell their goods as well as access to funding comparable to that recommended by international agencies for SMEs in the region. A representative of the association should be appointed to the government boards that oversee the arcades and markets provided for the traders to sell their goods. Taylor (1988) alluded to the formation of two associations in the late 1980s namely, the Jamaica Association of Higglers and the United Vendors Association (UVA), with the latter becoming the umbrella organization. The fact that 94% of the sample reported not belonging to an umbrella association suggests that the aims, objectives and service offering of the UVA require re-engineering so that the organization can enjoy significant membership among shuttle traders. It may be advisable for the re-engineering of the UVA to take into account features and aspects of the DHA, where appropriate.

Human resource development is critical to economic growth and the improvement of social conditions within Jamaica. A re-engineered UVA must engage vocational education institutes and community colleges to design and deliver special programmes that are aimed at facilitating the lifelong learning of shuttle traders. These programmes should include book-keeping and accounting, computer literacy, elements of cross-border trading and the use of information and communications technology for enhancing procurement, networking and marketing within the shuttle trade. Where possible, this training should be aimed at graduating the shuttle trader to full SME status and a reversal in the pattern of trade from the sale of imported goods to producing Jamaican products for export to CARICOM and extra-regional markets, beginning with markets located in countries where the Caribbean diaspora reside. The education programmes must also seek to unearth latent innovation talent among the shuttle traders and pre-pare them to access the business incubator programme in Jamaica.

From the standpoint of the government, it is essential that the size of the shuttle trade and all other cohorts of the informal economy, as well as the sources of its growth, be understood. Once the re-engineering of the UVA is completed, the government could seek to work with the association to periodically update the traders' demographic profile and collect data that will correct the under-reporting or non-reporting of the trade within the national economic statistics. Confidentiality should not be compromised whatever the system of data capture that is agreed upon. The updated profiles can also be used to develop, modify and deliver programmes that address the gaps observed in the profile. In addition, in keeping with the policy recommendations of Vuletin (2008), the Government of Jamaica could consider lowering and homogenizing tax rates across all sectors of the economy, as well as take steps to accelerate labour market reforms and enhance flexibility.

CARICOM has defined short- to medium-term goals for the progres-sive introduction of the CSME. Babb et al. (2004) posit that stronger link-ages among participants in the informal sector, government, farmers, and local institutions, in the context of the CSME, would be of benefit to all CARICOM economies. According to Babb et al. (2004, 4),

> National data collection and compilation of statistics on the volume and value of the small inter-island trade would enlighten planners on the extent of their investments and productivity and sensitize everyone to inefficien-cies in the system. Elevating their economic status nationally could lead to special provisions for enabling their trade to flourish, farmers to have more outlets for their produce, and their contributions to foreign exchange earn-ings to increase. The linkages that this informal sector has with the formal economy span banking, transportation on land, sea and air, government de-partments, agricultural production and ancillary services, employment and

savings. Family well-being, networks of support, and social stability are all linked to the trading activities of these hard working women and men.

The re-engineered UVA can explore opportunities provided in the CSME for the enhancement of the shuttle trade. The empirical data point to clothing and accessories as the most popular goods sold by traders. The attraction here may be pricing and the short lead time in bringing the most recent styles to Jamaica. At the same time, shuttle traders enjoy limited ability to achieve economies of scale. A possible opportunity therefore exists for bulk buying of clothing and accessories on behalf of traders within the construct of the CSME. Taylor (1988) found that traders value their independence. Every effort must be made by the re-engineered UVA to protect that independence as far as possible in the pursuit of any opportunity provided by CSME for the expansion of the trade.

Finally, enhancing the lot of shuttle traders in Jamaica must require a concerted effort on the part of the Government of Jamaica to progressively move the country away from its plantation economy and toward to the knowledge economy of the twenty-first century. Notwithstanding the above, observing the nature and characteristics of the shuttle trade can provide great insight for policymakers. Taylor (1988) noted that "Jamaican workers value their independence and being their own bosses, thus 'higglering' or trading provides an attractive occupation for women".

The benefits to be gained from incorporating these traders into the formal sector have been raised. From a government viewpoint, formalizing the traders may have benefits in terms of increased tax revenue for the government, as well as increased information and knowledge about the traders and their contribution to the economy. Even more formal recognition of employment may enhance their ability to obtain growth finance or capital from formal financial institutions. The persons who are employed by the traders may be entitled to formal benefits from the system as well. Formalizing the sector can contribute to linking the traders with the rest of the economy through investment and employment. For example, as discussed earlier, the majority of credit for this activity comes from family and friends as opposed to formal financial institutions. This may be due to the informal nature of the activity and the inability of traders to qualify for loans from the local banks. Other contributing factors may be a lack of understanding and trust in formal financial institutions due to the traders' low level of education. Further, many traders cited treatment by customs officers when importing goods as one of the major challenges they faced when operating. Formalizing the trade may enable traders to lobby for better treatment from customs officers.

Witter and Kirton (1990, 13) noted that "since the middle of the 1970s, there has been much public comment in the media on the social and environmental effects of sidewalk trading and on various aspects of its impact on the economy. The government has recognized the phenomenon and responded with measures, intended to regularize the activities of the sections of these traders." Taylor (1988) noted that in 1983 and 1986, centres known as arcades were constructed to accommodate traders. Further, the monitoring and improvement of markets for the traders were overseen by corporations established for this purpose. Witter and Kirton also noted that ICIs were "recognized, registered and given structural access to foreign exchange on the official market". These highlight the recognized importance and contribution of the shuttle traders. However, Ulysse (2007) noted that many traders prefer to hide from the formal economy. This may be attributed to fear or mistrust of the governing authorities because of the feeling of exploitation (via taxes) and strict policies to which they may have to adhere.

Problems with formalization that may be more perceived than real include the removal of a sense of freedom that traders have, taxes and regulation as well as persons who may be involved in illegal activities. In terms of specific government initiatives, understanding the shuttle trade may provide some insight in terms of the most appropriate policies to implement. In particular, in 2009, Jamaica officially opened its Small Business Incubator and Resource Centre, an arm of the Jamaican Business Development Centre. This was part of a government initiative to promote small-, medium- and micro-business development in Jamaica, as small business was cited as a possible avenue through which jobs could be created. However, if persons continue to operate in the informal sector even with alternative opportunities available, then policymakers may have to reconsider the incentives given to persons to formally register and operate their businesses.

In addition, as indicated by the survey, the most popularly traded good in the shuttle trade in Jamaica is clothing and accessories. Since there is an apparent demand for clothing and accessories and possibly an appetite for style and trend, promoting a local fashion industry in Jamaica may have extensive benefits for the Jamaican economy. An industry such as this can promote skills development, contribute to the GDP of the Jamaican economy and deal with some of the market failure in this industry, since clearly there is a demand for clothing not satisfied by the local Jamaican economy. Also, encouraging mass production of clothing may decrease prices and make items more cost competitive in addition to employing and creating linkages, such as industrial machine maintenance, transportation and other services.

Addressing the shuttle trade is not just a matter of formalizing or creating the right incentives for traders. The shuttle trade exists as a result of a deeper problem experienced by Jamaica, one entrenched in its historical roots. Jamaica can be considered a typical model of the plantation economy, as described by Lloyd Best. Of the three types of plantation models, including hinterlands of settlement, hinterlands of conquest and hinterlands of exploitations,[1] Jamaica (as well as other Caribbean islands) can be considered a hinterland of exploitation where the interest of the metropole was use of the economy for mass production for trade (Best 1968). This model is one in which the plantation was organized to produce for the purpose of exporting to the metropole. The system was so focused on the aforementioned that limited linkages were created with the remainder of the economy that was not aligned for this purpose. Beckford (1972) noted that this system is one which engenders persistent underdevelopment. One of the reasons cited was the fact that "the system creates a legacy of dependence because the locus of decision making concerning fundamental economic issues resides outside of plantation society, so that chronic dependency syndrome is characteristic of the whole population"(p. 215).

After the abolition of slavery, Jamaica was not relieved of the plantation mentality. During the boom period, what resulted was the formation of enclaves and a dual society where the enclaves were specialized in production for export, with limited productive linkages to the rest of the economy. The island continued to be dependent on imports for basic necessities as well as luxuries during the boom period. However, when the oil crisis occurred, the enclaves suffered considerably, as did the rest of the island, whose government found it difficult to continue spending on social programmes. Jamaica was led into the hands of foreign lending agencies and borrowed money to sustain its economy. Jamaica is therefore a very indebted country as a result of continuous assistance and bail-outs by monetary institutions such as the IMF and the World Bank. To amplify this problem, Jamaica has a high import bill, with many basic necessities coming from foreign territories. The distribution of income in Jamaica is very uneven and it appears that governing authorities past and present have continuously failed to address this issue. It can be argued that government policies to some extent have worsened the state of the Jamaican economy via its policies, actions and inactions.

Other economic issues need to be addressed since, as noted by Levitt (1991, 56), "The combination of chronic unemployment, declining living standards, deteriorating real incomes and reduced ability to purchase both necessities and comforts have changed the pattern of behaviour. It is no longer possible for a man or a woman dependent solely on a wage or salary income to hope ever to own a home. Hence, the increase in hustling, higgling, and reliance on multiple sources of income." The quote by Levitt confirms that the shuttle trade phenomenon in Jamaica cannot be treated in isolation. Beckford (1972) argues that for changes to be realized in plantation economies, development paths must involve changes in the institutional structure of the economy. In particular, economic, social and political arrangements must be altered away from the entrenched mentality to develop and grow. Therefore attitudinal change is firstly required for economic change to be realized in Jamaica. Although the government may be restricted due to debt servicing, the minds of the people of Jamaica need to be uplifted so that they take it upon themselves to propel development in the island.

Hong Kong and Singapore are examples of industrialized economies with limited land space or natural resources that have achieved high rates of economic growth, even in times of adverse international economic conditions (Brown 1989). These economies prove that it is not just about being endowed, but that an economy is a reflection of economic and social policy. With high rates of savings, heavy investment in education and the use of human resources, these economies were able to surpass even developed countries in rates of economic growth (Brown 1989).

The shuttle trade can be seen simply as a reflection of the inability of the economy to develop as it may have been able to if different policies were implemented and there was a more frugal use of resources during the 1960s boom. A look at the shuttle trade reinforces the need for Jamaica to examine and deal with its social and economic issues.

7

ICIs AND PRESCRIPTION MEDICINES IN THE CARIBBEAN: EVIDENCE FROM TRINIDAD AND TOBAGO

Pharmaceutical prices vary widely across differing economies, and this in turn provides an incentive for arbitrage where goods sold in high-priced markets can sidestep the established supply chain and low-priced goods can enter these markets. This chapter looks at the imports of pharmaceuticals via the suitcase trade into the Trinidad and Tobago economy. It offers an ideal example of the opportunity for informalization resulting from price discrimination and market failure. It is organized into seven sections. Section 7.1 traces the historical roots of the suitcase trader; this is followed by section 7.2 that explores price discrimination, suitcase trading and re-importation as a solution to rising cost. Section 7.3 lists other reasons for suitcase trade in medicines, while the handling of medicines and the suitcase trade are discussed in section 7.4. Section 7.5 examines the trade in pharmaceuticals, global, regional and national, while section 7.6 defines the nature of the suitcase trade in prescription (R_x) medicines in the Caribbean.

Suitcase traders participate in the pharmaceutical trade for a variety of reasons, including the high cost of starting up a business. Starting up a business in CARICOM normally requires that a firm or individual incur a variety of costs, including:

- licensing costs as may be relevant to some businesses;
- the cost of renting or acquiring the business premises on which the property is lodged;
- employing workers in accordance with minimum wages legislated in the economy;

- becoming familiar with the various government regulations and complying with them;
- obtaining relevant information about the goods and services available on the market;
- buying goods and services for the market; and
- establishing utility connections, such as electricity and water.

When suitcase traders enter the supply chain of pharmaceutical products, a number of issues become relevant, including the differences in prices between various economies, the actual handling of the pharmaceuticals and the possibility of counterfeiting. These issues are now discussed in turn.

7.1. Price Discrimination, Suitcase Trading and Re-importation as a Solution to Rising Cost

Pharmaceutical prices vary in different economies. The differences in the price of pharmaceuticals across economies reflect a combination of factors, including distinct demand patterns and differences in both government regulations and health care policies. Differences in prices across markets, however, give rise to the possibility of parallel trade, and as Lybecker (2004, 10) noted, "Parallel trade results in unregulated distribution pipelines and weakened regulatory controls of the supply chain both of which are characteristics that facilitate counterfeiting."[1]

Table 7.1 shows the different prices of drugs in different regions from data from eight pharmacies that sell Viagra online. The mean price of the Viagra drug sold by the listed online pharmacies is US$15.41, and prices range from US$8.00 in Israel to US$26.25 in Canada. Such price differences can typically be explained by four reasons, namely retail price discrimination, vertical pricing inefficiencies, free riding on distribution costs and differential price controls (Maskus 2001). Maskus also cites that the re-importation of pharmaceuticals occurs predominantly because of price discrimination.[2] Price discrimination occurs with differing levels of intensity. With first-degree price discrimination, the manufacturer has the ability to offer each buyer of this commodity a completely different price. When individuals are charged the optimal price that they are willing to pay for each unit of a commodity, then the price discriminating pharmaceutical company can extract the consumers' entire consumer surplus, as illustrated by the area DP_1A in figure 7.1.

Table 7.1: Prices for Viagra 100 mg from a Sample of Online Pharmacies

Online Pharmacy	Active Website	Base Country	Price per Pill (US$)
ShopRxToday.com	www.shoprxtoday.com	Cyprus	10.00
Advcare Pharmacy	www.adv-care.com	New Zealand	22.33
Drugstore.com	www.drugstore.com	United States	14.33
CanDrugstore.com	www.candrugstore.com	Canada	19.75
DoctorSolve.com	www.doctorsolve.com	Canada	26.25
BestPrice Pharmacy	www.bestpricepharmacy.com	Israel	8.00
Plane Drugs Direct	www.planetdrugsdirect.com	Australia	12.63
Supersavermeds.com	www.supersavermeds.com	India	10.00

Source: Compiled from the listed online sources, accessed January 2010.

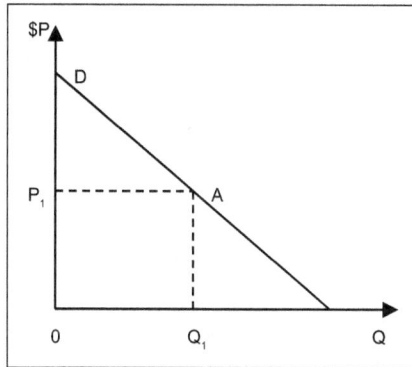

Figure 7.1 Illustration of first-degree price discrimination

With third-degree price discrimination, customers are charged different prices for the same units of a commodity for reasons not associated with the cost of production.[3] A brief illustration of third-degree price discrimination is provided in figure 7.2.

In Market 1, the demand curve of the firm is more inelastic when compared to Market 2. In Market 1, given the same marginal cost of production of MC_0, the price level is P_1 when compared to the price level P_2 in Market 2, which has a lower price elasticity of demand. Suitcase trading would force the price level in both markets to be the same. The price level charged by the monopolist would have to be between P_1 and P_2. This means that the consumers in Market 1 would pay less and those in Market 2 would pay

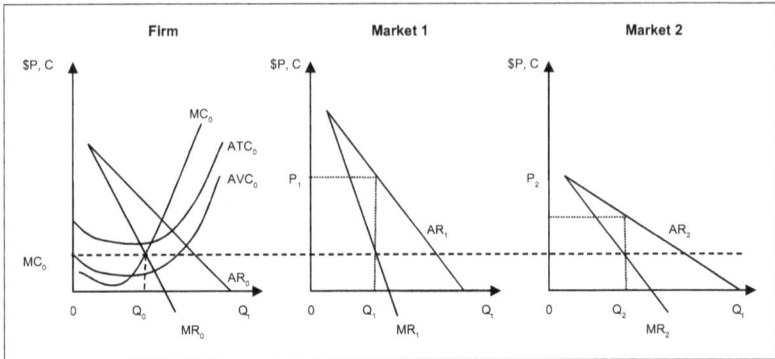

Figure 7.2 Illustration of third-degree price discrimination

more. It is difficult to ascertain *a priori* the welfare effects of this type of policy. However, what is clear is that there is some redistribution of income between the consumers in Market 1 and in Market 2.

Price discrimination raises producer welfare at the expense of consumer welfare, with the overall welfare effect conditioned by the volume of output under price discrimination when compared to a situation without price discrimination. However, if more goods are produced with price discrimination than without price discrimination, then more goods would reach a wider cadre of consumers than previously. Basically, with the suitcase trade (and parallel trade in general), low-priced goods designed for one market are purchased and sold in other high-priced markets. The suitcase trade in R_x pharmaceutical medicines can potentially reduce economic welfare by undermining pricing differentials that may exist among countries. It does this by reducing the capacity of pharmaceutical firms to charge Ramsey prices. Ramsey pricing involves the design of a pricing strategy that could maximize the revenues necessary to cover costs while at the same time trying to maximize consumer welfare. Ramsey prices are higher in price-inelastic markets and lower in price-elastic markets. Consequently, some economists argue that global social welfare would be higher in a Ramsey pricing environment than in an environment with uniform pricing. As Danzon (1998, 298) notes, "the level of [research and development] that can be sustained is greater with differential pricing than with uniform pricing, because manufacturer's revenues are higher with differential pricing".[4]

The economics literature provides some empirical evidence regarding the benefits of the parallel trade in R_x medicines. Two substantive studies are West and Mahon (2003) and Kananos et al. (2004). Assessing the welfare gains from parallel trading (and hence the suitcase trade) in R_x medicines is an extensive undertaking and beyond the scope of this book.

However, various benefits and costs attached to this type of trade are spelled out in table 7.2.

Apart from the economic benefits of arbitrage, suitcase traders can free ride on the fixed marketing and investment costs of the authorized distributors to market and distribute their products. Authorized distributors spend a considerable amount of money, especially as concerns prescription medicines marketing their products (Maskus and Chen 1999). These authorized distributors would obviously prefer protection from suitcase traders who can simply purchase these items from low-cost economies like India and China and distribute them in the local economy without having to incur the marketing and distribution costs of the authorized dealer (Chard and Mellor 1989). In fact it is because of the large economic outlays required that authorized dealers seek exclusive marketing rights.

Restricting parallel imports, including suitcase trading, can help to promote a greater degree of inter-brand competition and better after-sales services. Maskus (2001, 22) notes that "such restrictions on parallel imports may be pro-competitive, both through encouraging investment in inter-brand competition and through providing incentives to build markets and provide services". Parallel trade takes place for a variety of reasons, including differences in per capita GDP levels across economies. Countries may have different income levels, which may reflect different capacities to pay. This no doubt encourages dealers to buy in low per capita GDP economies and sell in economies with higher per capita GDP. Table 7.3 shows the per capita GDP of various CARICOM economies in relation to China and India for the period 1980–2008.[5] Certainly these markets, although small, have relatively superior per capita GDP and this can present an attractive option for dealers of counterfeit drugs.

Table 7.2: Benefits and Costs of the Suitcase Trade in Prescription Medicines

	Potential Benefits	Potential Cost and Risks
Pharmacies	Drugs at lower costs; drugs that are unavailable on the market from authorized dealers	Substandard drugs
Patients	Cheaper drugs, assuming the benefits of a lower price are passed onto the consumer; a wider variety of drugs	Substandard drugs
Suitcase traders	Widening of entrepreneurial talents; profits from niche market targeting	Legal implications of not having a licence

Source: West and Mahon (2003) and Kananos et al. (2004).

Table 7.3: GDP per Capita (Current US$) for China, India and Selected
CARICOM Countries, 1980–2008

	China	India	Jamaica	Barbados	Trinidad and Tobago
1980	193.02	267.41	1,256.16	3,455.84	5,764.54
1981	195.31	270.99	1,377.71	3,789.63	6,220.79
1982	201.44	275.13	1,496.98	3,943.40	7,121.55
1983	223.25	293.12	1,615.17	4,168.00	6,823.62
1984	248.29	279.68	1,041.08	4,521.40	6,671.97
1985	291.77	300.52	908.76	4,709.01	6,256.54
1986	279.19	315.09	1,179.27	5,145.06	4,023.15
1987	249.41	345.57	1,398.37	5,637.86	3,993.95
1988	280.97	359.43	1,624.66	5,969.73	3,720.32
1989	307.49	351.84	1,854.79	6,577.46	3,555.86
1990	314.43	373.70	1,921.43	6,587.01	4,142.06
1991	329.75	308.73	1,706.62	6,490.48	4,351.17
1992	362.81	278.15	1,459.10	6,111.71	4,453.64
1993	373.80	306.94	2,003.76	6,322.99	3,661.63
1994	469.21	353.29	2,007.37	6,669.92	3,921.57
1995	604.23	382.22	2,344.14	7,206.27	4,196.21
1996	703.12	409.32	2,600.60	7,722.67	4,508.72
1997	774.47	425.63	2,948.83	8,587.80	4,468.60
1998	820.86	423.80	3,419.20	9,317.47	4,685.32
1999	864.04	450.92	3,430.43	9,775.89	5,256.38
2000	949.18	452.97	3,479.06	10,168.05	6,269.92
2001	1,041.64	462.82	3,495.30	10,138.82	6,759.95
2002	1,135.45	483.66	3,697.01	9,846.50	6,875.89
2003	1,273.64	563.19	3,579.60	10,693.77	8,599.68
2004	1,490.28	649.17	3,841.78	11,134.38	9,969.44
2005	1,715.03	740.15	4,207.56	12,087.42	11,440.26
2006	2,027.34	824.37	4,502.02	12,568.44	14,376.79
2007	2,565.61	1,046.32	4,884.53	13,392.63	15,661.69
2008	3,263.47	1,068.01	5,603.37	13,867.20	17,864.99

Source: World Bank, *World Development Indicators* (2010).

7.2. The Handling of Medicines and the Suitcase Trade

The various arrows in the supply chain in figure 7.3 indicate the supply
process where drugs change hands from one source to another. Fenoff
and Wilson (2009) emphasized that the whole process is dependent on

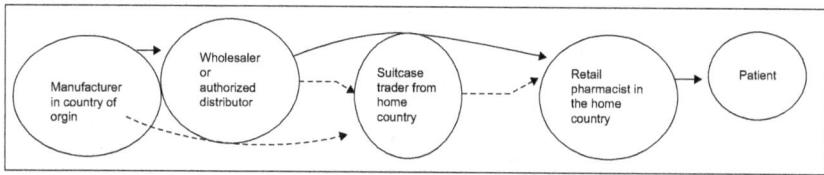

Figure 7.3 Supply chain for pharmaceuticals

a dense wholesale distribution network requiring numerous distributors as intermediaries. Typically, suitcase traders buy their drugs from wholesalers.

People in need of medicine in developing countries need access to medicine at prices that they can afford. This medicine must be complemented by an appropriate supply network and a suitable health infrastructure. Part of the dilemma associated with suitcase trading is that it greatly complicates the routes that medication takes from producer to consumer. Quality control becomes an issue when the traditional supply channel becomes disrupted. The handling of medicine by unofficial designates creates room for a wide category of complications. When medications are repackaged, the risk of further human error is also introduced. Such risk includes the possibility that some of the information may be printed in the wrong language or with the wrong trademark, and important information regarding side effects, batch number, directions for use, expiry date, and so on, may be left out for a variety of reasons. In addition, storage conditions may be violated. If the suitcase traders are involved in repackaging, deep-rooted problems may result in the event of a batch recall.

7.3. The Risk of Counterfeits and Suitcase Trading

Counterfeiting, according to Penn (1979), can be traced back to the ancient Egyptians and early Greeks. The US Federal Bureau of Investigation (FBI) referred to counterfeiting as the crime of the twentieth century (UNICRI 2003). The World Health Organization (WHO) defines a counterfeit drug as "one which is deliberately and fraudulently mislabeled with respect to its identity or source. Counterfeiting can apply to both branded and generic products and counterfeit products may include products with the correct ingredients or with the wrong ingredients, without active ingredients, with insufficient ingredients or with fake packaging" (1999, 4).

The Economic Intelligence Unit, in its issue dated 22 January 2010, drew attention to the fact that counterfeit medicines are imitation or copycat medicines. They are considered counterfeit because the medicine may be contaminated, it may contain the wrong active ingredients that make the medicine work or may even be made with the completely wrong amount of ingredients. There may also be the case where the medicine contains no active ingredients at all or is packaged in phony packaging. The issue, quoted from a report by Secure Pharma Chain (2009), further warned that "medicines that are counterfeit may not help the condition the medicine was intended to treat and may lead to dangerous side effects".

Despite a wide range of interventions by original distributors of medicines,[6] counterfeiting remains a serious problem and the full extent of the problem is still unknown. AccessRx.com cited that "the number of Food and Drug Administration (FDA) counterfeit drug cases opened from 2004–2007 was more than double 2000–2003, while the number opened in 2003 was itself five times that opened in 2000. In 2007, FDA counterfeit cases resulted in 71 arrests, 50 convictions and US$26.5 million in fines and restitution . . . in April 2008 the FDA had twenty open counterfeiting cases from just one of two regional California offices" ("Learn How to Avoid the Risks of Counterfeit Medications Online" http://www.accessrx .com/research/counterfeit-medications-online/).

Table 7.4 provides evidence of the growth in coverage of the problem of counterfeit medicines in the world and a 23% increase in the number of counterfeit medicines recorded between 2004 and 2005.[7] The most up-to-date data on the number of countries that were linked to incidents of coun-

Table 7.4: Evidence of the Growing Counterfeit Medicine Problem

	2004	2005	2009	% growth 2004–2005	% growth 2005–2009
Number of pharmaceutical products detected that are in counterfeiting, theft and diversion	560	687	808	23%	18%
	2004	2005	2008	% growth 2004–2005	% growth 2005–2008
Number of countries experiencing counterfeiting, theft and diversion	86	101	115	17%	14%

Source: Pharmaceutical Security Institute (various years).

terfeiting, theft and diversion increased by 17% over the 2004–5 period and a further 18% over the 2005–8 period.

The Pharmaceutical Security Institute website also recorded that in 2009 each of the seven regions listed in table 7.5 experienced a pharmaceutical crime incident, with Asia and Latin America being the top two regions in terms of frequency of pharmaceutical crime incidents (PSI 2009).

In terms of the top ten countries with incidences of counterfeit medicines, the most recent data, as shown in table 7.6 for 2005, highlights that the largest number of counterfeit cases of medicines (155) occurred in China, while Russia and the South Korea are next with 96 and 67 cases, respectively. The United States is fifth with 54 cases.

Table 7.5: Incidents of Pharmaceutical Crime by Region in 2009

Region	Number of Incidents
Asia	863
Latin America	570
Europe	347
North America	199
Eurasia	176
Near East	149
Africa	67

Source: www.PSI-Inc.org.

Table 7.6: Number of Cases of Counterfeit Medicines by Country

Country	Counterfeit Cases
China	155
Russia	96
South Korea	67
Peru	55
United States	54
Columbia	51
India	41
United Kingdom	39
Ukraine	28
Brazil	9

Source: Gren (2007).

Bosworth and Yang (2002) noted that between 1990 and 1995, the trade in counterfeiting drugs increased by 150% as compared to 49% for world trade in general. This perception has changed. Balfour (2005) estimated that as much as 7% of all global merchandise trade (US$512 billion) may be counterfeited; this estimate was not much different from the US$35 billion estimate provided by WHO (2005). Fenoff and Wilson (2009) revised the estimate for 2005 at US$39 million. Marshall (2009) cited the New York City-based Center for Medicine in the Public Interest as estimating the global trade in fake pharmaceuticals – including treatments for malaria, tuberculosis and AIDS – to reach US$75 billion a year in 2010. Table 7.7 summarizes these estimates.

The WHO (2006) identified that 10% of the world's drug supply is counterfeited. This estimate was revised in WHO (2008) and Primo-Carpenter (2009) to a range of 10%–15%, with as much as 30% of all the medicines in Africa and 70% in Nigeria being classified as counterfeit drugs.

The disruption of the supply chain by counterfeiters gives them leverage to contaminate the supply chain with counterfeit medicines. In the developing world, the high cost of medicines represents an obstacle to most patients in obtaining their medication. As a consequence, developing economy markets are targeted in a much more pronounced way than other markets by counterfeiters. Even so, in their quest for bigger profits, many retailers in the developing world may find it more profitable to buy from unregulated sources.[8]

The literature emphasizes that no country or no drug is immune to counterfeiting. Table 7.8 provides some brief newspaper-based commentaries on the existence of counterfeit medicines in the Caribbean.

Yankus (2006) identified the largest producers of counterfeit drugs as India, China, Russia, Nigeria, Mexico and Brazil. The WHO (2006b) noted that it conducted a study between January 1999 and October 2000 and

Table 7.7: Estimated Size of the World Counterfeit Drug Industry

Reference	Year	Estimated Size
Balfour (2005)	2005	US$36 billion
WHO (2005)	2005	US$35 billion
Fenoff and Wilson (2009)	2005	US$39 billion
Marshall (2009)	2009	US$75 billion

Table 7.8: Evidence of the Existence of Counterfeit Medicines in the Caribbean

Country	Researcher's Comments
Trinidad and Tobago	While the Chemistry Food and Drug Division has received no report of counterfeit drugs reaching this country, the President of the Pharmacy Board, Andrew Rahaman, could not "definitively" say this has not happened. *Newsday,* 13 March 2007.
Jamaica	Jamaica has been able to keep this problem of counterfeit and substandard medicines at bay with rigid regulations. *Jamaica Observer,* 13 March 2006.
Barbados	In November 2006, customs agents intercepted more than fifty shipments of counterfeit Tamiflu, the drug being stockpiled for a possible flu pandemic. The FDA reported that the drugs contained none of Tamiflu's active ingredient; instead, the fake capsules contained some vitamin C and not much else. Lesia Proverbs Division of Health Science Barbados Community College. http://www.commerce.gov.bb/FYI/news
Guyana	According to a Government Information Agency (2007), there is no information or evidence to support the belief that counterfeit drugs are being sold on the Guyana market. The absence of stringent measures would only allow the growing global scourge to be a major national problem. Guyana Government Information Agency, 11 July 2007. http://www.gina.gov.gy/archive/daily
The Bahamas	Walt Bogdanich, in Counterfeit Drugs path eased by Free Trade Zones, noted that a pharmacy from the Bahamas was associated with counterfeit versions of cholesterol, high blood pressure, acid reflux and arthritis pain medications. *New York Times,* 17 December 2007. http://www.nytimes.com/2007/12/17
Haiti	The World Customs Organization reported that 89 people were killed in Haiti in 1995, having taken a paracetamol-based syrup contaminated with glycol diethylene (a toxic chemical used in antifreeze). Blakeney (2004), Enforcement of Intellectual Property Rights: Challenges, Remedies and Public Awareness. http://counterfeiting.unicri.it/docs/wipo%20national%20seminar%20Ajman.pdf

Source: Compiled from various Caribbean newspapers.

found that approximately 60% of counterfeit medicines occurred in developing economies. The International Medical Product Anti-Counterfeiting Task Force, in an update of estimates, noted that in countries such as the United States, European Union, Australia, Canada, Japan and New Zealand, the equivalent of less than 1% of the value of drugs on the market are counterfeited (see table 7.9).

Table 7.9: Prevalence of Counterfeiting Drugs in the West and the
           Developing World

Country/ Region	Last WHO/IMPACT Estimate (%)	Other Authoritative Estimates
OECD		
United States	<1	
Europe	<1	Other sources site different figures as high as 10%
United Kingdom	<1	
Less developed countries		
Africa		
Nigeria	16	
Kenya	30	
Lebanon	35	
Asia		
Cambodia	13	
China	8 (over-the-counter only)	
India	10–20	
Indonesia	25	
Eurasia		
Russia	10	A different source places the figure higher at 12%
Former Soviet Republics	20	
Latin America		
Columbia	5	
Mexico	10	
Peru	15–20	
Venezuela	25	

Source: Bate (2008).

Developing economies are the ideal target for counterfeit drugs for a variety of reasons. In the first instance, these economies are characterized by a low level of consumer awareness. In particular, in developing countries the threat of counterfeit medicine is not widely publicized and with the prevalence of suitcase traders, many counterfeit drugs make their way to the market via unsuspecting local pharmacies. Cockburn et al. (2005) indicated that this situation is most acute on the African continent where rudimentary estimates are that up to 50% of the medicines distributed are counterfeit. In many developing countries, the rural communities are much more starved of medicinal goods than urban areas. This lack of an official supply chain creates a "missing market" and makes it much easier to infiltrate with counterfeit products, or replace poorly supplied sources with a more regular supply of counterfeit drugs.

Developing economies also tend to have weak detection systems, as these economies are often characterized by inefficient institutions or institutions lacking capacity of the appropriate order. One study by the International Medical Product Anti-Counterfeiting Task Force illustrated that in those economies with weak regulatory and legal oversight, there is a greater degree of counterfeiting (Morris and Stevens 2006). Several developing economies are characterized by the lack of a dedicated workforce with the capacity to deal with the problem. Further, weak institutional support and dated legislation, coupled with a high incidence of corruption, result in low levels of penalty (Stevens 2006). In some countries, pharmaceutical counterfeiting is just as profitable as narcotics, but carries a much lower penalty. The reason for this is that these fake drugs can be relatively cheaply manufactured in countries that lack the adequate enforcement regulation and as such there is a low degree of prosecutions and penalties for engaging in these kinds of activities.

Allen (2006) noted that in the face of the high profitability and low risk characteristic of the counterfeit drug trade, narcotics and arms traffickers are becoming involved in this trade. For example, Dorin and Dorin (2006, 28) indicated that "counterfeit medicines have become a more profitable and lucrative industry than narcotics. The current penalties for these criminals, if caught, are very light as opposed to those pertaining to illegal drugs (ranging anywhere from six months to one year). There have been reports that profits from the counterfeit medicines trade have been linked to organized crime and terrorist groups, including Hezbollah." Even more, many counterfeit drug producers use westernized addresses when sending their illegal products to developing country customers to create the impression of authenticity (Atemnkeng et al. 2007).

The growth of counterfeit pharmaceuticals may have been assisted by the rapid globalization of the world economy. The distribution of counterfeit drugs has become a very lucrative business, especially with the convergence and spread of information via the Internet. Green and Murray (2001), quoting John Dingell of the US House of Representative, noted that "with the introduction of Internet sites selling prescription drugs with almost no regulatory framework, the environment and the incentive for using fake drugs, making fake drugs and selling them directly to consumers is obvious".

The share of international trade (average exports and imports as a percentage of GDP) has increased considerably from 24% in 1960 to 57% in 2006, an increase of 33%. The WHO's *World Medicine Situation* (2004) noted that approximately two-thirds of the value of the medicines produced internationally is produced by firms with headquarters in five countries: the United States, United Kingdom, France, Japan and Germany. Table 7.10 shows that mainly developing economies (such as those in Africa) have very low access to medicines and the overall prevalence of very low access countries across the world was 29 out of 183. The modal group comprises countries with low to medium access to medicine, and 68 of the 183 countries fell into this group. Countries with low to medium access to medicines could potentially fall into the trap of being desperate and buy from available sources. Only 52 of the 183 countries have very high access to essential medicines.[9] In other words, 131 of the 183 countries have less than a high access to essential medicines. In general, when an economy has deficient access to essential medicines, it is likely to be more vulnerable to counterfeit medicines available on the market (WHO 2009).

Table 7.10: Distribution of Countries with Regular Access to Essential Medicines, 2004

WHO Region	Very Low Access (<50%)	Low to Medium Access (50–80%)	Medium to High Access (81–95%)	Very High Access (>95%)	Total Number of Countries for the Region
	Number of Countries	Number of Countries	Number of Countries	Number of Countries	
Africa	14	23	5	3	45
Americas	7	14	7	7	35
Eastern Mediterranean	2	7	5	8	22
European	3	12	6	25	46
South-East Asian	2	4	3	0	9
West Pacific	1	8	8	9	26
Total number of countries	29	68	34	52	183

Source: World Medicines Situation (2004).

7.4. Trade in Pharmaceuticals: Global, Regional and National

In terms of world trade in medicines, an overall picture may be drawn from reference to table 7.11, which uses SITC 541 and 542[10] as a base reference for pharmaceutical goods. As the data illustrate, global exports of medicines increased from US$39 billion in 1991 to US$415 billion in 2008, an increase of 964%. In addition, world exports of SITC 541 and SITC 542, as a percentage of total world exports, increased from 1.29% in 1991 to 2.76% in 2008, an increase of 1.47 percentage points.

Table 7.12 provides comparative data on the share of world exports and imports of SITC 54 for select developed and emerging countries. Germany, followed by the United States, lead this group in terms of exports, while the United States, followed by Germany, lead in terms of imports.

Table 7.11: Global Exports of Medicines, 1991–2008

Years	World Trade (Exports) in SITC 541 and 542 (US$b)	Total World Exports of All Commodities (US$b)	World Exports of SITC 541 and 542 as a % of Total World Exports
1991	39	3,024.57	1.29
1992	49	3,559.91	1.38
1993	51	3,552.87	1.44
1994	59	4,047.61	1.46
1995	71	4,843.42	1.47
1996	77	5,146.63	1.50
1997	83	5,335.68	1.56
1998	94	5,300.93	1.77
1999	105	5,508.19	1.91
2000	107	6,260.22	1.71
2001	133	6,016.49	2.21
2002	166	6,319.5	2.63
2003	201	7,375.49	2.73
2004	247	8,953	2.76
2005	273	10,153	2.69
2006	311	11,861	2.62
2007	368	13,481	2.73
2008	415	15,035	2.76

Source: UNCOMTRADE (various years).

Table 7.12: Comparative Shares of World Exports and Imports of SITC 54 for Selected Countries, 1991–2008

	Share of World Exports of SITC 54						Share of World Imports of SITC 54					
	United States	Canada	Germany	Japan	China	India	United States	Canada	Germany	Japan	China	India
1991	12.12	0.66	17.04	2.82	0.98	1.25	8.39	2.74	11.47	8.45	0.87	0.62
1992	11.07	0.79	15.17	2.78	1.82	0.88	8.05	2.69	9.79	7.66	0.99	0.65
1993	11.45	0.77	14.89	2.88	1.77	0.95	8.51	2.99	8.56	7.97	0.84	0.52
1994	10.52	0.86	14.86	2.63	2.02	1.00	8.28	2.80	9.32	7.36	0.70	0.52
1995	9.17	0.86	14.37	2.58	2.21	1.01	7.85	2.53	9.34	6.89	0.57	0.57
1996	9.48	0.89	13.86	2.44	1.96	1.05	9.16	2.59	9.16	5.76	0.45	0.39
1997	9.88	1.16	13.99	2.34	1.84	1.14	10.40	2.67	8.42	5.02	0.39	0.46
1998	10.24	1.11	15.08	2.03	1.79	0.99	11.50	2.83	8.79	3.94	0.56	0.40
1999	10.73	1.08	14.29	2.30	1.60	1.02	12.80	3.02	8.10	4.29	0.77	0.35
2000	12.22	1.14	12.07	2.54	1.67	1.17	13.3	3.40	7.88	4.27	0.85	0.34
2001	11.62	1.09	13.57	2.06	1.49	1.02	14.00	3.23	7.98	3.77	0.91	0.32
2002	9.70	0.93	10.52	1.69	1.40	1.06	14.20	2.80	10.36	3.10	0.82	0.34
2003	9.54	1.16	11.72	1.58	1.42	1.00	14.90	2.90	9.74	2.91	0.80	0.30
2004	9.72	1.21	13.80	1.44	1.31	0.93	13.90	2.74	10.32	2.80	0.75	0.27
2005	9.50	1.30	14.00	1.20	1.40	1.00	13.80	2.80	10.70	2.90	0.80	0.30
2006	9.40	1.50	14.50	1.00	1.40	1.10	14.50	2.90	10.90	2.70	0.80	0.40
2007	9.10	1.70	15.10	0.90	1.60	1.20	14.20	2.70	10.80	2.40	1.00	0.40
2008	9.20	1.50	16.30	0.90	1.90	1.40	14.40	2.60	11.20	2.60	1.30	0.40

Source: UNCOMTRADE (various years).

Table 7.13 shows the trends in the import and export of pharmaceutical products for CARICOM. Not surprisingly, CARICOM has a negative trade balance in the pharmaceutical products.

Figure 7.4 illustrates exports and imports of SITC 54 for Trinidad and Tobago for the period 1991–2007. Clearly and not surprisingly, Trinidad and Tobago is a net importer of pharmaceuticals and medications, such that imports increased by 124% while exports fell by 50% over the time period 1991–2007.

Imports of medicines into Trinidad and Tobago, however, increased by 167% over the period 1991–2007, whereas GDP per capita for Trinidad and Tobago increased 310% over the same period. Table 7.14 highlights the comparative trends in imports of medicines into Trinidad and Tobago and GDP per capita for Trinidad and Tobago in the period 1991–2007. The computed correlation coefficient is 0.98, confirming that these two variables are strongly positively correlated.

Table 7.13: Imports and Exports of SITC 54 for
CARICOM, 1991–2007 (US$b)

	CARICOM Exports	CARICOM Imports
1991	0.005	0.068
1992	0.011	0.082
1993	0.012	0.089
1994	0.010	0.099
1995	0.012	0.108
1996	0.013	0.120
1997	0.019	0.171
1998	0.025	0.180
1999	0.024	0.194
2000	0.029	0.225
2001	0.030	0.236
2002	0.020	0.204
2003	0.027	0.243
2004	0.019	0.235
2005	0.032	0.304
2006	0.043	0.349
2007	0.033	0.353

Source: UNCOMTRADE (various years).

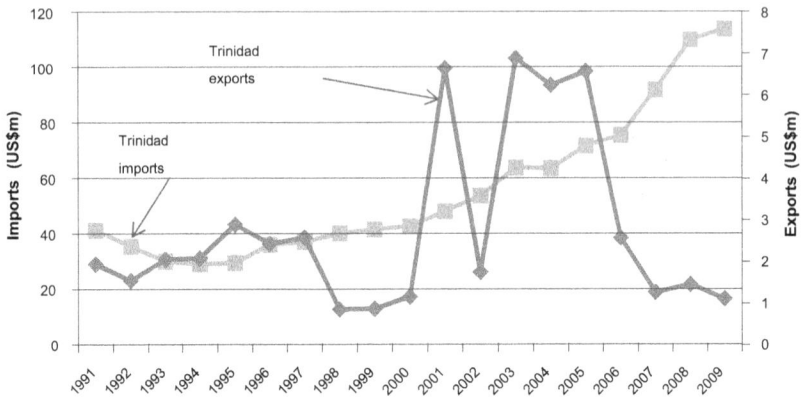

Figure 7.4 Exports and imports of SITC 54 for Trinidad and Tobago, 1991–2009
(US$m)
Source: Created using data from UNCOMTRADE (various years).

7.5. The Nature of the Suitcase Trade in Prescription Medicines in the Caribbean

In general, suitcase traders bring goods from low-priced economies like India, China and Pakistan and sell them in higher-priced economies where the trade is profitable, even when transport and accommodation costs are taken into consideration. Suitcase trading in the Caribbean then is really a form of arbitrage, in other words the practice of buying from low-priced markets and selling in high-price markets. Parallel imports have the potential to arbitrage away international price differences.

The increasing threat of counterfeit medicines for the Caribbean has been discussed in a number of different forums. Table 7.15 lists some of these forums.

Green and Murray (2001, 1) noted that "antiquated regulatory and enforcement systems . . . and a lack of corporate vigilance have resulted in an online environment where counterfeiting crimes go largely unpunished". Additionally, as Akunyili (2010, 12) indicated, "chief among the factors that encourage drug faking worldwide is corruption and conflict of interest. Corruption is a driving force for poor regulation, which encourages drug faking/counterfeiting. The efficiency of personnel is adversely affected by corruption and conflict of interests resulting in laws not being enforced and criminals not being arrested, prosecuted and convicted for crime."

Table 7.14: Trends in the Import of Medicines (SITC 54) and GDP per Capita in Guyana, Jamaica and Trinidad and Tobago

	Imports of SITC 54 (US$m)			GDP per capita (current US$)		
	Guyana	Jamaica	Trinidad and Tobago	Guyana	Jamaica	Trinidad and Tobago
1991	1.39	22.95	41.20	449.47	1,706.62	4,368.89
1992	3.00	21.36	35.39	490.35	1,459.10	4,472.20
1993	n/a	28.64	30.03	586.47	2,003.76	3,677.08
1994	n/a	32.14	29.00	714.47	2,007.37	3,938.22
1995	n/a	40.32	29.53	819.17	2,344.14	4,214.07
1996	n/a	44.79	36.06	929.08	2,600.60	4,527.92
1997	11.02	60.39	37.02	987.57	2,948.83	4,487.59
1998	7.00	64.24	40.15	947.46	3,419.20	4,705.16
1999	6.30	69.50	41.60	918.55	3,430.43	5,278.55
2000	12.01	82.27	42.66	942.36	3,479.06	6,296.28
2001	7.28	80.52	48.06	919.58	3,495.30	6,788.37
2002	8.65	78.79	53.72	952.07	3,697.01	6,904.88
2003	9.68	99.84	63.96	975.13	3,579.60	8,582.87
2004	9.75	96.95	63.69	1,030.51	3,841.78	9,808.45
2005	21.41	114.80	71.84	1,079.92	4,207.56	12,123.40
2006	20.27	123.35	75.63	1,196.64	4,502.02	13,882.63
2007	17.35	147.68	91.95	1,407.07	4,801.81	15,738.44
2008	38.24	196.05	110.17	1,518.44	5,438.48	19,475.41
2009	67.07	161.08	114.03	n/a	5,438.34	15,753.22

Source: UNCOMTRADE (various years).

It is well established that suitcase traders are responsible for the greater proportion of the counterfeit drugs moved around the world (Yar 2008). Typically, suitcase traders can provide counterfeit drugs or even generic drugs at prices that are lower than the originator firms. ICIs are often not aware that the prescription medicine they are selling is counterfeit. Instead, they simply believe that the cost differential is attributable to differences in the cost of production in the distinct geographical blocks.[11]

In a recent commentary, the Ministry of Health from Guyana noted that some suitcase traders acquired dated items at "knock-down prices" and proceeded to rename and or replace expiry dates. Also, Lascelles Chin of the Lasco Group of Companies from Jamaica recently warned

Table 7.15: Some Conferences/Seminars on Counterfeit Drugs in CARICOM

Country	Conference/ Seminar on Counterfeit Drugs
Trinidad and Tobago	First Caribbean Conference on Pharmaceutical Counterfeiting, April 2004
Dominican Republic	Fourth Pan American Conference, American Conference on Drug Regulatory Harmonization, 2005
Jamaica	Good Manufacturing Practices Workshop, April 2001
Jamaica	Caribbean Poison Information Network (CARPIN) Third Annual Scientific Conference, May–June 2008
St Lucia	OECS Pharmaceutical Procurement Service (OECS/PPS) Regional Consultations on Counterfeit Drugs, June 2008
United States	Third Pan-American Conference on Drug Regulatory Harmonization, April 2002

Source: Accessed from the related conference websites in April 2010.

of the need to be "careful of those who bring the suitcase medication". Countries like Guyana with many porous borders are especially vulnerable to counterfeit drugs as there are many points of entry other than the official ones.

7.6. A Preliminary Assessment of Suitcase Trade in Prescription Medicines in the Caribbean

There is no formal study on the extent and nature of the suitcase trade in R_x medicines in the Caribbean. To help provide some basic information on the extent and nature of the suitcase trade, a survey instrument was administered to pharmacists attending a seminar of private sector pharmacists on 12 April 2009.[12] Table 7.16 shows that on an average 2.93% of the weekly R_x expenditures by pharmacies relate to R_x goods provided by suitcase traders. On average, pharmacies spent approximately TT$43,078 per week on R_x goods. Given that there are 263 registered pharmacies in Trinidad and Tobago,[13] the annual expenditure on R_x medicines peddled by suitcase traders in Trinidad and Tobago to all pharmacies is estimated to be TT$18,680,425 +/- $122,975 with 95% confidence.

On average, 2.5 suitcase traders visit a pharmacy per week. The pie chart in figure 7.5 shows the reasons listed by private sector pharmacists as to why they buy R_x medicines from suitcase traders. Not surprisingly,

Table 7.16: Summary Measures of Data from the Suitcase Trade in
Prescription Goods

Summary Measure	Cost of goods provided by suitcase traders as a % of the weekly prescription expenditures by pharmacies	Summary Measure	Weekly expenditure by pharmacies on prescription goods (TT$)
Mean	2.930124	Mean	43,709.68
Standard Deviation	0.008864	Standard Deviation	7,634.106
Skewness	0.824465	Skewness	1.072673
Kurtosis	3.817750	Kurtosis	2.917024
Jarque-Bera	4.375761	Jarque-Bera	5.953801

Source: Authors' computations.

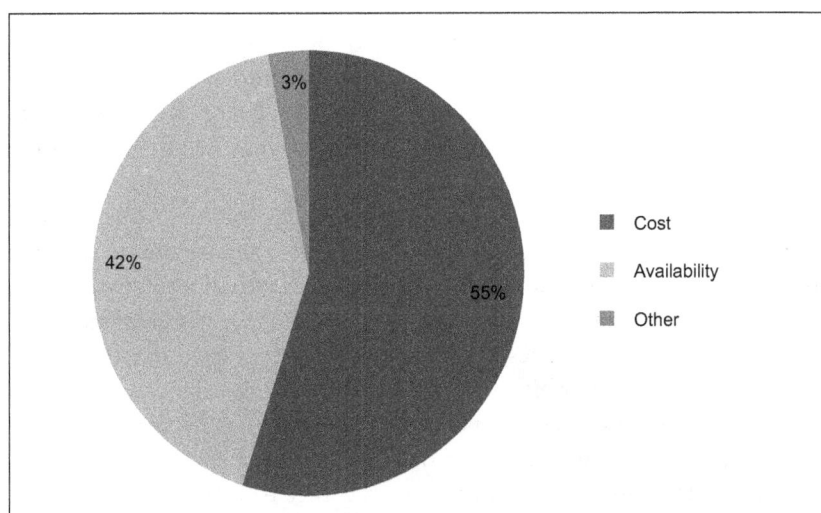

Figure 7.5 Reasons for buying counterfeit prescription drugs

the main reason for private sector pharmacies buying R_x medicines from
suitcase traders is cost (55%). However, 42% of private sector pharmacists
said that they bought some R_x medicines from suitcase traders because
these were not formally available on the market.

Discussion with key personnel from various pharmaceutical distribu-
torships operating in Trinidad and Tobago identified that they do not formally market certain drugs in Trinidad and Tobago for various reasons:

- These drugs are not approved for sale by the local Food and Drugs Division of the Ministry of Health.
- The gross profit margin of the drug has reduced to a level such that it is no longer profitable for the local distributor to supply the drug locally.
- The local distributor has flooded the market with the generic version of the drug; however, the higher income users of the drug maintain a preference for the original patented form of the drug.

Table 7.17 provides a classification of the main drugs circulated by suitcase traders from the Trinidad and Tobago economy. The table also lists the authentic local distributor and provides a sense of the average cost per unit from the official distributor and the suitcase trader.

7.7. Conclusion

To help deal with the suitcase trading of R_x medicines in the Caribbean, policymakers need to adopt what Fenoff and Wilson (2009) call evidence-based policy and intervention strategies. Such initiatives require policymakers to take several actions, some of which are detailed in the subsequent chapters.

Unlicensed sellers, their distributive network, the nature of the R_x medicines they sell and the various sections of the law that are breached in the context of the imports of counterfeit R_x medicines into the country must be identified. As medicines begin to flow between multiple wholesalers before arriving at local pharmacies, tougher oversight becomes necessary. Processes by which counterfeit drugs are distributed once they pass customs and other law enforcement agency personnel must be articulated. Appropriately trained personnel drawn from customs, the Pharmacy Board and other regulatory authorities must work together to identify and evaluate the current drug regulatory controls and quality assurance procedures to identify the various loopholes and close the related gaps. Where necessary, the country's parliament must pass legislative upgrades. Such initiatives will strengthen the regulatory and legal oversight over the imports of drugs into the country.

In an effort to reduce the amount of substandard and counterfeit drugs on the market, criminal and civil penalties on pharmacies found retailing these drugs sourced from unauthorized dealers must be severe enough that they act as a deterrent. The current penalties should be reviewed, assessed and where necessary, increased.

Table 7.17: Data on Main Drugs Sold by Suitcase Traders in the Trinidad and Tobago Economy

Drug	Authentic Local Distributor	Drug Use	Per Unit Cost from Official Distributor (TT$)	Average Cost per Unit from Suitcase Traders (TT$)
Amoxicilin	Bryden Pi	Antibiotic	2.15	2.00
Anafranil	Smith Robinson	Antidepressant	3.40	3.25
Ansaid	Suitcase traders only	Pain		5.10
Benzac	Alston Marketing Company Limited	Acne	45.35 for 60 g (10%)	35.00 for 5 g (5%)
Ciplox eye drop	Physician Pharmaceuticals	Antibacterial	28.50	22.00
Cytotec	Marketing and Distribution (M&D)	Abortificient		
Dermovate ointment	Smith Robinson and Agostini	Skin condition	48.00	37.00
Diazepam	Agostini	Muscle relaxant (substitute for Valium)	3.80	3.00
Dinnitel	Smith Robinson and/or Agostini	Appetite suppressant	1.50	1.00
Glucophage	Suncrest Pharmaceuticals	Diabetes	0.80	2.00

(Table 7.17 continues)

Table 7.17: Data on Main Drugs Sold by Suitcase Traders in the Trinidad and Tobago Economy (*continued*)

Drug	Authentic Local Distributor	Drug Use	Per Unit Cost from Official Distributor (TT$)	Average Cost per Unit from Suitcase Traders (TT$)
Kamagra	Suitcase traders only	Male enhancement, erectile dysfunction		9.00
Lipozene	Suitcase traders only			10.00
N.C. Derm	Suitcase traders only	Antibiotic		20.00
Norvasc	Marketing and Distribution and Hand Arnold	High blood pressure	10.18 for 10 mg; 6.30 for 5 mg	10.00 for 10 mg; 6.00 for 5 mg
Plavix	Agostini	Blood thinner	18.80	16.00
Tadalis	Suitcase traders only	Erectile dysfunction		18.80
Trental	Smith Robinson and Agostini	Blood circulation	2.60	1.90
Triple antibiotic ointment	Suitcase traders only	Minor cuts and bruises		14.00
Viagra	Marketing and Distribution	Erectile dysfunction	62.50	60.00
Voltaren	Smith Robinson	Anti-inflammatory analgesic	5.55 for 75 mg; 6.11 for 100 mg	5.55 for 75 mg; 6.11 for 100 mg
Wingora	Suitcase traders only	Erectile dysfunction		9.00

The regulatory authorities should make a detailed assessment of the capability and competence of law enforcement and customs personnel in detecting the movement of R_x medicines into the economy by suitcase traders. This will require particular focus on the strengths and weaknesses of law enforcement and customs personnel in intercepting and preventing counterfeit drugs from entering the country, strategic points of entry such as airports and sea ports, screening procedures, training provided in detecting counterfeit drugs and the technology employed in the detection of counterfeit drugs. The findings of the assessment will inform the ongoing training programme and the supporting technology requirements for the staff of customs, the Pharmacy Board and other regulatory authorities.

The Ministry of Health, the Food and Drug Division, the Pharmacy Board and the Government Information Service must network to raise the awareness of consumers, pharmacists and health care providers of counterfeit drugs and the related risks. Consumers must be advised, for example, to ask for pharmaceuticals and R_x medicines in the manufacturer's original packaging and to clearly scrutinize the appearance of the medicines and related packaging before purchase. Moreover, consumers should be alerted to the fact that if the price of pharmaceuticals and R_x medicines appear to be significantly lower than anticipated, then there is some probability that such medicines may be counterfeit. Further, every opportunity must be seized to use information and communication technologies in effecting such an increase in awareness. Educational programmes designed to raise awareness of counterfeit drugs must be periodically reviewed for effectiveness and the appropriate enhancements defined and implemented. Awareness must be backed up by training in identification of counterfeit drugs.

The resources of the Food and Drug Division must be evaluated in the context of its capacity to efficiently review and approve new drugs for sale and use in the country. Where necessary, these resources must be enhanced so that the division can deliver this critical aspect of its mission. Timely approvals of new drugs may reduce the perceived demand on the part of suitcase traders. The division must also assess demand reduction strategies on an ongoing basis.

Pharmacists and other health care dealers should be educated on the various problems posed by trading in pharmaceuticals and R_x medicines from unlicensed dealers. The Pharmacy Board may need to become more vigilant and involved and should seek to form partnerships with customs to improve screening and detection at the borders. Pharmacists must also be kept up-to-date on the technological developments made by drug and pharmaceutical manufacturers in special packaging and printing techniques that make counterfeiting both more difficult to perform and easier to detect.

Access to essential medicines used by various groups within the population of Trinidad and Tobago must be improved where necessary. Accordingly, suitable strategies must be devised and implemented to ensure that such groups have access to these medicines.

In the context of today's globalized environment, there is always room for international cooperation, particularly in the area of the regulation of pharmaceuticals and medicines. Trinidad and Tobago and all members of CARICOM should actively participate in the Pan American Network on Drug Regulatory Harmonization, which was established in 1999 to support processes on drug regulatory harmonization. This organization brings together national authorities of countries in the Americas, various pharmaceutical interest groups, industry, and academia.

Finally, given that the suitcase trade in counterfeit drugs thrives in a culture of corruption, it will also be necessary to effect positive change to such a culture. Anti-corruption initiatives must therefore be mainstreamed across all sectors of the Trinidad and Tobago economy.

8 TOWARD A FRAMEWORK FOR DEVELOPING ICIs

This chapter summarizes the results of the three empirical studies of shuttle traders in the Caribbean undertaken in this study, and discusses the possible effects of formalizing the informal trade in Caribbean economies. Further, it proposes strategies that can help in this formalization process if it is to be implemented.

As mentioned, the first study was undertaken among ICIs in Guyana in 2007. The traders in Guyana engage in the intra-Caribbean trade of mainly non-agricultural goods between Trinidad and Guyana. The sixty-two traders sampled were located principally in Georgetown. The second study was undertaken among hucksters in Dominica in 2008. The hucksters are unique in that (1) they trade primarily in agricultural goods between Dominica on the one hand and the French colonies of Martinique and Guadeloupe as well as the Caribbean islands of St Lucia, Antigua and St Kitts on the other; and (2) they are represented by the longest serving association of hucksters in the Caribbean. The forty-eight hucksters sampled were located in Roseau and Portsmouth. The third study was undertaken among shuttle traders in Jamaica in 2008. The traders in Jamaica purchase non-agricultural goods from outside of the Caribbean and sell these in Jamaica. The sixty-two traders sampled were located in Kingston.

As mentioned in the respective chapters, all three surveys used a common structured questionnaire that was developed to capture data on the demographics of traders, details of their trade, problems encountered in their trade and suggestions from the traders for improving their trade. The questionnaire was administered face-to-face. The survey design used in all three studies was purposive sampling. Table 8.1 provides a comparative summary

Table 8.1: Summary Attributes of Traders in Guyana, Dominica and Jamaica

Attribute	Guyana Most recent finding	Dominica Most recent finding	Jamaica Most recent finding	Guyana Holder (1988)	Dominica Lagro and Plotkin (1990)	Jamaica Taylor (1988)
% Females	73	52	90	100	64	93
Modal age group	21–30	41–60	41–50	20–25	31–46	26–35
Place of residence	Guyana	Dominica	Jamaica	Guyana	Dominica	Jamaica
% with highest level of education to at least Form 5	77	21	26	20	0	<55
Modal number of children	2	4	3	6 (avg)	7 (avg)	1–2
% operating as sole traders	85	8	71	80	19	72
Modal number of employees per non-sole trader	1	1	2	1	1	1–2
Average number of farmers supplying produce for the trade	n/a	11	n/a	n/a	6	n/a
% with prior supervisory or managerial experience	12	6	0	n/a	n/a	n/a
% who own a vehicle	66	67	61	n/a	11	17
% who have a fixed deposit/bank account	34	15	52	16	n/a	n/a
% who have life insurance coverage	26	15	10	n/a	n/a	n/a
% who own a house	45	69	74	18	6	n/a

% who belong to credit unions	2	33	6	n/a	11	n/a
Median length of service	8 years	15 years	15 years	2 years (avg)	9 years	>2 years
% of traders who buy and sell in a foreign country and in their home country	90	90	0	75	77	2
Average trip costs	US$500	US$709	US$1,520	n/a	n/a	US$1,487
Mean profits per trip	US$257	US$797	US$550	n/a	US$315/wk	US$727
% of traders with an alternative source of income	38	60	16	56	21	79
Alternative sources of income	Self-employment and working in family businesses	Farming and sale of dry goods and clothes	Rental of housing and operating taxis	Farming and public service	Farming	Self-employment and formal sector employment
% of ICIs who have no problems in conducting their trade	57	48	29	60	45	6
% who sought loans from local financial institutions	64	41	19	17	>45	4
Success rate for loan applications	75%	92%	42%	n/a	34%	n/a
Means of travel abroad	Air	Sea	Air	Air	Air and sea	Air
Form of transport of goods purchased abroad for the trade	Checked baggage	Checked baggage	Checked baggage	Checked baggage	Checked baggage	Checked baggage
Access to a traders' association	No	Yes	No	No	Yes	Yes

of the attributes of shuttle traders in Guyana, Dominica and Jamaica based on the findings of these three recent studies and those of three studies from the 1988–90 period.

The summary data for the three recent studies in table 8.1 indicate the following trends:

- A greater proportion of men than women are attracted to the huckster trade.
- The modal age of traders is lower among the ICIs in Guyana.
- A significantly smaller percentage of hucksters are sole traders.
- A significantly greater percentage of hucksters are involved in an alternative source of income.
- A small percentage of traders had supervisory or managerial experience prior to entering the trade.
- A significant percentage of traders in all three locations own a vehicle.
- A greater percentage of traders in Jamaica have a fixed deposit account.
- A greater percentage of traders in Guyana have life insurance coverage.
- A smaller percentage of traders in Guyana own a house.
- A significantly larger percentage of hucksters belong to a credit union.
- ICIs in Guyana spend fewer years in the trade.
- A smaller percentage of traders in Jamaica seek loans from local financial institutions and are also successful in their loan applications.
- Traders in Jamaica incur the highest average trip costs.
- Hucksters earn the highest mean profit per trip out of their home country.
- Hucksters primarily use sea transport while traders from Guyana and Jamaica use air transport.
- A smaller percentage of traders from Jamaica experience problems in conducting their trade.

Four principal trends emerge from comparison of the findings of the recent studies with those of the 1988–90 era:

- The modal age group for Dominica and Jamaica and median length of service for all three locations reflect the persistence of the trade.
- There is now a greater tendency for persons with at least a secondary education up to fifth form to be attracted to the trade.
- There is now a greater tendency for traders to own assets such as a vehicle and/or a home, as well as have a bank account or credit union membership.
- There is now a greater tendency to approach the financial institutions for funding.

The studies also point to a list of challenges faced by traders in the conduct of their trade. These include limited access to financing, the difficulty in completing documents required by the various public authorities, competition from other traders, ineffective interface with suppliers and airline staff, limited market access, small (if any) economies of scale and the effective supervision of their children. These challenges are consistent with those identified by other researchers such as Wedderburn et al. (2009) and others cited earlier in this book.

8.1. Options Available to Policymakers for Facilitating the Shuttle Traders

The options available to policymakers are twofold: facilitate the development of the trade and those who participate in it or formalize the trade. Facilitating the development of the trade and the traders will require several initiatives. This section documents three critical initiatives.

Firstly, a vibrant traders' association should exist in all countries in which the trade exists for the purpose of advancing the cause of traders. Stronger associations are better positioned to aggressively lobby the government and other stakeholders to protect local traders against foreign competition, to defend their rights to trade and the conditions under which the trade is executed, as well as to address ongoing trading issues. Based on the findings of the empirical surveys, a traders' association should be formed in Guyana, the DHA must be strengthened and the UVA must be revitalized in Jamaica to embody the capacity to represent the interest of all traders. More specifically, these associations should do the following:

- Lobby with customs, immigration, trade ministries, port health, airlines and sea freight companies and ensure that help desks are established as a minimum in each of these organizations. Such a lobby ensures that relevant information is disseminated in a coherent manner so that the trading policies and practices of each island are communicated to each trader. Further, this method can aid in the documentation process as each trader who visits the help desk can informally provide the clerk with details of their trade. It may be argued that several campaigns were launched for sensitizing immigration workers on the need to treat the travelling public with courtesy and professionalism. It is also conceivable that there may be ingrained prejudices among officers against traders from different islands. Accordingly, it will be necessary to sensitize all interfacing public officers to the peculiarities of communicating with informal traders and enforcing the laws of their country. Customs, immigration, port health and security administrations must also apply sanctions to officers who are willing to accept payments from the traders for some transactions.

- Lobby with the local government councils for the building or upgrading of facilities for the sale of goods, such as arcades or vendors' malls. This would provide traders with some permanency and would facilitate an increased level of sanitization, especially for traders of organic goods. It would also minimize health risks and aid in the security of the traders who occupy the building as well as ensure the security of their products. A point can also be made here that these facilities will reduce the incidence of shuttle traders ambushing passersby on the pavements and sidewalks in an effort to gain a sale.

- Lobby for representation on the boards that control the facilities that are used for the sale of goods by traders and for traders to jointly own these facilities. The traders' association represents the voice of all the informal traders who comprise its membership. In this regard, it would certainly be advantageous on the part of the traders to have an organizing body represented on these boards so that when issues such as storage facilities, utilities, the assignment of selling spots, and so on arise, they can be addressed expeditiously. On the matter of ownership, an important point to note is that traders who have the financial means will establish their own little stores or boutiques; consequently, payments for the ownership of these facilities will be the responsibility of the lesser earning or smaller-scale shuttle trader. Ultimately it should be the state's role to facilitate these traders.

- Lobby with vocational education providers to mount lifelong training for traders in the areas of bookkeeping and basic accounting, principles of business, computer literacy and, in particular, use of information and communications technology for networking, marketing and procurement, and cross-border trading.

- Focus on entrepreneurship and innovation. This area fosters diversity in the informal trade, one that moves away from traditional retailing toward the production and trading of new and creative types of commodities. It also promotes a new kind of business strategy, one that borders more on the formal side of trading. Through entrepreneurship and innovation, informal traders may be more inclined to pursue formal avenues to ply their trade as the motivation to finance the production and marketing of these new products take greater prominence in the larger frame.

- Make representation to financial institutions for the introduction of credit facilities and retirement planning schemes for traders. Traders encounter problems in accessing credit facilities. By making credit more accessible and cheaper, more traders will be able to receive loans, thereby improving the rate of application and even lowering default rates.

- Lobby the government for access to social security benefits for traders. One can argue that depending on the definition and classification of self-employed persons in many Caribbean countries, informal traders can contribute and benefit from national insurance and pension plans. Some effort must be expended, however, in changing the mindset of these traders especially the older individuals who may not be in a position to care for themselves when health and other problems arise.

- Establish an outreach to children of traders that focuses on academic excellence, extra-curricular activities, crossing the digital divide, career advice and planning, entrepreneurship and innovation.

- Encourage the government to provide a consultant to the huckster association whose job it is to advise the association on strategic planning, especially during times of economic constraint. Studies have shown that businesses that use strategic planning are better prepared for economic crises and also recover faster. Given the fact that shuttle traders' profitability depends heavily on the economic environment, strategic planning can be used to reduce some of the risk.

This first initiative brings the governments into the centre of facilitating the development of the trade. Governments should seek a better understanding of the shuttle trade, if only so that an intervention can be made via the trade toward sustainable economic growth and job creation in CARICOM countries. National databases of traders must therefore be established and maintained, as recommended by Babb et al.(2004). Indeed, Babb et al. noted that research personnel should be trained for data collection, database creation and database maintenance at specified periods. These activities, they argued, will over time form the basis of a market research agenda that supports all lobbying and advocacy on behalf of informal traders. Governments should also develop the legal framework to recognize the assets of traders and create a system of giving value to those assets so that traders can access capital from financial institutions.

This will contribute to removing the impediments to the traders' access to credit from these institutions.

The second initiative speaks of the development of traders into small- and medium-sized enterprises (SMEs). In order for this to occur, there needs to be a focus on more than just more access to financial services to hucksters. This development also requires training for traders, skills improvement in marketing and technological innovation and lastly, creating a more enabling environment for traders. While microfinance is important in allowing for the development of micro-enterprise, it cannot be done in a vacuum. There also needs to be a competitive market environment that allows firms to evolve and experience economies of scale and individual firms need to be at a certain level of maturity. As part of this maturity, microfinance institutions must satisfy international standards of performance. The most common standards as recently redefined and assessed in the framework of the Consultative Group to Assist the Poorest relate to outreach, sustainability and profitability, portfolio quality as well as efficiency and productivity. To a certain extent, the Grameen Bank Project in Bangladesh can be an example of what is needed for the shuttle traders in the region. The main idea behind this project was to extend banking facilities to poor men and women and to bring the disadvantaged, particularly women, into an organizational framework, giving them the opportunity to understand and manage their own financial lives. Given the description throughout the book that most of the traders in the region are women from poorer households, a project like this seems tailor-made to deal with the financing issues that most shuttle traders come up against.

If training programmes in business management, quality control methods and financial management are provided, the traders would be better equipped to adapt to the changing environment and make better decisions and increase the returns on their trading practices. These programmes, though ambitious, will require participation by some of the longstanding traders to generate buzz among other traders. Workshops should be implemented for training and even mentoring, particularly for those younger traders who may be unaware of the opportunities that exist outside the trade, especially given that the majority of this category of traders possesses menial academic qualifications. Such mentoring can result in younger traders being better able to inform and encourage their parents to incorporate more sustainable business strategies with their current trading practices.

Training for the development of traders into vertically integrated SMEs will require consultation among the traders' association, education providers, the Ministry of Trade, the Ministry of Education and the Ministry of

Labour and Co-operatives in each country. Such training can be conceptualized in concert with the paradigm of lifelong learning and flexible education. Flexible education is a learner-centred and client-focused approach that aims at fostering active learning through the use of information and communications technology (also called educational technologies) in improving course and programme design and in supporting and enhancing student learning. Flexible education has been portrayed in the literature as the high end of distance education, and includes but is not confined to online learning or e-learning. It encompasses mobile technologies and other new technological applications such as computer-based learning, web-based learning, virtual classrooms and digital collaboration. Studying by flexible education gives people in communities choices in terms of how, where, when and what to study.

A third initiative can follow from the second and recognizes the potential of the CSME for creating greater freedom of movement, thereby generating better economies of scale and wider market access for traders. Babb et al. (2004) singled out removing barriers "the following articles of the CSME policies articulated under agriculture, trade, shipping and free movement" as having direct implications for the livelihoods of shuttle traders: Article 34 (Removal of Restrictions on the Right of Establishment); Article 118 Trade Policy (Subsidies for Agriculture); Article 44 1(c) (Abolition of Exchange Controls); and Article 44 1(f) (Establishment of economical and efficient land, sea and air transportation services).

Traders associations and Ministries of Trade need to work with the CARICOM Secretariat to explore and clarify opportunities provided by CSME. Attention must be paid to shipping if free movement is to be a reality across the region. In this regard, the amount of documentation for shipping must be revised, and dedicated appropriately designed vessels must be identified and provided for the efficient and cost effective movement of agricultural goods across the region. The latter will close the existing resource gap in terms of the frequency, suitability and adequacy of sea transport for agricultural goods. Building on previous suggestions, this study recommends:

1. Development of a consortium comprising the Eastern Caribbean Central Bank, the Caribbean Development Bank, the Caribbean Regional Indicative Program of Cotonou (to be sustained in the Development Fund of the EPA with the European Union), in concert with other relevant agencies – such as the IDB and the World Bank – that provide financial support to regional development

efforts, to invest in two appropriately designed inter-island vessels specifically for use by shuttle traders. This venture will complement the proposed strategy above whereby help-desk facilities could be launched by all stakeholder agencies to facilitate traders who travel by air and sea. The inter-island vessels can enhance compliance with the documentation process, as only traders registered with approved associations will be allowed to travel via these facilities.

2. Institutions like the Central Planning Units, government Statistical Offices and Bureaus of Gender/Women's Affairs network with the more experienced organizations like the DHA, DEXIA, the National Development Foundation of Dominica, the Traffickers' Small Business Association, the UVA, the Ministry of Agriculture, the Ministry of Trade, Shipping Agents, Customs and Immigration, Port Health and Plant Quarantine across the region to define the way forward so that shuttle traders can optimize the benefit to them from CSME and in so doing sustain (if not enhance) their livelihoods.

8.2. The Informal Trade: Effects of Formalization

This brings us the second option: integrating the shuttle trade and the formal economy (formalization/semi-formalization of the trade). Discussion on integrating the informal sector and the formal economy stems from the issue that the informal sector engages in survival activities. The growth of this sector is contingent on the ease with which these activities can be integrated into the mainstream economic system. It is therefore important to document the past attempts made by various Caribbean economies to formalize the shuttle trade.

Perhaps the only credible formalization attempt was made by the Jamaican government in the 1980s. In an effort to offer some legitimacy to the informal trade, the Jamaican prime minister and minister of finance and planning, Edward Seaga, established a no-funds import licence in 1980 so that foreign higglers would be able to obtain foreign exchange from local banks. This measure was in response to the declining Jamaican economy and protest by the established business sector for the government to enforce controls on foreign informal traders. The core objective of this measure, which formally took effect in 1982, was to compile a list of all foreign informal traders so that they could be registered by December of that year. This action proved to be difficult as they not only had to pay import duties, but also back taxes on all previous importing activities. Soon after, the state amended this policy in two ways: they allowed informal traders to legally obtain an annual quota of foreign currency, and they implemented an import quota that permitted the importation of certain commodities up to a period of six months. This period was consistent with the timeframe within which higglers could obtain foreign currency. This licensing system proved to be a failure as it infringed on their buying practices and the flexibility of these traders in satisfying market demand. Tremendous protest ensued, which drew national and academic support. In June 1983, the policy was subsequently abandoned (Ulysse 2007).

Accordingly, this study recommends that if emphasis is placed on integrating the informal sector into the overall economic system, it should be undertaken in a three pronged approach. The first approach involves the provision of support systems primarily for the development of micro-enterprises that must be afforded easier access to markets and productive resources. These systems range from credit facilities to boosting training and marketing activities. The second approach deals with the welfare and poverty aspects associated with engaging in informal trading. In particular, it consists of poverty alleviation policies in the larger frame, but also targets family and small business needs since it is clear that capital commodities (such as vehicles) serve dual purposes: commercial business use and private use. The third approach focuses on the regulatory framework, even though it acknowledges that inadequate employment created by a failure in the economic system rather than regulatory inadequacies is what causes informal activities. Notwithstanding, we must not lose sight of the fact that improving regulations will cause faster integration of informal activities in the modernization process. This approach must deepen any strategy that is aimed at altering the regulatory framework in a manner conducive to the integration of the informal sector.

The question arises as to why attempt to integrate the informal sector with the formal economy and what the implications are of this arrangement for both sectors. In general terms, such integration could be approached if it fits into an overarching intervention of promoting growth conducive to the pursuit of poverty reduction. This includes employment-generating growth, coupled with massive investment in human capital. In this regard, the authors expand on the suggestions provided in chapters 4, 5 and 6 and offer the following strategies for consideration in the context of formalizing the shuttle trade, including discussion of the implications of each of these strategies for the trade.

Provide Credit Assistance

An important constraint to entrepreneurs doing business in the informal sector is a lack of credit. Given this fact, governments as well as non-governmental organizations should provide credit assistance. There are different ways in which this credit should be provided to make it easier for hucksters to gain access to it. These include channelling the credit through women's associations, requiring no collateral, guaranteeing the loans and monitoring both repayment and the use of the credit. To make access even easier for hucksters, a further distinction can be made whereby enterprises are separated into different categories and then the specific needs of each category are addressed.

There should also be more of a participatory approach to providing credit since some businesses, for example, require more working capital, thus feedback will allow the association to meet each business need before credit is provided. In many cases, existing lending agencies are mandated to address financing needs of certain categories of persons that have legally established enterprises so that secured loans are given. The Caribbean lacks financing facilities for entrepreneurs who engage in the informal trade. In terms of informal traders, they engage in mostly retailing activities so that their assets are in the form of merchandise. For the most part, they do not possess fixed assets as a means of collateral. In addition, these traders are highly transient so that even if financing were to be arranged, there is no way for agencies to be assured that these individuals would make the payments and make them in the agreed time period as they may trade in different locations at different times of the year.

Link with Credit Unions

Another method that can be employed to widen access to a wider variety of micro-credit institutions is that of developing linkage strategies to existing credit unions like the peoples' banks and community banks. Many women who want to access credit through normal means face the barrier of burdensome loan applications forms, which can be discouraging. This issue should be dealt with by clarifying the forms, or training bank officials to assist the women in these details. The World Bank Poverty Assessment Workshop based in Lagos, Nigeria recommended developing a social fund that is administered outside of the government and financed both publically and privately. It is important that the fund be outside of the government's bureaucratic channel so it better reaches local groups who require the capital.

Provide Technical Training

Another important hindrance to traders in the informal sector is a lack of technical training that tends to hold back traders from maintaining pace with technological progress. A specific case was noted by Haan (2002) who pointed out the need in the African informal sector for the provision of training. Delving into how the training should be provided, it is important for it to be different from the norm of centre-based courses with a permanent staff, and be more flexible to meet the needs of the hucksters; it should also be demand-driven. Another aspect of the training pointed out by Haan (2002) is that any focus on young people entering the informal sector should be about the training of technical skills and business. Such a change in focus has important consequences for the design and delivery of skills training.

The study did not provide a definite answer in terms of what kind of training provider is best for the informal sector, however it did note that the public sector holds no advantage in how they organize and deliver training to informal sector traders. Although they still have existing facilities, staff, training content and experience, a host of criticisms applies to each of these. Most importantly, their operations are being adversely affected by the fact that their budgets over the years have been severely diminished. Following a similar pattern highlighted above are the church-based training providers. The research found few non-governmental organizations that provided interesting training activities to traders, and private sector technical training providers have only recently begun coming on board.

Provide Different Kinds of Training

The informal sector is highly segmented, and this should be reflected in the way in which the offerings of skills training is organized and delivered. There are different ways in which training can be provided depending on the strategies of the providers and the target group. For instance, they can direct their training at the high end of the informal sector, meaning providing courses for wage employment in small workshops. They could also focus on self-employment in micro-enterprises, which requires preparing trainees for starting their own business, or they could contribute to the promotion of income-generating activities. The first option will require some changes by the training providers already in existence to make the training more effective, as they are able to better respond to the demands for skills by the local traders. Other changes will be required by training providers, especially in urban areas.

Provide On-the-job Training and Courses

Outside of credit assistance, government and non-governmental organizations can also help entrepreneurs in the informal sector by providing on-the-job training or even short courses. These courses will allow entrepreneurs to become more familiar with new methods, machines, equipment, processes and management training. Petty entrepreneurs rarely keep records and this is a major reason for their poor performance. Another aspect of this issue that should be looked at is the gender dimension as the urban informal sector has become more female dominated. Focusing on this growing group of traders will allow for improvement of their skill level, which in turn will increase the productivity and income level of the group specifically and all traders as a whole. Providing financial and management programme is only one step; the more difficult step would be to convince traders who normally keep their assets very liquid and use mental recording of sales transactions to participate in these programmes.

Make Technology more Accessible and Affordable

According to Byrne and Strobl (2004), an important determinant of income, productivity and employment, as well as a major supply side factor for traders in the informal sector, is technology. For regional traders, however, acquiring technological inputs in the past has been difficult, along with the fact that those suppliers of technological inputs were heavily dependent on imports and only minimally on local fabrication. Another reason for the constraint in adopting new technologies experienced by traders is the lack of access to credit and training. This problem is further compounded by structural and institutional imperfections, which tend to limit productivity and income.

What is needed is intervention in the form of policy to control inflation and make technological inputs more accessible and affordable. Local production of spare parts should also be encouraged. Generally, the informal trade in the Caribbean comprises commodities with quick turnovers such as clothes, accessories and agricultural produce. The integration of technology in the trading of these items is of little value to profitability. Items produced via enhanced technical means will certainly be more difficult to sell as little will be known of the products and traders will need to charge a competitive price to compensate for capital outlay. This translates into higher prices for consumers and overall lower profits for the shuttle trader.

Review and Revise Structural Adjustment Programmes

The negative impact of structural adjustment programmes on the informal sector needs little elaboration. These programmes include a component that involves rationalizations and privatization of government-owned enterprises. There has been retrenchment in the formal sector, which in turn has directly led to growth of the informal sector. The informal sector has also grown due to high levels of unemployed graduates, particularly the urban informal sector, and high levels of unemployed women due to competition for resources. Another issue arising out of structural adjustment programmes is inflationary pressures that have eroded profits and increased the prices of technological inputs and raw materials, as well as the prices of final products and services. Most of these programmes included deregulation, but unlike what was theorized, there have been no beneficial effects on the agricultural sector, leading to a heightened element of migration from the rural areas to the informal sector. All these factors have made it more difficult for women as they became more marginalized due to the fact that structural adjustment programme policies tend to be gender blind. The appropriate policy approach must be both sectoral and gender sensitive, incorporating different budgetary allocations to disadvantaged sectors and groups.

Review Time and Cost Required to Setting up a Business

There are different obstacles to be dealt with when operating formal businesses and informal businesses. Firstly, formal employers bear a larger responsibility in the form of the number of regulatory costs that unregistered firms can typically avoid. These costs include licences, bureaucratic approvals, bribes and other fees. For example, to set up a formal business in Lima, Peru, the estimated time period would be ten months (costing over thousands of dollars in lost profits) and one would have to pay about US$200 in fees (de Soto 1989). In comparison, according to Chickering and Salahdine (1991), the estimated time to set up a business in Florida is 3.5 days and in New York it is 4 days.

Further dissecting this issue, Djankov et al. (2002) estimated the costs of entry in eighty-five countries and found that they range from 2.63% of per capita GDP in Canada to 463% of per capita GDP in the Dominican Republic. Pratap and Quintin (2006) noted that the most important cost to potential formal sector businesses is likely the profit and payroll taxes they will be required to pay. For developing countries this is even more of a burden, as the narrowness of the tax base causes governments to set high tax rates. In addition, Hart (1971) pointed out some other adverse factors faced in trying to enter the formal business realm, such as environmental and zoning rules and restrictions in the use of imported inputs.

Obtain Updated Data

Finally, formal producers must typically comply with the stipulations of the labour code including minimum wage restrictions, severance payments and social security requirements. Given this fact, the immense impact that reductions in barriers can have on transforming from an informal business to a formal business is obvious. This in turn can strengthen the link between the informal sectors and the formal sectors. One area where there is little information is the measurement of informal sector wealth levels. To do a proper analysis of the wealth inequality that exists across households and countries, better data are needed.

Another aspect of the sector that needs further investigation is the role of women's contribution to the development of the informal sector regionally. This can be done by examining the role of technological inputs in employment and income generation for women entrepreneurs, thus allowing for the introduction of gender issues in economic development. As a matter of policy, periodic surveys can be conducted in Caribbean economies where the trade is most prominent under the purview of CARICOM so that the sector can be properly profiled over a period of time. Further, these surveys can be conducted several times per year, particularly in peak trading periods. In this way, researchers can be relatively certain of the generalizations made about the sector over a five- to seven-year period.

Suggestions for Governments

A critical examination of the strategies presented above suggests that governments in the region would need to review the positive and negative aspects of the shuttle trade as a prerequisite action for formalizing the shuttle trade. Policies must be designed to strengthen the positive virtues of this trade and suppress the various negative attributes. These negative aspects include the loss of government revenue, the under-reporting of national economic statistics, possible misallocation of public funds due to the unknown size and structure of the sector, rent-seeking behaviour and adherence to health and sanitation standards. The positive aspects are the creation of employment and income, human capital formation and, eventually, sustainable livelihoods and contribution to government revenues resulting from the indirect taxes applied to the informal activities of this shuttle trade. The psychological positive benefits include the realization of the desire for independence, enhanced self-esteem, the potential to earn income and provide for families, and the capacity to identify and exploit business opportunities in a stagnant economic market. In this regard, policies to assist the shuttle trader cannot be static and must be adaptable in different environments and under varied considerations.

Given the cumbrous nature of starting a formal business in the region, governments need to improve on the processes for so doing as a precondition for formalizing the shuttle trade. The evidence suggests substantial variation in procedures to start up a business between developed and Caribbean countries. For example, in the United Kingdom and Singapore it takes six procedures to start a business (Doingbusiness.org). Relatively speaking, it is tedious to start a business in CARICOM; thus in Guyana, it takes forty-six procedures and in Trinidad and Tobago it takes forty-three procedures to start a business.

In those economies in which a high tax burden is the dominant causal factor for the persistence of the shuttle trade, one policy option is the lowering of the effective tax rate and homogenizing this rate across all sectors of the economy. This option has found some support in the work of Sookram et al. (2006), who documented the socioeconomic, demographic and attitudinal characteristics of households participating in informal sector activities like the shuttle trade in an emerging economy like that of Trinidad and Tobago. Their conclusions suggest the following:

- Household members are motivated to undertake informal sector activity such as the shuttle trade because they believe that (1) taxes are too high, (2) their incomes are too low, (3) they have dependents to support, and (4) tax evasion will go undetected.
- The perception of shuttle traders of the risk of detection by the tax authority is determined largely by the extent of the prevailing government bureaucracy.
- Tax morale is probably low in most emerging economies.
- Individuals such as shuttle traders believe they are paying too much tax, relative perhaps to what they receive in return and relative to what they perceive as low incomes. They also perceive that non-payment of taxes goes undetected (and therefore unpunished), a perception that they hold to be true for the wealthier members of society.

- Any policy measure for adjusting effective tax rates should start with a strengthening of the trust in government and government institutions. Taxpayers must believe that (1) they are getting value for their tax dollars, (2) the tax net is all-inclusive, and (3) they are not being unduly punished by the tax authority.

Further support for the link between effective tax rates and tax evasion can be found in the findings of Thomas-Hope et al. (2009) from their analysis of the underground economy in Guyana over the period 2001–8. These researchers found "a significant positive relationship between taxes (with a lag of one year) and real currency holdings suggesting that higher taxes may encourage tax evasion" (p. 25).

Although lowering tax rates or even implementing a new tariff for the informal sector is an admirable suggestion, the question can then arise as to whether the incentives from this lower or special tax rate will outweigh the benefits of evading taxes completely. Further, one of the desirable characteristics of the informal trade is its ease of entry and exit. Indeed, there is a fluidity of the participation in the trade, so the argument remains, why pay a tariff, duty or licence when the duration of traders' participation in the trade is uncertain? Even further, in many Caribbean countries the persistence of tax evasion on the part of the formal sector remains an issue, thus the possibility of extracting taxes from the informal sector will certainly be an uphill battle. Another possible option is negotiations by the traders' association to reduce charges paid by informal traders on baggage. In particular, traders have three options with respect to the shipment of their goods by air-checked baggage, excess baggage and cargo. The checked baggage option is standard; excess baggage carries with it a charge per bag or charge per kilogram and a priority/no priority status. The traders' association should be in a position to gather data on the volumes of cargo moved by the traders by air in a calendar year. Such data can be used to negotiate with the airlines a discount on the charge per bag or per kilogram and a high priority for the traders' excess baggage.

For countries in which inflation is the dominant causal variable, the policy recommendation is to tighten monetary policy and stabilize prices. For countries in which labour market rigidity is the dominant causal variable, the policy recommendation is to accelerate labour market reforms and enhance flexibility. In a broader context, policymakers in the Caribbean should implement labour market policies that strive to create an environment that enhances productivity and promotes flexibility, while at the same time providing effective safety nets and increasing real incomes.

Labour market reform will require that measures be taken on both the demand and supply sides of the market, as well as in the areas of remuneration and labour market institutions. More specifically, the following policy measures can be considered as part of labour market reform in the Caribbean:

- Use a national production programme as the basis of developing an employment-creation programme. This programme would include diversification of the economy, providing the environment within which SMEs can provide some potential for job creation (in particular, financing and technical support), forming pan-Caribbean enterprises in the context of the CSME to allow SMEs to explore markets in the Caribbean diaspora and non-traditional markets in Latin America and Africa, and creating the environment for greater FDI to supplement regional financial resources and penetrate international markets.
- Strengthen the dialogue among the social partners to define the overall macroeconomic framework for the reform.
- Revise the labour laws and work practices to reflect the changes in the commodities and the labour market.
- Develop measures to stem or take advantage of the brain drain. This would include maximizing the benefits of remittances, training persons for the export of services, and focusing on diaspora relations and joint services provision in destination countries.
- Develop a labour market information system to supply information on labour market needs, outcomes and behaviours.

The development of these policy measures should be approached in a holistic and integrated manner since the main challenges facing the region are inter-related.

The transition of the shuttle trade from the informal sector to the formal sector raises the issue of mobility. The barriers to mobility can be found in the country's social institutions, its cultural norms, its legal and institutional climate, its geography, its migration policies and in its lack of infrastructure. These barriers bring into sharp focus issues such as discrimination, limitations to access to capital and increasing returns on capital, race relations, ethnicity, physical disability, portability of the social security system, restrictive property rights or lack thereof, aging, Internet connectivity and the information and communications infrastructure, among others. Each of these can impact the shuttle trade as it seeks to transition to formality. A situation analysis of the country's labour market should be undertaken to identify these barriers to mobility and measure their impact on the shuttle trade. The findings of such an analysis will allow for the necessary policy changes and legislative changes to be identified, designed and implemented to the benefit of the traders.

8.3. Formalization/Semi-formalization of the Informal Sector: Possible Application to the Caribbean

Informal traders currently pay customs duties at the port of entry, do not pay income tax, and do not contribute to the National Insurance System or the National Health Insurance System. In most countries, informal traders are not provided with an adequate location to sell their wares. Against this backdrop, the following is a critical minimum list for formalizing this sector:

1. An association of informal traders must be established in each country.
2. The association must be empowered, authorized and resourced to register all informal traders in the country; collect data on imports and sales from the traders on a quarterly basis; arrange seminars for traders in areas such as customs declaration and immigration; provide advice and assistance to traders in terms of visa requirements; lobby with local and national government bodies for adequate and appropriate space for the sale of goods and products by traders; compile data on the trade for submission to national government; collect fees on a weekly, fortnightly and monthly basis from traders for use of the space provided for their trade; remit fee income as necessary to the local and national government; and lobby with financial institutions for financial facilities for traders.
3. The association will be required to receive on an ongoing basis the concerns of traders and lobby the relevant bodies with a view to addressing these concerns.
4. The association will be required to hold an annual general meeting to report to its members in accordance with its by laws or articles of incorporation.
5. The national government can provide a tax holiday to registered traders in its fiscal package.
6. The national government, after consultation with the traders' association, should define a plan of action to graduate registered traders to the SME classification by the end of the tax holiday. Such a

plan will include a training programme for registered trader, coordinated by the traders' association in conjunction with the ministry responsible for SME development.

7. Once graduated, traders will be eligible to access all the fiscal, financial, marketing and business development support available to SMEs.

8. A team of specially trained persons from the traders' association and the ministry responsible for SME development should be appointed to facilitate the transition of registered traders who have completed the SME training.

9. Registered traders will be required to contribute to the National Insurance System, with the level of contribution pegged to the lowest income category in the National Insurance System. This measure qualifies traders for benefits under this system.

10. Registered traders should be encouraged to contribute to a retirement scheme such as the Unit Trust Corporation Universal Retirement Fund in Trinidad and Tobago as a form of retirement savings. The traders' association should be responsible for marketing such a scheme to traders. The level of contribution to the scheme can be increased as traders expand their businesses and generate higher levels of income.

In closing, this chapter has provided a comparative summary of the key findings of the three empirical surveys undertaken in Guyana, Dominica and Jamaica. It has also explored two options available to governments, namely facilitating the development of the shuttle trade and those who participate in it on the one hand, or integrating the shuttle trade into the formal economy. Policy strategies were subsequently proffered for each option. It therefore remains to be seen whether Caribbean countries will indeed attempt to undertake formalization or semi-formalization strategies, or whether the respective governments will engage in facilitative activities. Either way, Caribbean traders stand to benefit.

Appendix

Questionnaire for Shuttle Traders Survey

Country: _____ Questionnaire Ref. No._____

Greetings!

1. Sex : 1. Male   2. Female
2. What is your age group?
   1. Less than 21   2. 21–30   3. 31–40
   4. 41–50   5. 51–60   6. Over 60
3. What is your home country? _____
4. What is your highest level of education?
   1. No formal   2. Primary
   3. Secondary (up to Form 3)   4. Secondary (up to Form 5)
   5. Secondary (up to Form 6)   6. Technical/Vocational
   7. Tertiary
5. What is your marital status?
   1. Married   2. Common-law   3. Divorced
   4. Single   5. Widowed
6. How many children do you have? 1. _____; 2. Boys _____; 3. Girls _____
7. Which of the following assets do you own?
   1. House   2. Vehicle
   3. Fixed Deposits   4. Money Market Units
   5. Credit Union Shares 6. Life Insurance
8. How long have you been engaged in the suitcase trade? _____ years

9. Were you employed before entering the suitcase trade?
   1. Yes   2. No   IF NO, GO TO Question 12

10. In which sector were you employed?   1. Private   2. Public

11. What was your occupation before entering the suitcase trade?
    1. None   2. Domestic
    3. Labourer/Other   4. Clerk
       Elementary Occupation
    5. Technician   6. Service Sector Staff
    7. Technician   8. Craft Worker
    9. Agricultural Worker   10. Plant/Machinery Operator
    11. Supervisor   12. Manager/Professional

12. How many assistants do you employ? _____

13. What goods do you trade on a regular basis?
    1. Manufacturers   2. Appliances   3. Cosmetics
    4. Jewellery   5. Toys   6. Haberdashery
    7. Novelty Goods   8. Fashion Accessories 9. Garments
    10. Shoes/footwear 11. Condiments/Confectionery
    12. Other: SPECIFY _____

14. Which ONE is your dominant line of goods?
    1. Manufacturers   2. Appliances   3. Cosmetics
    4. Jewellery   5. Toys   6. Haberdashery
    7. Novelty Goods   8. Fashion Accessories 9. Garments
    10. Shoes/footwear 11. Condiments/Confectionery
    12. Other: SPECIFY _____

15. Do you encounter problems/difficulties in conducting your trade?
    1. Yes   2. No   If NO, GO TO Question 18

16. From which of the following things, persons or groups do you face the
    most problems/difficulties?
    1. Trade Ministry Regulations   2. Customs Officers
    3. Immigration Officers   4. Local Health Officers
    5. Competition from other traders 6. Bureau of Standards
    7. Family Members   8. Cargo Forwarding Firms
    9. Airlines   10. Space on Cargo Ships
    11. Completing Documents   12. Damage to cargo
    13. Reservations on Airlines   14. Cargo Space on Airlines
    15. Ground Transportation   16. Other: SPECIFY_____

17. With which of the following persons do you sometimes have problems?
    1. Trade Ministry Officers   2. Customs Officers
    3. Immigration Officers   4. Local Health Officers
    5. Female Traders   6. Bureau of Standards Staff
    7. Male Traders   8. Shipping Firm Staff
    9. Airlines Reservation Staff   10. Customers
    11. Truckers   12. Suppliers

13. Airline Airport Staff   14. Airline Cargo Staff
15. Hotel/Guest House Staff   16. Income Tax Officers
17. Other: SPECIFY_____

18. Which of the following groups of persons buy your goods?
    1. Hotels   2. Restaurants   3. Supermarkets
    4. Small Shops   5. Street vendors   6. General public

19. Which <u>ONE</u> is the dominant group which buys your goods?
    1. Hotels   2. Restaurants   3. Supermarkets
    4. Small Shops   5. Street vendors   6. General public

20. Did you try to obtain any loans from any financial institutions to assist with trade?
    1. Yes   2. No   IF NO, GO TO Question 22

21. Did you succeed?   1. Yes   2. No
    IF NO, why were you rejected? _____
    _____

    How many trips do you usually make in a typical month? _____

22. How many are by   a. sea _____   b. air _____?

23. On average, how many days do you spend on a trip?_____

24. Where do you stay most of the time on your trip?
    1. Hotel   2. Guest House   3. Bed & Breakfast
    4. Relative   5. Friends   6. Other

25. On average, how much do you spend in US$ per trip cost for airfare, accommodation, food, freight charges, ground transportation, telephone calls & incidentals?
    1. Less than $250   2. $251–$500   3. $501–$750
    4. $751–$1,000   5. $1,001–$1,250   6. $1,251–$1,500
    7. $1,501–$2,000   8. $2,001–$3,000   9. $3,001–$4,000

26. On average, how often per month do you ship your purchases as unaccompanied baggage/cargo?
    1. Not at all   2. once   3. twice
    4. 3 times   5. 4 times   6. 4+ times

27. How many months per year do you trade? _____

28. How many suppliers do you have? _____

29. How many of these suppliers do you have a written agreement with? _____

30. Where do you sell your goods (in which markets, street, people's mall, etc)?
    _____
    _____

31. Name the countries in which you trade.
    1. _____ 2. _____

32. What do you do with the produce you are not able to sell? _____
    _____

33. What kind of records do you keep?
    1. Manual   2. Computerized

34. On average how much do you earn per week (in US$) after expenses are
    taken out?
    1. Less than $250   2. $251–$500   3. $501–$750
    4. $751–$1,000   5. $1,001–$1,250   6. $1,251–$1,500
    7. $1,501–$2,000   8. $2,001–$3,000   9. $3,001–$4,000
    10. $4,001–$5,000   11. Above $5,000

35. What are your peak months for business? _____

36. Do you have any additional sources of income? 1. Yes   2. No
    If YES, what are those sources?_____
    _____

37. Are you a member of any traders' association? 1. Yes   2. No
    If NO, Why not?_____
    _____

38. What do you think can be done to assist traders such as yourself?
    _____
    _____
    _____
    _____
    _____

THANK YOU FOR YOUR CONTRIBUTION TO THIS SURVEY

Notes

Introduction

1. The Voice and Accountability index was developed by World Bank Group and is a measure of "various aspects of the political process, civil liberties and political rights, measuring the extent to which citizens of a country are able to participate in the selection of governments". The voice and accountability values are indexed to have a mean of zero and a standard deviation of one. Positive scores indicate better governance and negative scores indicate weaker governance. A total of 99% of all scores range between −2.5 and 2.5.
2. For Thomas et al. (2009), the underground economy includes the informal sector as well as parallel and black market activities.
3. The countries included were Antigua and Barbuda, Argentina, Barbados, Belize, Brazil, Chile, Colombia, Costa Rica, Cyprus, Dominica, Dominican Republic, Ecuador, El Salvador, Fiji, Grenada, Guatemala, Guyana, Honduras, Jamaica, Malta, Mexico, Nicaragua, Panama, Paraguay, Peru, St Kitts and Nevis, St Lucia, St Vincent and the Grenadines, the Bahamas, Trinidad and Tobago, Uruguay, and Venezuela.
4. See also Turgot's reflections (1770, 28) where he notes "If the parties are not in accord, it will be necessary that they should approach one another by yielding a little on one side and a little on the other, offering more and contenting themselves with less."
5. It is possible to argue that at some point in the past all trade conducted was shuttle trade.

Chapter 1

1. Remittances from overseas raise the standard of living of those left behind. In this regard, we can mention the work of Lewis (1954). Lewis detailed how

a labour surplus economy could use an abundant stock of labour to develop. Importantly, when workers leave the labour surplus economy, it raises the ratio of capital per worker in the developing economy.

2. Given that in CARICOM member states the construction of housing characteristically involves a large domestic component, it means that the associated domestic multiplier of housing expenditure on growth and employment in these less developed countries would be higher when compared if remittances were expanded on goods, which facilitate a large import leakage.

3. CARICOM members are Antigua and Barbuda, the Bahamas, Barbados, Belize, Dominica, Grenada, Guyana, Haiti, Jamaica, Monserrat, Trinidad and Tobago, St Kitts and Nevis, St Lucia, St Vincent and the Grenadines, and Suriname.

4. From the West Indian Federation (1958) to CARICOM (1973).

5. SITC 3 comprises mineral fuels, lubricants and related materials.

6. The trade intensity index captures all the factors influencing trade between two countries. The index compares the extent of trade between two trade partners with the expected level of trade. The index is calculated as follows: $T_{ij} = (x_{ij}/X_{it})/(x_{wj}/X_{wt})$, where x_{ij} and x_{wj} are the values of country i's exports and of world exports compared to country j, and where X_{it} and X_{wt} are country i's total exports and total world exports respectively. Trade intensity indices above 1 indicate a high level of bilateral trade flows.

7. An impression of whether a member state of an intra-regional trading agreement sells an export basket to the intra-regional market that has broadened over time can be gleaned through the use of a specialization index (S). Such an index may be calculated as follows: $S_j = \sum_{i=0}^{9} (Xsitc_{ij}/X_j)^2$, i=0,......,9. Where $Xsitc_i$: the exports of $sitc_i$ (i equals the 0.....9 single digit exports sectors) and j = 1 or 2, (1 represents intra-CARICOM exports and 2 represents extra-CARICOM exports). Thus, $Xsitc_{11}/X_1$ represents the export of SITC 1 to CARICOM as a proportion of the total intra-CARICOM exports of the relevant CARICOM member state, and $Xsitc_{12}/X_2$ represent the same economy's extra-regional exports of SITC 1 as a proportion of the total extra-regional exports of the relevant CARICOM member state. The index can range anywhere between 0 and 1. A value tending toward 1 is indicative of extreme dependence on a single commodity, while a score approaching zero is reflective of a higher degree of diversification.

8. Over time, however, as the legal framework develops, the free movement of labour would apply to all persons.

9. Antigua and Barbuda and St Kitts and Nevis have yet to implement phase 4.

10. Geographically, the Windward Islands are those islands of the Caribbean Sea between Dominica and Grenada.

11. The European Union countries have their suppliers with whom they prefer to trade, and to meet their objectives they depend on the provisions of Article 115 of the Rome Treaty to meet their objectives. For example, Spain accesses the majority of their banana imports from the Canary Islands, France from their former colonies abroad and the United Kingdom's and Portugal's

preferred providers are Madeira and the islands of the Caribbean respectively. The Latin American banana producers cater to the entire Belgian, German and Danish markets, as well as over 90% of the Dutch and 85% of the Irish market (ECLAC 2002).

12. The Latin American producers dominate the world trade in bananas, accounting for some 75% of world exports. The major players in the banana trade, however, are the United States transnational corporations, United Brands (Chiquita), Standard Fruit (Dole) and Del Monte. With respect to the European Union market, which is second in size only to the United States, the three United States banana transnational corporations hold 66% of the European Union market, distributed with 43% to Chiquita, 13% to Dole and 10% to Del Monte (Bardhan 1997).

13. In terms of bananas, the beneficiary countries with the European Union are Belize, Grenada, Jamaica, Dominica, St Lucia and St Vincent and the Grenadines. For rum, sugar and molasses, the beneficiaries are Belize, Guyana, Jamaica, St Kitts and Nevis, and Trinidad and Tobago.

Chapter 2

1. Shops are *owned* by men but *operated* by women.
2. Markets were established in Jamaica from as early as 1669 under British rule.
3. Some of this trading pattern with female domination is partly due to African ancestoral linkages. Among tribes in Nigeria like the Yoruba, women are in control of the funds and capital associated with petty trading (Simmonds 1987).
4. With slavery, women and men were labour units, with women having the additional benefit of reproductive capability. The reproductive role of slave women became more significant when the slave trade came to an end.
5. In Grenada, for example, the Grenada legislature passed an act in 1767 which stopped higglers from selling goods house to house.
6. The market higglers brought produce into town, but as Sheller (2007, 11) notes, they took news and information into the rural districts in the process: "In largely non-literate societies, women's concentration in the towns and markets gave them an advantage in gathering oral information, while their economic and familial ties throughout the country enabled them to disseminate important information more quickly than official channels."
7. Kaiser Jamaica Bauxite Company Limited, established in 1952; JBM/ Lydford Mine, formally Jamaica Reynolds Bauxite Partners, established in 1952; Jamalco began production of bauxite in 1963.
8. The term ICI originated in 1982. It was first used by then Jamaican prime minister Edward Seaga. Previously ICIs were referred to as foreign higglers, travelling higglers, international higglers or suitcase traders. It was a label that would officially create "a hierarchy of distinction among traders". As a

result of the economic crisis during this period, the need arose for women to take greater control of the economic destiny of their families by participating in the informal sector, having operated as higglers since the days of slavery. These conditions presented them with an economic opportunity that they seized. The term ICI was a formal recognition of the difference from that of the traditional higgler. It emphasized the distinct demands of international trade over that of local market practices. Higglers represented the peasant with its stigma of backwardness or lack of sophistication. There was also the town or urban higgler who had limited experience when compared to the ICI who travelled extensively in support of her trade.

9. Le Franc and Downes (2001) stress that the reduction in the levels of poverty can be attributed to the large extent of remittance flows associated with high emigration levels. They note that after emancipation, Jamaicans emigrated on a large scale to the United States, Canada, the United Kingdom, Panama and other Central American countries. These emigrants were a source of remittances to their families whom they left behind. Le Franc and Downes (2001) have shown a strong negative relationship between remittance flows and poverty levels. They also show a bi-directional relationship between the informal sector and poverty.

10. Close ties exist between Jamaica and the Cayman Islands. The United Kingdom took formal control of both territories in 1670 under the Treaty of Madrid. After 1670, the Cayman Islands were dependencies of Jamaica. When Jamaica gained its independence in 1962, the Cayman Islands broke its administrative ties with Jamaica and chose to become a dependency of the United Kingdom. By 1999, 40% of the population of the Cayman Islands was of Jamaican descent, and by 2004–5, 50% of the expatriates were Jamaican.

11. The Colón Free Trade Zone is one of the largest in the world. It was created in 1948, and in 2005 had an export (and re-export) level in excess of US$ 6.5 billion.

12. The government built up a crippling external debt burden and this was worsened by an increase in arrears to several international creditors. The state at this point was very resource-starved and repaired its relationship with the IMF/World Bank to gain valuable foreign exchange.

13. Between 1989 and 1992, the government introduced a variety of complementary measures. The objectives of the enterprise resource planning were to source external funding and to implement economic measures to ensure the continuity of funding. This was simply because in the past Guyana had a track record of default. It meant that Guyana had to satisfy various requirements of the multilaterals before it could access credit.

14. See Sergeant and Forde (1991) for a review of the government's involvement in the industrial sector of Trinidad and Tobago. It should also be noted that the New World Group expressed their discontent with the Lewisian proposition of "industrialization by invitation" and cited the multi-national corporation as being representative of the metropolis and merely extending the colonial legacy (Best 1968). Identifying with the problems induced by slavery

and indentureship, the New World Group suggested that an end to persistent poverty lay in de-emphasizing foreign capital. Two of the main proponents of this perspective, Best and Levitt (1969), argued that Lewis' propositions were ill-suited to the needs of the Caribbean and his model was alien to the operational structure of the production unit in the West Indies – the plantation. In this context, they looked upon the Lewisian industrialization by invitation strategy as destined to fail and they took serious issue with it, clamoring for greater government control over the commanding heights of the economy.

15. Assume that the economy consists of two parts: a tradable (T) and a non-tradable (NT) part. Further, let the T sector consist of two parts, booming tradable (BT) and non-booming tradable (NBT). An increase in the price of oil would stimulate economic activity in the BT sector, which would now expand. This sector would draw resources from the NBT and NT sectors. This is the resource movement (R^m)effect. When benefiting economic agents, including the government spending their resources, there would be an increase in demand for NT and this in turn would promote the movement of resources out of the NBT sector to the NT sector. This is the spending effect.

16. Chen et al. (1999, 603) noted that "when opportunities in wage employment in either the modern or agricultural sector are scarce, men and women turn to the informal sector".

Chapter 3

1. Pigou (1938), in the public interest theory of regulation, infers that unregulated markets are characterized by market inefficiencies such as market failure, monopolies and externalities, and so asserted that regulation is in the interest of the people. Proponents of the public interest theory of regulation (who are some of the other proponents) support screening by government of new entries on the market to ensure they meet criteria necessary to properly serve the population.

Chapter 4

1. Other contributing factors were adverse weather conditions and worsening terms of trade.

2. The weak performance was due to a difficult political situation at home. Public sector growth driven by overseas development assistance for infrastructural projects has helped the economy.

3. Heckscher Ohlin Trade is otherwise known as inter-industry trade.

4. The single digit SITCs are: SITC 0: food and live animals; SITC 1: beverages and tobacco; SITC 2: crude materials and inedible oils except fuels; SITC 3:

minerals, fuels, lubricants and related materials; SITC 4: animal and vegetable oils and fats; SITC 5: chemicals; SITC 6: manufactured goods classified by materials; SITC 7: machinery and transport equipment; SITC 8: miscellaneous manufactured articles; SITC 9: miscellaneous transactions and commodities.

5. This is mostly because of the increase in the price of crude oil.
6. Drysdale (1967) derived the trade complementarity index by decomposing the bilateral trade intensity index into a special country trade bias index and a trade complementarity index. Yamazawa (1970, 63) also noted that "if the effects on trade intensity of the degree of complementarity in comparative advantage structures are separated from the effects of other factors, it enables us to identify traditional trade-determining factors and their over time changes". The bilateral trade intensity index following Yamazawa (1970) is given as:

$$I_{ij} = C_{ij} * B_{ij}$$

Where:

$$I_{ij} = \frac{X_{ij}}{X_{iw}} / \frac{X_{wj}}{X_{ww}} , \quad C_{ij} = \sum_k \left(\frac{X_{ww}^k}{X_{ww}} \right) * \left(\frac{X_{iw}^k}{X_{iw}} / \frac{X_{ww}^k}{X_{ww}} \right) * \left(\frac{X_{wj}^k}{X_{wj}} / \frac{X_{ww}^k}{X_{ww}} \right) ,$$

and

$$B_{ij} \equiv \frac{X_{ij}}{X_{ij}} = \frac{X_{ij}}{\sum_k X_{ij}^k} = 1 / \sum_k \left(\frac{X_{ij}^k}{X_{ij}} \right) * \frac{1}{B_{ij}^k}$$

X_{iw}^k is country i's export of commodity K to the world; X_{wj}^k is the world exports of commodity K going to country j; and X_{ww}^k is total world exports of commodity K.

Chapter 5

1. Dominica obtained its independence in 1978 from the United Kingdom.
2. Complainants in Ecuador, Guatemala, Honduras, Mexico and the United States requested consultations with the European Community on 28 September 1995 (WT/DS16). They alleged that the European Community's regime for importation, sale and distribution of bananas was inconsistent with GATT Articles I, II, III, X, XI and XIII, as well as provisions of the Import Licensing Agreement, the Agreement on Agriculture, the TRIMs Agreement and the GATS. On 11 April 1996, the five complainants requested the establishment of a panel, which subsequently found that the European Community's banana import regime and the licensing procedures for the importation of bananas in this regime were inconsistent with the GATT (www.WTO.org).
3. Popularly referred to as 9/11.
4. See www.dominica2day.com.
5. Namely cars, trucks and pick-up vans.

6. Namely haberdashery shops, rumshops and snackettes.
7. Information provided by the general manager of the DHA in August 2008 interview.
8. Information provided by the General Manager of the DHA in August 2008 interview.
9. Markets were listed as Antigua and Barbuda, Guadeloupe, St Maarten NA, and St Martin FWI.
10. Travellers carry goods from country A, sell it in country B, buy goods in country B and return to country A where they sell the goods purchased in country B. The cycle restarts and travellers return with cash to country A to buy more goods.
11. Namely lower freight costs, discounted airfares, a pension for older traders to prevent the market from being flooded with traders, market quotas, a rotational system that will not require each huckster to travel every week, improved storage facilities, better handling of produce by the boat crew, financial compensation for dumped produce and sheltered areas at the markets to protect produce from the sun and heat.

Chapter 6

1. See Best (1968) for an elaboration of the three models of plantation economies.

Chapter 7

1. The term parallel trade is mainly used in Europe.
2. Maskus (2001) discussed these points in relation to parallel imports in general.
3. Second-degree price discrimination is an intermediate case the discussion of which may be skipped without loss of continuity.
4. The Ramsey price rule concerns what price a monopolist should set to maximize social welfare, subject to a constraint on profit. For any monopoly, the price markup should be inverse to the price elasticity of demand: the more elastic demand for the product, the smaller the price markup.
5. Loken and Chaudhuri (2008), in an article entitled *Counterfeit Drugs: Problems and Solutions for the Indian Pharmaceutical Industry,* noted that "India is a major producer of counterfeit drugs and that the production of counterfeit drugs in India has led to significant negative publicity around the world". Bogdanich (2007) noted that "pharmaceutical ingredients exported from China are often made by chemical companies that are neither certified nor inspected by Chinese drug regulators . . . because the chemical companies are not required to meet even minimal drug-manufacturing standards, there is little to stop them from exporting unapproved, adulterated or counterfeit ingredients. The substandard formulations made from those ingredients often

end up in pharmacies in developing countries and for sale on the Internet, for cheap medicine."

6. Hall (2010) discussed one of the most recent measures being used to protect consumers from counterfeit medicines: "The new measure . . . comes in the form of a sticker that will be placed on boxes of medicine to help consumers identify counterfeit medicine. The sticker, reading 'Living Proof', contains a unique alphanumeric code, which patients can use to check the medicine's authenticity by calling a helpline. The code can be revealed by scratching a gray panel on the box and cannot be reused once it is verified."

7. List also includes theft and diversion.

8. The production of counterfeit drugs takes place in a cross-section of economies, with India allegedly accounting for 35% of all counterfeit drugs (Datta 2003). Production of these illicit medications takes place in a variety of differing plant sizes (Yar 2008). Yar identified that counterfeiters range from large industrial-scale enterprises that manufacture sophisticated drugs with higher quality packaging and may have transnational linkages (Castells 1998). Chatterjee (2001) noted that some manufacturers make both counterfeit and legitimate drugs but also supplement the low returns from the production of generic drugs with the counterfeit production of high value branded medicines.

9. Very low access is a situation where the percentage of the population with regular access to essential medicines is less than 50%. Low to medium access is a situation where the percentage of the population with regular access to essential medicines is between 50% and 80%. Very high access is a situation where the percentage of the population with regular access to essential medicines is greater than 95%.

10. Medicines (excluding GRP542) and medicaments.

11. Stevens (2006, 3) noted that "the recent news that the government of North Korea is in the business of manufacturing and selling counterfeit prescription drugs puts the problem into a dramatic new perspective. It is nothing short of international health care terrorism."

12. The group consisted of forty-nine private sector pharmacists, of which thirty-two responded.

13. Data provided by the Pharmacy Board of Trinidad and Tobago in May 2010.

References

Akunyili, D.N. 2010. "Is the Time Ripe for an International Anti-counterfeiting Commission?" *National Agency for Food and Drug Administration and Control (NAFDAC)* 12.

Alderslade, J., J. Talmage, and Y. Freeman. 2006. *Measuring the Informal Economy: One Neighbourhood at a Time.* http://www.brookings.edu/~/media/Files/rc/reports/2006/09communitydevelopment_alderslade/20060905_informaleconomy.pdf.

Alesina, A., and G.M. Angeletos. 2005. "Corruption, Inequality and Fairness". http://www.nber.org/papers/w11399.pdf.

Allen, T. 2006. *Counterfeit Drugs: Infected with Greed; Counterfeit Drugs Are Flooding Hospitals and Markets Worldwide.* http://www.inthesetimes.com/article/2845/counterfeit_drugs_infected_with_greed/.

Alleyne, D. 2007. "The Impact of Remittances on Poverty and Inequality in Jamaica: What Is the Evidence?" *Global Development Studies* 4(3–4): 188–216.

Ambursely, F., and R. Cohen. 1983. *Crisis in the Caribbean.* London: Heinemann.

Atemnkeng, M., K. de Cock, and J. Plaizier-Vercammen. 2007b. "Quality Control of Active Ingredients in Artemisinin-derivative Antimalarials Within Kenya and DR Congo". *Tropical Medicine and International Health* 12(1): 68–74.

Babb, C., J. Babb, and U. Whittaker. 2004. "Feasibility Study on Supporting Women Traders in the Eastern Caribbean". Study commissioned by the UNIFEM Caribbean Office.

Balassa, B. 1965. "Trade Liberalization and Revealed Comparative Advantage". *Manchester School* 33: 99–123.

Balfour, F. 2005. "Fakes!" *Businessweek,* February 6.

Bardhan, P. 1997. *The Role of Governance in Economic Development.* Paris: Organisation for Economic Co-operation and Development.

Barrientos, A., and S.W. Barrientos. 2002. "Extending Social Protection to Informal Workers in the Horticulture Global Value Chain". Social Protection Discussion Paper No. 0216. Washington, DC: World Bank.

Barro, R.J., N.G. Mankiw, and X. Sala-i-Martin. 1995. "Capital Mobility in Neoclassical Models of Growth". *American Economic Review* 85(1): 103–15.

Bate, R. 2008. "Making a Killing: The Deadly Implications of the Counterfeit Drug Trade." http://www.aei.org/docLib/20080520_MakingaKillingnew.pdf.

Beckford, G. (1972) 1999. *Persistent Poverty*. Oxford: Oxford University Press. Reprint, Kingston: University of the West Indies Press.

Bennett, C. 1995. *Comprehensive Multicultural Education: Theory and Practice* (3rd ed.). Needham Heights, MA: Allyn and Bacon.

Best, L. 1968. "Outlines of a Model of the Pure Plantation Economy". *Social and Economic Studies* 17(3): 283–323.

Best, L., and K. Polanyi Levitt. 1969. "Externally Propelled Industrialization and Growth in the Caribbean". 4 vols., with A. Brown, G. de Benedetti, E. Carrington, G. Dedestyre, N. Girvan, A. Harewood and P. Hein. McGill Centre for Developing Area Studies. Manuscript.

Blakeney, M. 2004. *Enforcement of Intellectual Property Rights: Challenges, Remedies and Public Awareness*. www.wipo.int/edocs/mdocs/arab/en/wipo.

Bogdanich, W. 2007. "From China to Panama: A Trail of Poisoned Medicine". *New York Times*. May 6. http://www.nytimes.com/2007/05/06/world/06poison.html.

Bolles, A.L. 1992. "Common Ground of Creativity". *Cultural Survival* 16(4): 34–38.

Bosworth, D., and D. Yang. 2002. "The Economics and Management of Global Counterfeiting". http://www.ulb.ac.be/cours/solvay/vanpottelsberghe/resources/resources/rsaem_39.pdf.

Brown, D. 1989. "Trade and Welfare Effects of the European Schemes of the Generalized System of Preferences". *Economic Development and Cultural Change* 37: 757–76.

Brown, V. 1994. "Higgling: The Language of Markets". In *Higgling-Transactors and Their Markets in the History of Economics* (annual supplement to *History of Political Economy*), edited by N. de Marchi and M.S. Morgan, 66–93. Durham: Duke University Press.

———. 1998. *Adam Smith's Discourse. Canonicity, Commerce and Conscience*. New York: Routledge.

Byrne, D., and E. Strobl. 2004. "Defining Unemployment in Developing Countries: Evidence from Trinidad and Tobago". *Journal of Development Economics* 73 (February): 465–76.

CARICOM. CARICOM Secretariat. 2009. *Cooperation Agreement between the Secretariat of the United Nations and the Caribbean Community Secretariat*. http://www.CARICOM.org/jsp/secretariat/legal.

———. 2010. *The CARICOM Single Market and Economy (CSME)*. http://www.caricom.org/jsp/single_market/freemovementskills_socialsecurity.pdf.

Carr, M., and M.A. Chen. 2002. "Globalization and the Informal Economy: How Global Trade and Investment Impact on the Working Poor". Working Paper on the Informal Economy 2002/1. ILO, Geneva. http://www.ilo.org/wcmsp5/groups/public/---ed_emp/documents/publication/wcms_122053.pdf.

Castells, M. 1998. *The Information Age: Economy, Society and Culture*. Vol. 3, *End of Millennium*. Oxford: Blackwell.

CDB (Caribbean Development Bank). 2006. *Social and Economic Indicators*. http://www.caribank.org/.

———. Various years. *Country Poverty Assessment Reports*. Available at http://www.caribank.org/.

Chard, J.S., and C.J. Mellor. 1989. "Intellectual Property Rights and Parallel Imports". *World Economy* 12(1): 69–83.

Charmes, J. 1998. *Women Working in the Informal Sector in Africa: New Methods and New Data*. Paris: Scientific Research Institute for Development and Co-operation.

Chatterjee, P. 2001. "India's Trade in Fake Drugs: Bringing the Counterfeiters to Book". *Lancet* 357: 1776.

Chen, M., J. Sebstad, and L. O'Connell. 1999. "Counting the Invisible Workforce: The Case of Homebased Workers". *World Development* 27: 603–10.

Chickering, L.A., and M. Salahdine. 1991. *The Silent Revolution: The Informal Sector in Five Asian and Near-Eastern Countries*. San Francisco: ICS Press.

CIA. Various years. *CIA World Factbook*. https://www.cia.gov/library/publications/theworld-factbook/.

Clarke, C. 1957. *The Conditions of Economic Progress*. London: Macmillan.

Cockburn, R., P. Newton, E. Agyarko, D. Akunyili, and N. White. 2005. "The Global Threat of Counterfeit Drugs: Why Industry and Governments Must Communicate the Dangers". *Policy Forum PLOS Medicine* 2(4): 100.

CSME (Caribbean Single Market and Economy) Unit. 2005. *The CSME: A Route to Greater Wealth and Prosperity*. http://www.jis.gov.jm/special_sections/CARICOM.

Danzon, P.M. 1998. "The Economics of Parallel Trade". *Pharmaco Economics* 13(3): 293–304.

Datta, P.T.J. 2003. "India Turning Capital for Counterfeit Drugs". *Financial Times*. 3 August.

De Albuquerque, K., and J.L. McElroy. 1999. "A Longitudinal Study of Serious Crime in the Caribbean". *Caribbean Journal of Criminology and Social Psychology* 4: 32–70.

De la Roca, J., M. Hernandez, M. Robles, M. Torero, and M. Webber. 2002. "Informal Sector Study for Jamaica". Group of Analysis for Development, Inter-American Development Bank. Typescript.

De Soto, H. 1989. *The Other Path: The Invisible Revolution in the Third World*. New York: HarperCollins.

Dillip, R., and S. Mohapatra. 2009. *Revised Outlook for Remittance Flows 2009–2011: Remittances Expected to Fall by 5 to 8 Percent in 2009*. World Bank Other Operational Studies, No. 10990. Washington, DC: World Bank.

Djankov, S., I. Lieberman, J. Mukherjee, and T. Nenova. 2002. "Going Informal: Benefits and Costs". World Bank, Washington, DC. Typescript.

DHA (Dominica Hucksters Association). 2008. *DHA Annual Report 2007*. Rosseau: DHA.

Dorin, S.A., and A.F. Dorin. 2006. "Terrorism and Viagra? Medicinal Drugs Sold over the Internet". *San Diego Physician*, August.

Downes, A.S. 2000. "Human Resources Development in the Caribbean: Overcoming the Unemployment Problem". *Journal of Education and Development in the Caribbean* 4(1): 19–39.

Drysdale, P.D. 1967. "Australian-Japanese Trade". PhD Thesis, Australian National University.

ECDPM (European Centre for Development Policy Management). 2003. *Discussion Paper 40: How to Make EPAs WTO Compatible? Reforming the Rules on Regional Trade Agreement.* http://www.ecdpm.org/.

ECLAC (Economic Commission for Latin America and the Caribbean). 1988. "Preliminary Overview of the Latin American Economy, 1987". *Notes on Economy and Development* 455/456 (December): 36.

———. 1989. "The Informal Sector and Women in the Caribbean: Notes for Reflection". Discussion paper. Port of Spain.

———. 2005. "Economic Survey of Latin America and the Caribbean, 2004–2005". LC/G.2279-P, Santiago, Chile. United Nations publication, Sales No.E.05.II.G.2.

———. 2006. "Social Panorama 2006". ECLAC–UN, Santiago de Chile, Chile.

———. 2009. Regional Workshop on Informal Sector Surveys in the Caribbean Sub-Region". Regional Workshop on Informal Sector Surveys in the Caribbean Sub region Castries, St Lucia. November 12–13.

———. 2010. "Preliminary Overview of CARICOM Economies 2009–2010: Striving for Productive Diversification after the Great Recession". ECLAC–UN, Port of Spain.

———. Various years. Cepalstat database. http://websie.eclac.cl/infest/ajax/cepalstat. asp?carpeta=estadisticas&idioma=i.

Eder, M., A. Yakovlev, and A. Carkoglu. 2003. "The Suitcase Trade between Turkey and Russia: Microeconomics and Institutional Structure". Working Paper WP4/2003/07, Moscow State University, Higher School of Economics. http://www.hse.ru/data/432/973/1224/WP4_2003_07.pdf.

EIU (Economic Intelligence Unit). 2009. "Guyana Factsheet". http://www.economist. com.

Ellis, P. 1986. *Women in the Caribbean.* London: Zed Books.

Faal, E. 2003. "Currency Demand, the Underground Economy, and Tax Evasion: The Case of Guyana". IMF Working Papers, WP/03/7. IMF, Washington, DC.

Feenstra, R.C., and G. Hanson. 1996. "Foreign Investment, Outsourcing, and Relative Wages". In *The Political Economy of Trade Policy: Papers in Honour of Jagdish Bhagwati,* edited by R.C. Feenstra, G.M. Grossman, and D.A. Irwin, 89–127. Cambridge, MA: MIT Press.

Feige, E. 2005. "Overseas Holdings of US Currency and the Underground Economy". *Macroeconomics* 0501022, EconWPA.

Fenoff, R., and J. Wilson. 2009. "Africa's Counterfeit Pharmaceutical Epidemic: The Road Ahead". http://news.msu.edu/media/documents/2010/02/2da48fe 7-2cc2-41d2-8604. 0df3f0f704ab.pdf.

Gërxhani, K. 2004. "The Informal Sector in Developed and Less Developed Countries: A Literature Survey". *Public Choice* 120(3–4): 267–300.

Girault, C. 1984. "Commerce in the Haitian Economy." In *Haiti: Today and Tomorrow: An Interdisciplinary Study*, edited by C. Foster and A. Valdman, 173–79. Landham, MD: University Press of America.

Global Politician. 2005. "Trading from a Suitcase: Shuttle Trade and Global Black Market". http://www.globalpolitician.com/2381-trade.

Gonzáles, A.P. 1998. "The Vulnerability of Small Island Developing States and the Future of ACP-EU Cooperation: The Search for New Instruments". Paper presented to the Small Island Developing States (SIDS) Conference, Brussels, 1–2 September.

———. 2002. "CARICOM, the European Union and International Linkages in External Trade Negotiations".Working Paper Series 2, no. 4 (April). Miami European Union Center, University of Miami,

Green, J.V., and B.H. Murray. 2001. *Online Distribution of Counterfeit Pharmaceuticals.* Arlington, VA: Cyveillance, Inc. http://www.cyveillance.com/web/downloads/Online_Pharmaceuticals.pdf.

Greenaway, D., and C. Milner. 2003. "A Grim REPA". *GEP Research Paper 03/30.* http://www.nottingham.ac.uk/economics/leverhulme/research_papers/03_30.pdf.

Greenidge, K., C. Holder, and S. Mayers. 2009. "Estimating the Size of the Informal Economy in Barbados". *Business, Finance and Economics in Emerging Economies* 4(1): 197–226.

Gren, J. 2007. "International Trade Issues Related to Counterfeit Medicines". US–Asian Business Council Anti-Counterfeiting Medicine Conference Week, 15–19 January, Indonesia, Philippines and Thailand. www.us-asean.org/life_sciences/anti c/Jeffrey_Gren.ppt.

Griffith, W.H. 2002. "A Tale of Four CARICOM Economies". *Journal of Economic Issues* 36(1): 79–105.

Grubel, H.G., and P. Lloyd. 1975. *Intra-Industry Trade: The Theory and Measurement of International Trade in Differentiated Products.* London: Macmillan.

Haan, H.C. 2002. *Training for Work in the Informal Sector: New Evidence from Eastern and Southern Africa.* Turin, Italy: International Training Centre of the International Labour Organization.

Hall, R. 2010. *Living Proof.* http://waterinmajorca.wordpress.com.

Handa, S., and C. Kirton. 1999. "The Economics of Rotating Savings and Credit Associations: Evidence from the Jamaican 'Partner' ". *Journal of Development Economics* 60(1): 173–94.

Hart, K. 1971. "Informal Income Opportunities and Urban Employment in Ghana". Geneva: ILO.

———. 1973. "Informal Income Opportunities and Urban Employment in Ghana". *Journal of Modern African Studies* 11(1): 61–89.

Heeks, R. 1999. "Information and Communication Technologies, Poverty and Development". Development Informatics Working Paper Series, Institute for Development Policy and Management, University of Manchester. http://www.man.ac.uk/idpm/diwpf5.htm.

Holder, Y. 1988. "Women Traders in Guyana". ECLAC, Caribbean Development and Cooperation Committee.

Homiak, J. 1986. "The Hucksters of Dominica". *Grassroots Development* 10(1): 28–37.

Hosein, R., M. Franklin, and C.S. Joseph. 2010. *The Caribbean Diaspora: An Untapped Resource for Impacting Economic Developments through Investments in the Caribbean.* http://sta.uwi.edu/conferences/09/salises/documents/M%20 Franklin.pdf.

Hussmanns, R. 2001. "Informal Sector and Informal Employment: Elements of a Conceptual Framework". Paper presented at the Fifth Meeting of the Expert Group on Informal Sector Statistics (Delhi Group), New Delhi, September 19–21.

———. 2004. "Measuring the Informal Economy: From Employment in the Informal Sector to Informal Employment". Working Paper no. 53, ILO Bureau of Statistics, Geneva.

IDB (Inter-American Development Bank). 2006. "The Informal Sector in Jamaica". *Economic and Sector Studies Series.* RE3-06-010.

———. 2009. *Development in the Americas Report.* Washington, DC: IDB.

IFAD (International Fund for Agricultural Development). 2000. *Report and Recommendation of the President to the Executive Board on a Proposed Technical Assistance Grant for Agricultural Research and Training by a Non-CGIAR Supported International Centre: International Network for Bamboo and Rattan (INBAR): Development and Diffusion of Technologies for Smallholder Bamboo- and Rattan-Based Producers – Phase II.* Rome: IFAD.

ILO (International Labour Organization). 2002. *Women and Men in the Informal Economy: A Statistical Picture.* Geneva: ILO.

———. 2010. *Caribbean Studies and Working Papers.* No. 6. Geneva: ILO.

IMF (International Monetary Fund). 1998. *Shuttle Trade.* Eleventh Meeting of the IMF Committee on Balance of Payments Statistics. Washington, DC, October 21–23. https://www.imf.org/external/bop./pdf/98-1-3.pdf.

———. 2002. *Assessing Sustainability.* Prepared by the Policy Development and Review Department in consultation with the Fiscal Affairs, International Capital Markets, Monetary and Exchange Affairs, and Research Departments.

———. 2011. World Economic Outlook, "Slowing Growth, Rising Risks". http://www.imf.org/external/pubs/ft/weo/2011/02/pdf/text.pdf.

Kairi Consultants. 2007. *Analysis of the 2005 Survey of Living Conditions for Trinidad and Tobago.* http://www.vision2020.info.tt/pdf/Policies%20and%20 Procedures/Policy%20Documents/Analysis%20of%20the%20Trinidad%20 and%20Tobago%20Survey%20of%20Living%20Conditions.pdf.

Kananos, P., J. Costa-i-Font, S. Merkur, and M. Gemmill. 2004. "The Economic Impact of Pharmaceutical Parallel Trade in European Union Member States: A Stakeholder Analysis". LSE Health and Social Care, London School of

Economics and Political Science. http://archives.who.int/prioritymeds/report/append/829Paper.pdf.

Kar, S., and S. Marjit. 2001. "Informal Sector in General Equilibrium: Welfare Effects of Trade Policy Reforms". *International Review of Economics and Finance* 10(3): 289–300.

Kossek, B. 1993. "Women Slaves and Rebels in Grenada". In *Alternative Cultures in the Caribbean*, edited by Thomas Bremer and Ulrich Fleischmann. Frankfurt: Vervuert Verlag.

Lagro, M. 1988. *Women Traders in Saint Vincent and the Grenadines*. Port of Spain, Trinidad: ECLAC.

———. 1990. *The Hucksters of Dominica*. Port of Spain, Trinidad: ECLAC.

Lagro, M., and D. Plotkin. 1990. *The Agricultural Traders of St Vincent and the Grenadines, Grenada, Dominica, and St Lucia*. Port of Spain, Trinidad: ECLAC.

Le Franc, E., and A. Downes. 2001. "Measuring Human Development in Countries with Invisible Economies: Challenges Posed by the Informal and Remittance Sectors in Jamaica". *Social and Economic Studies* 50(1):169–98.

Le Franc, E., D. McFarlane-Gregory, and A. Taylor. 1985. *The Informal Distribution Network in the Kingston Metropolitan Area*. Kingston: Institute of Social and Economic Research, University of the West Indies.

———. 1987. "Petty Trading and Labor Market Mobility: Higglers in the Kingston Metropolitan Area". Paper presented at Caribbean Studies Association Conference, Belize.

Levitt, K. 1991. *The Origins and Consequences of Jamaica's Debt Crisis, 1970–1990*. Kingston: Consortium Graduate School of Social Sciences, University of the West Indies/University of Guyana.

Lewis, W.A. 1950. "The Industrialization of the British West Indies". *Caribbean Economic Review* 2(1): 1–51.

Lewis, W.A. 1954. "Economic Development with Unlimited Supplies of Labour". *Manchester School of Economic and Social Studies* 22: 139–91.

Little, P.D. 1999. *Selling to Eat: Petty Trade and Traders in Peri-Urban Areas of Sub-Saharan Africa*. Research Paper prepared for the Broadening Access and Strengthening Input Market Systems-Collabourative Research Support Program (BASIS-CRSP). http://pdf.usaid.gov/pdf_docs/Pnacl390.pdf.

Loayza, N. 1996. "The Economics of the Informal Sector: A Simple Model and Some Empirical Evidence from Latin America". World Bank Policy Research Working Paper, no. 1727. Washington, DC.

Loken, M., and A. Chaudhuri. 2008. "Counterfeit Drugs; Problems and Solutions for the Indian PharmaceuticalIndustry". http://www.pacmed.ca/Resources/Counterfeit_Drugs.

Lund, F., and J. Nicholson. 2006. "Tools for Advocacy: Social Protection for Informal Workers". *WIEGO*, Cambridge, and Homenet Thailand, Bangkok.

Lybecker, K.M. 2004. "Economics of Re-importation and Risks of Counterfeit Pharmaceuticals". *Managed Care* 13: 10–13.

Mantz, J.W. 2003. "Lost in the Fire, Gained in the Ash: Moral Economies of Exchange in Dominica". PhD Dissertation., University of Chicago.

———. 2007. "How a Huckster Becomes a Custodian of Market Morality: Traditions of Flexibility in Exchange in Dominica". *Identities: Global Studies in Culture and Power* 14: 19–38.

Marshall, A. 2009. "The Fatal Consequences of Counterfeit Drugs". http://www.smithsonianmag.com/people-places/Prescription-for-murder.html?c=y&p.=2.

Maskus, K.E. 2001. *Parallel Imports in Pharmaceuticals: Implications for Competition and Prices in Developing Countries*. Final report to the World Intellectual Property Organization.

Maskus, K.E., and Y. Chen. 1999. "Vertical Price Control and Parallel Imports: Theory and Evidence". World Bank Policy Research Working Papers. http://elibrary.worldbank.org/doi/pdf/10.1596/1813-9450-2461. Washington, DC.

Massiah, L. 1989. "Women's Lives and Livelihoods: A View from the Commonwealth Caribbean". *World Development* 17: 965–78.

Maurin, A., S. Sookram, and P.K. Watson. 2006. "Measuring the Size of the Hidden Economy in Trinidad and Tobago 1973–1999". *International Economic Journal* 20(3): 321–41.

McCormick, B., and J. Wahba. 2003. "Return International Migration and Geographical Inequality: The Case of Egypt". *Journal of African Economies* 12: 500–532.

McFee, D. 2007. *A Comparison of the Haggling Experience in Trinidad and Tobago and Guyana*. Paper presented at the Trinidad and Tobago Chamber of Industry and Commerce Conference on Small and Medium Enterprises (SMEs), Port of Spain, March.

McLean, P. 1988. "Swaziland Manpower and Development Project, Development Communications". Third quarterly report, Mbabane, Swaziland.

Mintz, Sidney W. 1974. *Caribbean Transformations*. Chicago: Aldine.

———. 1995. "Slave Life on Caribbean Sugar Plantations". In *Slave Cultures and the Cultures of Slavery*, edited by S. Palmie. Knoxville: University of Tennessee Press.

Mlachila, M., P. Cashin, and C. Haines. 2010. "Caribbean Bananas: The Macroeconomic Impact of Trade Preference Erosion". Working Paper WP/10/59, IMF, Washington, DC.

Momsen, J.H. 1988. "Gender Roles in Caribbean Agriculture". In *Labour in the Caribbean*, edited by Malcolm Cross and Gad Heuman, 141–58. London: Macmillan.

Morris, J., and P. Stevens. 2006. *Counterfeit Medicines in Less Developed Countries: Problems and Solutions*. London: International Policy Network. http://www.fightingdiseases.org/pdf/ipn_counterfeit.pdf.

Mukhina, I. 2010. "New Losses, New Opportunities: (Soviet) Women in the Shuttle Trade, 1987–1998". *Journal of Social History* 43(2): 341–59.

Mulakala, A. 1991. "Women as Agents of Transformation: The Inter-island Traders of Agricultural Produce in the Caribbean". MA "Thesis, University of the West Indies.

Nadvi, K. 2004. "Globalization and Poverty: How Can Global Value Chain Research Inform the Policy Debate?" *IDS Bulletin* 35(1): 20–30.

OECD (Organisation for Economic Co-operation and Development). 2002. *Measuring the Non-Observed Economy: A Handbook.* http://www.oecd.org/dataoecd/9/20/1963116.pdf.

———. 2009. *Informal Is Normal? Towards More and Better Jobs in Developing Countries.* Paris: OECD Development Centre Studies.

Olofin, S., and A. Folawewo. 2009. *Trade Reforms, Informal Sector Activity and Employment.* www.wto.org/english/res_e/reser_e/...e/olofin_paper_e.doc.

Osarenkhoe, A. 2009. *The Oxymoron of Informal Sector: A Framework for Conceptualizing Informal Sector as Enabler of Economic Development in Developing Countries.* http://www.freepatentsonline.com/article/Journal-International-Business Economics/208535028.html.

Oxford Advanced Learner's Dictionary. 1974. 3rd ed. Oxford: Oxford University Press.

Pagano, M., ed. 2001. *Defusing Default, Incentives and Institutions.* Washington, DC: John Hopkins University Press.

Peake, L., and D.A. Trotz. 1999. *Gender, Ethnicity and Place: Women and Identities in Guyana.* London: Routledge.

Pearson, R. 1993. "Gender Issues in Industrialization". In *Industrialization and Development,* edited by J. Hewitt, H. Johnson, and D. Wield, 222–47. New York: Oxford University Press.

Peltzman, S. 1976. "Toward a More General Theory of Regulation". *Journal of Law and Economics* 19 (August): 211–40.

Penn, R.G. 1979. "The State Control of Medicines: The First 3,000 Years". *British Journal of Clinical Pharmacology* 8: 293–305.

Phillips, S. 2002. "Social Capital, Local Networks and Community Development". In *Urban Livelihoods: A People-Centred Approach to Reducing Poverty,* edited by C. Rakodi and T. Lloyd-Jones, 133–50. London: Earthscan.

Pigou, A.C. 1938. *The Economics of Welfare.* London: Macmillan.

Portes, A., M. Castells, and L. Benton, eds. 1989. *The Informal Economy: Studies in Advanced and Less Developed Countries.* Baltimore: Johns Hopkins University Press.

Pratap, S., and E. Quintin. 2006. *The Informal Sector in Developing Countries: Output, Assets and Employment.* Research Paper No. 2006/130. Helsinki: World Institute for Development Economics Research.

Primo-Carpenter, J. 2009. *Matrix of Drug Quality Reports in USAID-Assisted Countries.* http://www.usp.org/pdf/EN/dqi/ghcDrugQualityMatrix.pdf.

PSI (Pharmaceutical Security Institute). 2006. *Pharmaceutical Security Institute Situation Report.* Vienna, VA: Pharmaceutical Security Institute Inc.

———. 2009. *Pharmaceutical Security Institute Situation Report.* Vienna, VA: Pharmaceutical Security Institute Inc.

Roopnarine, L. 2006. "Return Migration of Indentured East Indians from the Caribbean to India, 1838–1920". *Journal of Caribbean History* 40(2): 308–24.

Sadovskaya, E.Y. 2007. "Chinese Migration to Kazakhstan: A Silk Road for Cooperation or a Thorny Road of Prejudice?" *China and Eurasia Forum*

Quarterly 5(4): 147–70. http://www.isdp.European Union/files/publications/cefq/07/es07silkroad.pdf .

Sahin, A., Y. Akdi, and C. Atakan. 2008. "An Investigation on the Shuttle Trade Dynamics of a Small Open-economy". *International Journal of Economic Sciences and Applied Research* 1(2): 1–12.

Secure Pharma Chain. 2009. *Counterfeit Medicines: Filled with Empty Promises.* November 29. http://securepharmachain.blogspot.ca/#uds-search-results.

Schiff, M., and W. Chang. 2001. "Market Presence, Contestability, and the Terms-of-Trade Effects of Regional Integration". World Bank Policy Research Working Paper Series no. 2532. Washington, DC.

Sergeant, K., and P. Forde. 1991. "The State and Divestment in Trinidad and Tobago: Some Preliminary Findings". Paper presented at the annual conference of the Regional Programme of Monetary Studies, Research Department of the Central Bank.

Sheil, R. 2006. "Teachers, Nurses to Have Free Movement in CSM". *Jamaica Gleaner.* 5 July. http://www.jamaica-gleaner.com/.

Sheller, M. 1997. "Democracy after Slavery: Black Publics and Peasant Rebellion in Post Emancipation Haiti and Jamaica". PhD Diss., New School for Social Research.

———. 2007. "Virtual Islands: Mobilities, Connectivity, and the New Caribbean Spatialities". *Small Axe* 11(3).

Simmonds, L. 1987. "Slave Higglering in Jamaica, 1780–1834". *Jamaica Journal* 20(1): 31–38.

Smikle, C., and H. Taylor. 1978. *Higgler Survey, Jamaica.* Kingston: Agricultural Planning Unit.

Smith, A. 1776. *An Inquiry into the Nature and Causes of the Wealth of Nations.* London: Methuen.

Sookram, S., P.K. Watson, and F. Schneider. 2006. "Structure and Size of the Household Sector of the Hidden Economy in Trinidad andTobago". *Applied Economics* 41 (27): 3545–59.

Stevens, P. 2006. "Counterfeit Drugs: Getting to the Root of the Problem". MedicalProgressToday.com, March 24. http://www.medicalprogresstoday.com/spotlight/spotlight_indarchive.php?id=1182.

Taylor, A. 1988. "Women Traders in Jamaica: The Informal Commercial Importers". ECLAC, Subregional Headquaters for the Caribbean.

Thomas, C.Y. 1989. "Foreign Currency Black Markets: Lessons from Guyanese Experience". *Social and Economic Studies* 38(2): 137–84.

Thomas, C.Y., N. Jourdain, and S. Pasha. 2011. "Revisiting the Underground Economy in Guyana, 2001–2008". *Transition* (40): 60–86.

Thomas, J. 2002. *Decent Work in the Informal Sector: Latin America.* London: London School of Economics/ILO.

Thomas, J.J. 1995. *Surviving in the City: The Urban Informal Sector in Latin America.* London: Pluto.

Thomas-Hope, E., C. Kirton, P. Knight, N. Mortley, and M.A. Urquhart. 2009. "Development on the Move: Measuring and Optimising Migration's Economic and Social Impacts. A Study of Migration's Impacts on Development in Jamaica and How Policy Might Respond". Institute for Public Policy Research and Global Development Network, London.

Treisman, D. 1998. *The Causes of Corruption: A Cross-national Study.* http://www.isr.umich.edu/cps/pewpa/archive/archive_98/19980019.pdf.

Trinidad and Tobago. Ministry of Finance. Various years. *Annual Economic Survey.* Port of Spain: Government of Trinidad and Tobago.

———. Various years. *Review of the Economy.* Port of Spain: Government of Trinidad and Tobago.

Trouillot, M. 1988. *Peasants and Capital: Dominica in the World Economy.* Baltimore: Johns Hopkins University Press.

Turgot, A.R.J. 1770. *Reflections on the Formation and the Distribution of Riches.* New York: Macmillan.

Ulysse, G.A. 2007. *Down Town Ladies, Informal Commercial Importers, A Haitian Anthropologist, and Self-Making in Jamaica.* Chicago: University of Chicago Press.

UNICEF. 2000. *Situation Assessment and Analysis of Jamaican Children and Their Families,* 2000. UNICEF.

UNICRI (United Nations Interregional Crime and Justice Research Institute). 2003. *Global Counterfeiting: Background Document.* http://counterfeiting.unicri.it/docs/ Global%20counterfeiting%20background.pdf.

UN (United Nations). Various years. *Human Development Report.* New York: UN.

UN Commodity Trade Statistics. 2010. http://comtrade.un.org/.

United Nations Economic and Social Commission for Asia and the Pacific. 2006. *Poverty and the Informal Sector: Role of the Informal Sector in Poverty Reduction.* Committee on Poverty Reduction, 29 November–1 December. Bangkok.

Varadharajan, S. 2004. "Explaining Participation in RoSCAs: Evidence from Indonesia". Working Paper, Cornell University.

Vuletin, J.G. 2008. "Measuring the Informal Economy in Latin America and the Caribbean". IMF Working Paper no. 08/102. Washington, DC.

Wedderburn, C., P.E. Chiang, and R. Rhodd. 2009. "The Informal Economy in Jamaica: Is It Feasible to Tax This Sector?" *Journal of International Business and Cultural Studies* 6.

West, P., and Mahon, J. 2003. "Benefits to Payers and Patients from Parallel Trade". York Health Economics Consortium, York, May 2003. http://www.yhec.co.uk.

Wharton, T.C., and Wasley T.C. II. 2009. "Consideration of One Area of Persistent Poverty in the United States". *Social Development Issues* 31(1).

WHO (World Health Organization). 1999. "Counterfeit Drugs: Guidelines for the Development of Measures to Combat Counterfeit Drugs". Department of Essential Drugs and Other Medicines, World Health Organization, Geneva. http://whqlibdoc.who.int/hq/1999/WHO_EDM _QSM_99.1.pdf .

———. 2005. *WHO Fact Sheet.* http://www.wpro.who.int/media_centre/fact_sheets/fs_20050506.htm.

———. 2006. *Counterfeit Medicines: An Update on Estimates.* http://www.who.int/medicines/services/counterfeit/impact/TheNewEstimatesCounterfeit.pdf.

————. 2008. *Counterfeit Drugs Kill!* http://www.who.int/impact/FinalBrochure WHA2008a.pdf.

————. 2009. *General Information on Counterfeit Medicines.* http://www.who.int/medicines/services/counterfeit/overview/en/.

WIEGO (Women in Informal Employment: Globalizing and Organizing). 2001. "A Policy Response to the Informal Economy". WIEGO, Cambridge, MA.

Witter, M., and P. Anderson. 1991. "The Distribution of Social Cost of Jamaica's Structural Adjustment 1977–1989". In *Consequences of Structural Adjustment: A Review of the Jamaican Experience*, edited by Elsie Le Franc. Kingston: Canoe Press.

Witter, M., and C. Kirton. 1990. *The Informal Economy in Jamaica: Some Empirical Exercises*. Kingston: Institute of Social and Economic Research, University of the West Indies.

World Bank. 1990. *World Development Report 1990: Poverty*. New York: Oxford University Press.

————. 2008. *Ghana: Job Creation and Skills Development Draft Report*. Vol. 1, Main Document. Washington, DC: World Bank.

————. 2009. "Informality in Latin America and the Caribbean". Policy Research Working Paper no. 4888. World Bank, Washington, DC.

————. 2010. *Doing Business*. http://www.doingbusiness.org/.

————. Various years. *World Development Indicators*. http://publications.world-bank.org/WDI/.

Worrell, D. 1985. "Monetary Mechanisms in Open Economies: A Model for the Caribbean". In *The Economics of the Caribbean Basin*, edited by Michael Connolly and John McDermott. New York: Praeger.

————. 1987. *Small Island Economies: Structure and Performance in the English-speaking Caribbean since 1970*. New York: Praeger, 1987.

WTO (World Trade Organization). 1997. "European Communities: Regime for the Importation, Sale and Distribution of Bananas: Complaint by Guatemala and Honduras". WT/DS27/R/GTM; WT/DS27/R/HND: Report of the Panel. 22 May. http://www.wto.org/english/tratop_e/dispu_e/27rgtm.pdf.

Yamazawa, I. 1970. "Intensity Analysis of World Trade Flows". *Hitotsubashi Journal of Economics* 10(2): 61–90.

Yankus, W. 2006. *Counterfeit Drugs: Coming to a Pharmacy Near You*. http://www.acsh.org/docLib/200608171_counterfeitdrugw.pdf.

Yar, M. 2008. "The Other Global Drugs Crisis: Assessing the Scope, Impacts and Drivers of the Trade in Dangerous Counterfeit Pharmaceuticals". *International Journal of Social Inquiry* 1(1): 151–66. Available at http://www.socialinquiry.org/articles/IJSI V1N12008%20-%20008.pdf.

Yeats, A.J. 1998. "Just How Big Is Global Production Sharing?" Policy Research Working Paper Series no. 1871. World Bank, Washington, DC.

Yukseker, D. 2004. "Trust and Gender in a Transnational Market: The Public Culture of Laleli, Istanbul". *Public Culture* 16(1): 47–65.

Index

Note: The letters *f*, *t*, and *n* indicate that the entry refers to a page's figure, table or note, respectively.

www.ingramcontent.com/pod-product-compliance
Lightning Source LLC
Chambersburg PA
CBHW061146220326
41599CB00025B/4368